MW01008418

Moral Psychology with Nietzsche

4/24/19

To Josh,

With gratitude for all your help

Yours,

[illegible]

Moral Psychology with Nietzsche

Brian Leiter

OXFORD
UNIVERSITY PRESS

OXFORD
UNIVERSITY PRESS

Great Clarendon Street, Oxford, OX2 6DP,
United Kingdom

Oxford University Press is a department of the University of Oxford.
It furthers the University's objective of excellence in research, scholarship,
and education by publishing worldwide. Oxford is a registered trade mark of
Oxford University Press in the UK and in certain other countries

First Edition published in 2019

Impression: 1

Published in the United States of America by Oxford University Press
198 Madison Avenue, New York, NY 10016, United States of America

British Library Cataloguing in Publication Data
Data available

Library of Congress Control Number: 2018959696

ISBN 978-0-19-969650-5

Printed and bound in Great Britain by
Clays Ltd, Elcograf S.p.A.

for William
scientist, polyglot, a "deep well"

Preface and Acknowledgments

One happy consequence of writing on Nietzsche is that one does not need to persuade readers that Nietzsche is important or interesting: he is a brilliant writer, a magnet for interest across all fields of humanistic and social scientific inquiry. An unhappy problem for the Nietzsche scholar is that Nietzsche's writing style is often too seductive, that too many readers fail to take seriously his views about style: namely, that it is also meant to *exclude* those not really prepared for his insights or those not patient enough to uncover his meaning. Probably because of the seductive writing style, Nietzsche, compared to the other major figures of nineteenth-century philosophy, continues to attract more juvenile commentary than most, though the scholarly situation is much better now than a generation ago. As I noted in the Second Edition of my *Nietzsche on Morality* (Leiter 2002; 2015: x), "the secondary literature has matured considerably, to the point that it now compares favorably, I believe, with the secondary literatures on figures like Kant and Marx, something that was not true when I finished the first edition in late 2001."

This volume picks up on many themes broached, but treated more briefly, in my 2002 book. Chapter 3 of the earlier book dealt with Nietzsche's critique of "moral agency," but many of the papers I have written since then have tried to probe Nietzsche's moral psychology more deeply, and ventured into territory neglected almost entirely in the earlier book, such as Nietzsche's treatment of the affects, of the unconscious, and of freedom. Much of that work from the intervening years has migrated, often transmogrified, into the present volume. I have been particularly interested since the earlier book in the extent to which the best empirical evidence, in fact, vindicates Nietzsche's speculative psychology, and that will be a recurring theme throughout this volume.

I owe a general (and sometimes very specific) intellectual debt to the community of philosophically smart and serious Nietzsche scholars which has formed over the last generation, and that now gathers annually at the meetings of the International Society for Nietzsche Studies I established with colleagues in 2015, including Lanier Anderson, Jessica Berry, Maudemarie Clark, David Dudrick, Michael Forster, Ken Gemes, Andrew Huddleston, Christopher Janaway, Peter Kail, Paul Katsafanas, Simon May, Al Prescott-Couch, Bernard Reginster, Mattia Riccardi, John Richardson, Simon Robertson, and Gudrun von Tevenar. I owe special thanks to Gemes for years of friendship and penetrating philosophical and scholarly insight about Nietzsche (and especially for his comments on Chapter 4). Graduate students in philosophy at both the University of Texas at Austin and the University of Chicago have been a continual source of insight, stimulation, and challenge for me; many are now established scholars in their own right, as I'm sure the others will be in the years to come. So warm thanks for good questions and insights to Nir Ben-Moshe, Jessica Berry (again!), Reid Blackman, Lawrence "Dusty" Dallman, Jaime Edwards, Roger Eichorn, Guy Elgat, Matt Evans, Joshua Fox, Tes Hash, Claire Kirwin, Joel Mann, Christopher Raymond, Neil Sinhababu, Dan Telech, and Ariela Tubert (with apologies to those I may have forgotten). Dan Telech also provided typically excellent research assistance as I prepared the volume for publication and offered invaluable substantive comments on the penultimate draft. Other PhD students at the University of Chicago have taught me a lot even when they have done no work on Nietzsche. I should mention especially Nethanel Lipshitz, whose excellent dissertation on the basis of equality problem has taught me a great deal.

I also discussed many of the issues treated in this volume with a wide array of philosophers, many not primarily interested in Nietzsche. With apologies, again, to those I have forgotten, I am grateful to Mark Alfano, Justin Clarke-Doane, Justin Coates, Nicolas Delon, John Doris, David Enoch, Max Etchemendy, Richard Holton, Tom Hurka, Pierre Keller, Joshua Knobe, Martin Kusch, Don Loeb, Samantha Matherne, Ram Neta, Alastair Norcross, Martha Nussbaum, Jesse Prinz, Peter Railton, Eric Schwitzgebel, Ralph Wedgwood, and Howard Wettstein. I must thank Delon, in particular, for written comments on large parts of the penultimate manuscript, and especially for his objections to arguments in Chapter 5, to which I have probably not adequately responded.

In the late fall of 2017, when I asked the philosophers Don Rutherford and Manuel Vargas whether they and some colleagues and students at the University of California, San Diego might be willing to read some of the manuscript and "crucify me" (as I put it), they generously agreed. Penultimate drafts of Chapters 1, 2, 3, and 5 benefitted immeasurably from the careful attention and criticism of Don and Manuel, as well as from their colleagues David Brink, Michael Hardimon, Dana Nelkin, Samuel Rickless, and Eric Watkins, and UCSD PhD students Dallas Amico, Noel Martin, and Leo Moauro. In addition, I am grateful to Pierre Keller, one of the most knowledgeable and insightful scholars of Kant and the post-Kantian traditions in European philosophy in North America, who came down from the University of California, Riverside to participate in the workshops, and who pressed on me the places where Nietzsche may have remained more of a NeoKantian than I am inclined to suppose. I suspect I will have not responded to his doubts adequately, though I have tried to take them seriously. I must also thank Rutherford for his later feedback on Chapter 6, though he should not, of course, be presumed to agree with what I say there. I am also grateful to Riverside PhD student Avery Snelson, who took off an afternoon from working on his dissertation on Nietzsche, to press me on a number of textual and interpretive matters while I was in San Diego.

Peter Momtchiloff, the philosophy editor at OUP to whom so many are indebted, was, as always, patient, but also nudged and encouraged me at the right times. Lorrie Ragland, my secretary for the last decade, has provided invaluable support in a multitude of ways that has facilitated completion of this project.

Some arguments and ideas in this book appeared previously, though almost everything has been revised, often so extensively that the original is probably unrecognizable. Portions of the introduction draw on material that originally appeared as "Nietzsche's Naturalism Reconsidered," in K. Gemes and J. Richardson (eds.), *The Oxford Handbook of Nietzsche* (Oxford: Oxford University Press, 2013). Chapters 1 and 2 include ideas and arguments from articles that originally appeared as "Nietzsche's Metaethics: Against the Privilege Readings," in *European Journal of Philosophy* 8 (2000): 277–97, and as "Moral Skepticism and Moral Disagreement in Nietzsche," in R. Shafer-Landau (ed.), *Oxford Studies in Metaethics, Volume 9* (Oxford: Oxford University Press, 2014); both are revised quite a bit, including with responses to critics of my views; reproduced by permission of Oxford University Press. Chapter 3 is a revised version of a paper of the same name that appeared in *Social Philosophy & Policy* 30: 237–58, ©2013, reprinted with permission. Chapter 4 incorporates some material from "Normativity for Naturalists," *Philosophical Issues: A Supplement to Nous* 25 (2015): 64–79, and also incorporates some ideas from a forthcoming paper on perspectivism (that paper in full is slated to appear in a volume on relativism in German philosophy, edited by Martin Kusch and colleagues from the University of Vienna).

Chapter 5 draws on material that originally appeared in "Nietzsche's Theory of the Will," *Philosopher's Imprint* 7 (2007): 1–15, which also was reprinted in K. Gemes and S. May (eds.), *Nietzsche on Freedom and Autonomy* (Oxford: Oxford University Press, 2009). Chapter 5, and also Chapter 6, draw on material that first appeared in "Who is the Sovereign Individual? Nietzsche on Freedom," in S. May (ed.), *The Cambridge Companion to Nietzsche's* On the Genealogy of Morality (Cambridge: Cambridge University Press, © 2011, reprinted with permission), as well as some material that first appeared as "The Paradox of Fatalism and Self-Creation in Nietzsche" in C. Janaway (ed.), *Willing and Nothingness: Schopenhauer as Nietzsche's Educator* (Oxford: Oxford University Press, 1998). Chapter 7 was co-authored with Joshua Knobe and appeared in a collection I co-edited with Neil Sinhababu on *Nietzsche and Morality* (Oxford: Oxford University Press, 2007); all reproduced by permission of Oxford University Press. I am very grateful to Joshua for allowing me to include this essay here, since it was very much a joint effort. I have revised this chapter primarily to insure consistency with the rest of the volume.

I am grateful to the publishers for permission to reuse this material here.

Sheila, my best friend for a very long time now, has continued to be incredibly generous and supportive of my work (including being exceptionally tolerant of my habit of doing a lot of writing in the evenings). I am grateful to her for all that, and much more—most importantly, for Sam, William, and Celia, who have not only made our lives so much better but deepened my understanding of moral psychology. My last book was dedicated to Sam, our first child who is now poised to graduate college and pursue his own professional, intellectual, and political aspirations. This book is dedicated to our second child, William, a science enthusiast with philosophical curiosity, and a gifted learner and speaker of languages, a facility I not only admire but have had occasion to consult at times when working on this book. (Celia, I promise you are up next for a dedication!) From all three, I learned the truth of Schopenhauer's doctrine, one Nietzsche (despite occasional noises to the contrary) ends up sharing, namely, that "a man does not alter, and his moral character remains absolutely the same all through his life." I have learned much from each of theirs, and look forward to seeing them each unfold in the years ahead. It has been the most extraordinary experience of my life to be part of that.

B.L.

Chicago, USA
May 2018

Contents

Introduction

Nietzsche's Naturalistic Moral Psychology

1. Moral Psychology, Philosophy, Naturalism

"Moral psychology" has become something of a term of art in Anglophone philosophy over the last several decades, though it warrants some elaboration here for the benefit of those not current with that often narrow literature. The label picks out a set of interrelated issues of central philosophical concern for millennia, going back at least to Plato, and figuring prominently in most of the major philosophers of modernity, including Nietzsche. The "psychology of morality" would, indeed, be a good first approximation of the subject matter, that is, the psychological explanation of what is involved in both making moral judgments and acting morally (or acting in a way the agent takes to be apt for moral assessment). But what is the distinctive contribution of *philosophy* as distinct from *empirical psychology* to moral psychology?

Answering that question when thinking about Nietzsche requires us to be careful with our terminology, since for Nietzsche, "genuine philosophers" (BGE 211) are those who create or "legislate" values, in contrast to those "philosophical laborers"—Nietzsche names Kant and Hegel as exemplary cases—who simply "press into formulas... some big set of valuations—that is, former *positings* of values, creations of value which have become dominant and are for a time called 'truths'" (BGE 211). There may only be two "genuine philosophers" by this criterion, namely, Plato and (perhaps) Nietzsche himself, but Nietzsche's "honorific" sense of what it is to be a philosopher is largely irrelevant for purposes of my aims in this volume. I mean to elaborate on the "philosophical" contribution to moral psychology in a more mundane sense, namely, the contribution that clarity about the concepts in play and their inferential relations can contribute to thinking about the psychology of morality. In particular, a psychological account of moral judgment and purported moral agency has to be clear about, among other things, the nature of morality and of moral judgments, what would be involved in agency and distinctively *moral* agency (which is always in the modern tradition understood to be *free* agency), and the workings of a mind in which such agency is possible. "Moral psychology," in short, encompasses issues in metaethics, philosophy of mind, and philosophy of action, including questions concerning the objectivity of morality, the relationship between moral judgment and emotion, the nature of the emotions, free will and moral responsibility, and the structure of the mind as that is relevant to the possibility of moral action and judgment.

Nietzsche is, along with Hume, one of the two great naturalists of modern moral philosophy,[1] a theme I have defended, with some success, in my earlier work (Leiter 2002), so much so that one recent scholar claims that, "Most commentators on Nietzsche would agree that he is in a broad sense a naturalist in his mature philosophy" (Janaway 2007: 34).[2] I hope that assessment of current scholarly opinion is correct, but it marks a dramatic change from an earlier consensus from the 1960s through the 1980s when resolutely anti-naturalistic readings (sometimes obvious *mis*readings) by Martin Heidegger, Jacques Derrida, Sarah Kofman, Richard Rorty, and Alexander Nehamas were particularly influential. Nietzsche's naturalism, as I have argued, is centrally *methodological* (hereafter M-Naturalism), calling for continuity with the methods of successful sciences (in the nineteenth century, this meant especially physiology and biology).[3] This continuity entails some substantive commitments, such as the denial of supernatural entities which play no explanatory role in the successful sciences, as well as skepticism about freedom of the will, which Nietzsche, like many nineteenth-century writers, took to be undermined by the sciences. Crucially, though, M-Naturalism requires the philosopher seeking to understand human beliefs, attitudes, and behavior to develop a speculative psychology of human beings and human nature. This aligns Nietszche quite closely with Hume, as many scholars have now noted (cf. Kail 2009), though Hume had only Newtonian science as a paradigm, while Nietzsche had the benefit of extensive familiarity with developments in nineteenth-century science on which to draw, both substantively and speculatively (Emden 2014; cf. Leiter 2017). Recall Barry Stroud's useful formulation of Hume's speculative M-Naturalism:

[1] Spinoza is another, and one relevant in the case of Nietzsche because of his way of reconciling fatalism and freedom, a topic to which we return in Chapter 6. But Spinoza's panpsychism was utterly foreign to Nietzsche, although central to Spinoza's conception of the natural.

[2] Janaway, in an otherwise illuminating study, makes several errors in his discussion of my version of Nietzsche's naturalism: in the end, his view of Nietzsche's naturalism is just a version of mine. For an extended discussion, see Leiter (2015a: 244–64). I address briefly a couple of these points, below.

[3] After 1830 in Germany, "Physiology...became the basis for modern scientific medicine, and this confirmed the tendency, identifiable throughout the whole of the nineteenth century, towards integration of human and natural sciences" (Schnädelbach 1983: 76). In his 1843 *Philosophy of the Future*, Feuerbach could write that, "The new philosophy makes man, along with nature as the basis of man, into the one and only universal and highest object of philosophy: anthropology, including physiology, becomes the universal science" (Sec. 54). The 1850s saw an explosion of books drawing on the new sciences, and articulated the German Materialists' naturalistic view. As one scholar has written: "[T]he German materialists...took the German intellectual world by storm during the 1850s" (Vitzthum 1995: 98). A critic of materialism writing in 1856 complained that, "A new world view is settling into the minds of men. It goes about like a virus. Every young mind of the generation now living is affected by it" (quoted in Gregory 1977: 10). We know from Thomas Brobjer's research (Brobjer 2008: 44, 123, 133–4) that Nietzsche, as a young man, had read Feuerbach and was also a regular reader of the journal *Anregung für Kunst, Leben und Wissenschaft* which, in the early 1860s, published many articles about materialism, including by Büchner. The crucial event for Nietzsche was his discovery in 1866 of Friedrich Lange's recently published *History of Materialism*, a book which opened up for him the whole history of philosophical materialism up to and including German Materialism, as well as introducing him to the profound developments in modern natural science, especially biology, chemistry, and physiology (cf. Brobjer 2008: 32–6; Emden 2014: 21–32).

[Hume] wants to do for the human realm what he thinks natural philosophy, especially in the person of Newton, had done for the rest of nature.

Newtonian theory provided a completely general explanation of why things in the world happen as they do. It explains various and complicated physical happenings in terms of relatively few extremely general, perhaps universal, principles. Similarly, Hume wants a completely general theory of human nature to explain why human beings act, think, perceive and feel in all the ways they do...

[T]he key to understanding Hume's philosophy is to see him as putting forward a general theory of human nature in just the way that, say, Freud or Marx did. They all seek a general kind of explanation of the various ways in which men think, act, feel and live... The aim of all three is completely general—they try to provide a basis for explaining *everything* in human affairs. And the theories they advance are all, roughly, deterministic. (Stroud 1977: 3, 4)

Hume modeled his theory of human nature on Newtonian science by trying to identify a few basic, general principles that would provide a broadly deterministic explanation of human phenomena, much as Newtonian mechanics did for physical phenomena. Yet the Humean theory is still *speculative*, because its claims about human nature are not confirmed in anything resembling a scientific manner, nor do they even win support from any contemporaneous science of Hume's day.

Nietzsche's speculative M-Naturalism obviously differs from Hume's in some respects: Nietzsche, for example, appears to be a skeptic about nomic determinism based on his professed (if not entirely cogent) skepticism about laws of nature (cf. BGE 21–22). Yet Nietzsche, like Hume, has a sustained interest in explaining why "human beings act, think, perceive and feel" as they do. The crux of this speculative naturalism derives from ideas popular among German Materialists in the 1850s and after: that human beings are fundamentally bodily organisms, creatures whose physiology explains most or all of their conscious life and behavior. Nietzsche adds to this Materialist doctrine the proto-Freudian idea that the unconscious psychic life of the person is also of paramount importance in the causal determination of conscious life and behavior.[4] Thus, Nietzsche accepts what I have called (Leiter 1998) a "Doctrine of Types," according to which,

Each person has a more-or-less fixed psycho-physical constitution, which defines him as a particular type of person.[5]

Call the relevant psycho-physical facts here "type-facts." Type-facts, for Nietzsche, are either *physiological* facts about the person, or facts about the person's unconscious drives or affects. Nietzsche's claim, then, is that each person has certain physiological

[4] Nietzsche's "official" view seems to be that physiology is primary, but he mostly concentrates on psychological claims, most obviously because he is no physiologist! There were, of course, other anticipations of the Freudian idea, ones that Nietzsche likely encountered, e.g., Fechner (1848). (Thanks to Dan Telech for calling the Fechner article to my attention.)

[5] Are individuals born with these traits or do they acquire them? Nietzsche's texts are unclear on this point. But it is clear that particular traits and wax and wane in importance in an individual's life depending on circumstances. (Thanks to Mark Alfano for pressing me on this issue.) For more discussion, see Chapter 7.

and psychic traits that constitute the "type" of person he or she is. While this is not, of course, Nietzsche's precise terminology, the ideas are omnipresent in his writings.

A typical Nietzschean form of argument, for example, runs as follows: a person's theoretical beliefs are best explained in terms of his moral beliefs;[6] and his moral beliefs are best explained in terms of natural facts about the type of person he is (i.e., in terms of type-facts). So Nietzsche says, "every great philosophy so far has been... the personal confession of its author and a kind of involuntary and unconscious memoir"; thus, to really grasp this philosophy, one must ask "at what morality does all this (does *he*) aim" (BGE 6)? But the "morality" that a philosopher embraces simply bears "decisive witness to *who he is*"—i.e., who he *essentially* is—that is, to the "innermost drives of his nature" (BGE 6). Indeed, this explanation of a person's moral beliefs in terms of psycho-physical facts about the person is a recurring theme in Nietzsche. "[M]oralities are... merely a sign language of the affects" (BGE 187), he says. "Answers to the question about the *value* of existence may always be considered first of all as the symptoms of certain bodies" (GS P:2). "Moral judgments," he says, are "symptoms and sign languages which betray the process of physiological prosperity or failure" (WP 258). "[O]ur moral judgments and evaluations... are only images and fantasies based on a physiological process unknown to us" (D 119), so that "it is always necessary to draw forth... the *physiological* phenomenon behind the moral predispositions and prejudices" (D 542). A "morality of sympathy," he claims, is "just another expression of... physiological overexcitability" (TI IX:37). *Ressentiment*—and the morality that grows out of it—he attributes to an "actual physiological cause [*Ursache*]" (GM I:15). Nietzsche sums up the idea well in the preface to the *Genealogy*: "our thoughts, values, every 'yes,' 'no,' 'if' and 'but' grow from us with the same inevitability as fruits borne on the tree—all related and each with an affinity to each, and evidence of one will, one health, one earth, one sun" (GM P:2).

Like Hume, then, Nietzsche proffers a speculative psychology (based on his Doctrine of Types), though as I argue in Chapter 7 (co-authored with Joshua Knobe), Nietzsche's speculations seem to fare rather well in light of subsequent research in scientific psychology. And this speculative psychology (as well as the occasional physiological explanations he offers in passing) appear to give us causal explanations for various human phenomena, which, even if not law-governed, seem to have a deterministic character, i.e., they presuppose that the phenomena in question have causal determinants (cf. Leiter 2002: 5). Readers should remember how omnipresent causal claims are in Nietzsche's philosophical writing. When he says in *Daybreak*, for example, that "[O]ur moral judgments and evaluations... are only images and fantasies based on a physiological process unknown to us" (D 119), so that "it is always necessary to draw forth... the *physiological* phenomenon behind the moral predispositions and prejudices" (D 542), he is making a causal claim, i.e., the claim that certain physiological

[6] More precisely, as we will see in Chapters 3 and 5, the explanation operates in terms of the underlying drives that produce particular moral beliefs.

processes *cause* moral judgments through some presumably complicated process that yields them as "images" and "fantasies" brought about by these causes. When he says in the *Genealogy* that *ressentiment*, and the morality that grows out of it, has an "actual physiological cause [*Ursache*]" (GM I:15) his meaning is, of course, unmistakable. When he devotes an entire chapter of *Twilight of the Idols* to what he calls "the four great errors," errors that almost entirely concern causation—"confusing cause and effect," the "error of false causation," the "error of imaginary causes" he calls them—it is clear that he wants to distinguish *genuine causal relations* from the mistaken ones that infect religious and moral thinking. When he returns to the same theme in *The Anti-Christ*, he again denounces Christianity for trafficking in "imaginary causes" and for propounding "an imaginary *natural* science," one that depends on anthropocentric concepts and lacks, as Nietzsche puts it, "any concept of natural cause" (A 15; cf. A 25)—science consisting, on his account, of "the healthy concepts of cause and effect" (A 49). Psychological and physical causation are essential for Nietzsche's entire moral psychology and revaluation of values.[7]

2. Misunderstanding Nietzsche's Naturalism

Some misunderstandings of Nietzsche's naturalism, which frames his moral psychology, have arisen among scholars, even among those friendly to the idea that Nietzsche is some kind of philosophical naturalist. Christopher Janaway, for example, complains that,

> [N]o scientific support or justification is given—or readily imaginable—for the central explanatory hypotheses that Nietzsche gives for the origins of our moral beliefs and attitudes. For a prominent test case, take Nietzsche's hypothesis in the *Genealogy*'s First Treatise that the labeling of non-egoistic action, humility, and compassion as "good" began because there were socially inferior classes of individuals in whom feelings of *ressentiment* against their masters motivated the creation of new value distinctions. This hypothesis explains moral phenomena in terms of their causes, but it is not clear how it is *justified* or *supported by* any kind of science, nor indeed what such a justification or support might be. (2007: 37)

This challenge ignores that Nietzsche, like Hume, was a *speculative* M-Naturalist, as Nietzsche had to be given the primitive state of psychology in the nineteenth century. A speculative M-Naturalist simply does *not* claim that the explanatory mechanisms essential to his theory of why humans think and act as they do are supported by existing scientific *results*. To be sure, what Nietzsche does do is appeal to psychological mechanisms—such as the seething hatred mixed with envy characteristic of *ressentiment*—for which there seem to be ample evidence in both ordinary and historical experience, and weave a narrative showing how these simple mechanisms could give rise to particular human beliefs and attitudes. It is, moreover, quite easy to see what

[7] On the central role of causation in Nietzsche, *contra* skeptics, see the discussion in Leiter (2013a: 587–92).

empirical evidence would bear on this: e.g., evidence that a psychological state usefully individuated as *ressentiment* serves diagnostic or predictive purposes. Even in the First Essay of the *Genealogy*, Nietzsche elicits a variety of kinds of evidence of his own in support of the existence of this psychological mechanism: for example, the facts about the etymology of the terms "good" and "bad"; the general historical fact that Christianity took root among the oppressed classes in the Roman empire; and the rhetoric of the early Church Fathers. Here we see Nietzsche arguing for a characteristically scientific kind of inference: namely, to believe in the causal role of a particular psychological mechanism, for which there is ample independent evidence, on the basis of its wide explanatory scope, i.e., its ability to make sense of a variety of different data points.

In my earlier reading of Nietzsche as a philosophical naturalist, I emphasized two respects in which naturalism was either subordinated to or displaced by other philosophical concerns. Even though, as I argued, "the bulk of [Nietzsche's] philosophical activity is devoted to variations on this naturalistic project" (Leiter 2002: 11)—that is, to explaining morality in naturalistically respectable terms—it is equally clear that Nietzsche's "naturalism is enlisted on behalf of a 'revaluation of all values,'" that is the project of trying "to free ... nascent higher types from their 'false consciousness,' i.e., their false belief that the dominant morality is, in fact, *good for them*" (Leiter 2002: 26, 28; cf. 283). That means, of course, that even when Nietzsche's texts are informed by his M-Naturalism, he has important reasons to employ a variety of rhetorical devices aimed at unsettling readers from their existing moral commitments.

In addition to the fact that Nietzsche's M-Naturalism is an instrument in the service of the revaluation of values, there is also the important point, noted at the start, that he actually uses the term "philosopher" as an honorific to designate those who "create" values (Leiter 2002: 11) That activity is *not* part of the naturalistic project, except in two relatively weak senses. First, it should presumably observe the stricture of "ought implies can," i.e., not valorizing any capacities and achievements that are, in fact, beyond the ken of creatures like us. Second, it views the sciences as a resource which can illuminate the *effects* of different kinds of value on different kinds of people (GM I:Note is a striking example).[8] But the *legislation* of values is a creative exercise, and the values so created are just that: creations, not features discovered in a pre-existing reality.

"The Humean Nietzsche," we can say, is the Nietzsche who aims to explain morality naturalistically (in the senses already discussed). We may contrast him with "the Therapeutic Nietzsche" who wants to get select readers to throw off the shackles of morality (or "morality in the pejorative sense" [MPS], as I have called it [2002: 74–80]). The "revaluation of values" involves enlisting the Humean Nietzsche for the Therapeutic Nietzsche's ends, though the Therapeutic Nietzsche has (as I argued in

[8] I should note that I take the doctrine of eternal return to be an ethical doctrine, and thus part of the project of "creating" new values, and so it has only a tangential connection to Nietzsche's naturalism, except insofar as it observes the strictures of "ought implies can."

Leiter [2002: 159, 176]) a variety of other rhetorical devices at his disposal beyond the Humean Nietzsche's understanding of morality: for example, exploiting the genetic fallacy (leading his readers to think that there is something wrong with their morality because of its unseemly origin) or exploiting their will to truth (by showing that the metaphysics of agency on which their morality depends is false). That the Therapeutic Nietzsche should avail himself of such non-rational devices is hardly surprising, indeed, follows from the Humean Nietzsche's understanding of persons. As I noted in Leiter (2002: 155): "Nietzsche's naturalism, and the prominent role it assigns to non-conscious drives and type-facts, leads him to be skeptical about the efficacy of reasons and arguments. But a skeptic about the efficacy of rational persuasion might very well opt for persuasion through other rhetorical devices."

Janaway (2007) laid considerable emphasis on what I am calling the Therapeutic Nietzsche, arguing, plausibly, that Nietzsche wanted to engage his readers emotionally or "affectively," because such engagement was a necessary precondition for altering the reader's views about evaluative questions.[9] As Janaway puts it: "without the rhetorical provocations, without the revelation of what we find gruesome, shaming, embarrassing, comforting, and heart-warming we would neither comprehend nor be able to revalue our current values" (2007: 4; cf. 96–8). Whether this affective arousal is necessary for *comprehending* Nietzsche's critique is less clear than that it is necessary for bringing about a revaluation, as I argue in Chapter 4. But Janaway draws an unwarranted conclusion from his observation: he thinks it is wrong to treat "style"—that is, the rhetorical devices central to Nietzsche's therapeutic aims—as "mere modes of presentation, detachable in principle from some elusive set of propositions to which his philosophy might be thought to consist," since to do so, "is to miss a great part of Nietzsche's real importance to philosophy" (2007: 4). "Nietzsche's way of writing," Janaway explains, "addresses our affects, feelings, or emotions. It provokes sympathies, antipathies, and ambivalences that lie in the modern psyche below the level of rational decision and impersonal argument." This, Janaway says, is "not some gratuitous exercise in 'style' that could be edited out of Nietzsche's thought" (2007: 4).

These, and similar passages in Janaway's book,[10] conflate the Humean and Therapeutic Nietzsches. There can be no doubt that Nietzsche's practical objective is to transform the complacent consciousness of (at least some of) his readers about the received morality, and it seems equally clear that he thinks the only way to do that is by engaging them emotionally. Yet the proposition that readers will only change their most basic moral commitments if their underlying affective states are aroused and

[9] He wrongly thinks this is inconsistent with my naturalist reading, as I discuss in Leiter (2015a: 244–59).

[10] See esp. p. 212, where Janaway (2007) claims, without any support, that "it is beyond question that Nietzsche regards the *Genealogy* as providing greater *knowledge* [emphasis added] about morality than any combination of the traditional *Wissenschaften* could have attained unaided," which would only be true if one conflates the therapeutic aims with Nietzsche's philosophical theses about morality. I return to some of these issues in Chapter 4.

altered is, itself, a philosophical position that can be stated unemotionally. What Janaway fails to establish is that one cannot, in fact, separate out the Humean Nietzsche's philosophical positions (about agency, motivation, the origins of morality, i.e., his "moral psychology") from the mode of presentation that is essential to the Therapeutic Nietzsche's aims. This books offers such a separation, for the benefit of scholars and students; philosophical exposition of this kind is, of course, no substitute for reading Nietzsche, but it should make that reading even more meaningful.

To see why such an approach is, *contra* Janaway, perfectly sound, consider the related case of Freudian psychoanalysis. Unlike Nietzsche's, of course, Freud's books had no therapeutic aim: therapy took place in the psychoanalyst's office. Freud's books, by contrast, expressed the cognitive content of his philosophical or theoretical positions: about the structure of the mind, the interpretation of dreams, the course of human psychic development and—most importantly for our purposes—the centrality of the mechanism of transference to therapeutic success. Yet a correct theoretical description of transference is no substitute for the patient's actual *experience* of transference in the therapeutic setting, when he projects onto the analyst the heretofore repressed feelings that had been the source of his suffering, thus permitting the patient to recognize the reality of those feelings at last.

I assume no one denies that one can separate the theoretical account of transference as a therapeutic mechanism from the actual experience of cure via psychoanalysis culminating (more or less) with the moment of transference. Nietzsche differs from Freud in many respects, but only one that matters in this context: his books are both the expression of his theoretical positions *and* the therapeutic method, in Janaway's sense. The Humean Nietzsche's theoretical positions—e.g., what he thinks explains the genesis of our current morality, how he understands the mechanisms of human psychology, what he takes to be the causal consequences of moral beliefs, and so on—are both explicit and implicit in a text that also aims to produce a therapeutic effect on certain readers, i.e., to free them from their false consciousness about the dominant morality. Just as successful therapeutic transference requires the patient to experience the repressed feelings directed at the analyst, so too a successful revaluation of values requires engaging the reader sub-consciously at the affective level, so that he feels revulsion, disgust, and embarrassment about his existing moral beliefs. From none of this, however, does it follow that one cannot separate out philosophical or cognitive content from the therapeutic technique, that we cannot separate the Humean and Therapeutic Nietzsches. The Therapeutic Nietzsche does, indeed, depend on "artistic devices, rhetoric, provocations of the affects, and explorations of the reader's personal reactions" (Janaway 2007: 52) and much of the corpus is given over to the therapeutic project, but this does not change the fact that the therapeutic project is pursued within and informed by the framework of the Humean Nietzsche's picture of persons and morality, which also permeates the corpus. The latter is a recognizably naturalistic conception, one which, in fact, explains why rational discursiveness—in contrast to the stylistic devices Janaway emphasizes—is an ineffective therapeutic technique.

The goal of this book is to set out the main features of the Humean Nietzsche's naturalistic moral psychology[11] and to defend, philosophically and empirically, the soundness of his speculative claims. This book is moral psychology *with Nietzsche* because I think Nietzsche is mostly right, so getting clear about his views, and seeing the arguments and empirical evidence that support them, advances the subject.

3. How Could Nietzsche Be a Successful Philosophical Naturalist?

Philosophical naturalists always incur an evidential burden that most philosophers do not: their claims must answer to the facts as they unfold in the course of systematic empirical inquiry. Kantians can make up their moral psychology from their sanctimonious armchairs, invoking an interest only in the "concept" or "possibility" of moral motivation, but naturalists actually care about how human beings *really* work. Hume does not fare that well by this more demanding evidential standard (though he fares better than Kant, to be sure), since some of his speculation about human nature seems to involve wishful thinking about human moral propensities: yes, many people do have sympathetic dispositions in certain circumstances, but so too, as Nietzsche likes to emphasize, they often reveal pleasure in cruelty. Nietzsche is certainly not prone to wishful thinking, but does he actually fare any better? How does his speculative M-Naturalism look more than a century later?

One important reason that philosophers should take Nietzsche seriously, as I will argue in several chapters in this volume, is because he seems to have gotten, at least in broad contours, many points about human moral psychology *right*. Consider:

(1) Nietzsche holds that heritable type-facts are central determinants of personality and morally significant behaviors, a claim well-supported by extensive empirical findings in behavioral genetics (see Chapter 7).
(2) Nietzsche claims that consciousness is a "surface" and that "the greatest part of conscious thought must still be attributed to [non-conscious] instinctive activity" (BGE 3), theses overwhelmingly vindicated by recent work by psychologists on the role of the unconscious (e.g., Wilson 2002) and by philosophers who have produced synthetic meta-analyses of work on consciousness in psychology and neuroscience (e.g., Rosenthal 2008; see Chapter 5).
(3) Nietzsche claims that moral judgments are post-hoc rationalizations of feelings that have an antecedent source, and thus are not the outcome of rational reflection or discursiveness, a conclusion in sync with the findings of the ascendant "social intuitionism" in the empirical moral psychology of Jonathan Haidt (2001) and others (see Chapter 3).

[11] Some approaches to moral psychology lay more emphasis on the emotions then I will in this volume, in part for reasons that will become clear in Chapter 3. See Alfano (2018) for such an approach to Nietzsche's moral psychology.

(4) Nietzsche argues that free will is an "illusion," that our conscious experience of willing is itself the causal product of non-conscious forces, a view recently defended by the psychologist Daniel Wegner (2002) (see Chapter 5).

If Nietzsche were more widely read by academic psychologists—too many years of Heideggerian and Derridean misreadings appear, alas, to have put them off Nietzsche—then he would be recognized as a truly prescient figure in the history of empirical psychology.

Naturalists, to be sure, are hostages to empirical fortune, and Nietzsche's remarkable track record may turn out to be less impressive in fifty or a hundred years. But prophecy about the empirical sciences is not my interest here. For Nietzsche's remarkable psychological insight raises a new, and different kind of, puzzle about the M-Naturalism I have ascribed to him and whose conclusions I defend in this volume. To put it simply: Nietzsche seems to have been *right* about much of human moral psychology notwithstanding his failure to employ any of the *methods* of the empirical psychology that has confirmed much of his work. What kind of *methodological* naturalism is that?

Scott Jenkins posed a succinct version of this objection in commenting on the empirical evidence that Knobe and Leiter (2007) (a revised version of which is Chapter 7 here) adduced in support of Nietzsche's moral psychology. Jenkins writes (2008):

> Knobe and Leiter examine a wide range of psychological studies (including studies of twins' behavior, the effects of child-rearing practices on personality, and the relation between moral behavior and reports of moral attitudes) and argue that a person's behavior in moral contexts can be explained primarily through appeal to heritable "type-facts," while moral upbringing (the Aristotelian view) and conscious decision-making (the Kantian view) quite surprisingly play almost no role in such explanations. This empirical evidence, they argue, demonstrates that Nietzsche's theory of different psychological types, with their characteristic moral and theoretical commitments, at the very least deserves serious attention from philosophers interested in moral psychology. Knobe and Leiter do a very good job of making their case, and their work suggests an interesting question concerning Nietzsche's work—How, exactly, did he arrive at a theory that is confirmed by recent empirical investigations if not by way of considering the data that support the theory?

We need to distinguish, in this context, between what counts as *confirmation* of a theory from what might lead a genius like Nietzsche to have perceived a possible truth about human moral psychology. Empirical psychology has evolved methods for testing and confirming hypotheses that were not in use in the nineteenth century[12]—hence the need for a naturalistically-minded philosopher like Nietzsche to *speculate*. But, by the same token, it is not as though Nietzsche lacked *evidence* on which to base his speculative moral psychology. His evidence appears to have been of three primary

[12] While the use of systematic experimentation, rather than mere introspection, seems a rather clear advance, parts of empirical psychology have been plagued by failures of replication, and the social and medical sciences more generally have suffered from a specious notion of "statistical significance." See, e.g., the devastating critique in Colquhoun (2014).

kinds: first, his own observations, especially of the behavior of others; second, the psychological observations of others recorded in a wide array of historical, literary, and philosophical texts over long periods of time, observations which, in some respects, tended to reinforce each other (consider, e.g., the realism about human motivations detailed by Thucydides in antiquity and, in the modern era, in the aphorisms of La Rochefoucauld, both authors whom Nietzsche admired); and third, his reading about contemporaneous scientific developments, many of which—even if amateurish or simply wrong by today's standards—did represent systematic attempts to bring scientific methods to bear on the study of human beings and which, in some of their broad outlines, have been vindicated by subsequent developments. By the standards of contemporary methods in the human sciences, we would not deem insights arrived at based on this evidence to be well-confirmed, but that certainly does not mean it is not, in the hands of a genius like Nietzsche, adequate for insights that survive scrutiny by our contemporary methods. This is precisely one of the reasons why Nietzsche is a great *speculative* M-Naturalist in the history of philosophy: with unsystematic data and methods he could nonetheless arrive at hypotheses that turn out to win support by more systematic data and methods. Of course, unlike our contemporary social scientists, Nietzsche is not just a Humean, but a Therapist, and so weaves these hypotheses into a powerful critical project that aims to transform consciousness about morality. Some of our contemporary naturalists in moral psychology have perhaps similar aims, but nothing like Nietzsche's rhetorical talent, or his fearless readiness to abandon conventional wisdom about morality. Contemporary cognitive science should lead us to have a renewed appreciation for the penetrating insight of Nietzsche's speculative M-Naturalism, but cognitive science is no match for the rhetorical power of the Therapeutic Nietzsche, who sees not only how human beings actually work but also how to exploit these facts in a way that upsets the complacent moral consciousness of some of his readers.

4. Nietzsche's Naturalistic Moral Psychology: An Overview

Remember that Nietzsche is not a critic of *all* "morality," explicitly embracing, for example, the idea of a "higher morality" which would inform the lives of "higher men" (cf. Schacht 1983: 466–9); in doing so, he often employs the very same German word—*Moral*—for both what he attacks and what he praises. Moreover, Nietzsche aims to offer a revaluation of existing values in a manner that appears, itself, to involve appeal to evaluative standards of some sort. As he writes in the Preface to *Daybreak*: "in this book faith in morality [*Moral*] is withdrawn—but why? *Out of morality* [*Moralität*]! Or what else should we call that which informs it—and *us*?... [T]here is no doubt that a 'thou shalt' [*du sollst*] speaks to us too" (D 4). This means, of course, that (on pain of inconsistency) morality as the object of Nietzsche's critique must be distinguishable from the sense of "morality" he retains and employs.

Yet Nietzsche does not confine his criticisms of morality to some one religiously, philosophically, socially, or historically circumscribed example. Thus, it will not suffice to say that he simply attacks Christian or Kantian or European or utilitarian morality—though he certainly at times attacks all of these. To do justice to the scope of his critique, we should ask what characterizes "morality" in Nietzsche's pejorative sense—hereafter, "MPS," the label I introduced in earlier work (Leiter 2002: 74)—that is, morality as the object of his critique. For Nietzsche does believe that all normative systems which perform something like the role we associate with "morality" share certain structural characteristics, even as the meaning and value of these normative systems varies considerably over time. In particular, all normative systems have both *descriptive* and *normative* components, in the sense that: (a) they presuppose a particular account of human agency, in the sense that for the normative claims comprising the system to have intelligible application to human agents, particular metaphysical and empirical claims about agency must be true; and (b) the system's norms favor the interests of some people, often (though not necessarily) at the expense of others.

As I argued in earlier work (2002: 81–125)—an account I will presuppose here—any particular morality will be the object of Nietzsche's critique (i.e., an MPS) if it presupposes certain descriptive claims about the self and agency (e.g., that the will is free, that the self is transparent to introspection) *or* if it endorses norms that are harmful to those Nietzsche deems "the highest men." While Nietzsche offers criticisms of both the descriptive and normative claims of MPS, what ultimately defines MPS as against unobjectionable normative systems is for Nietzsche the distinctive normative agenda. Thus, while Nietzsche criticizes the description of agency that is typically part and parcel of MPS (see Chapter 5), he also holds that "[i]t is *not* error as error that" he objects to fundamentally in MPS (EH IV:7): that is, it is *not* the falsity of the descriptive account of agency presupposed by MPS, per se, that is the heart of the problem, but rather its distinctive normative commitments. Thus, strictly speaking, it is true that an MPS would be objectionable even if it did not involve a commitment to an untenable descriptive account of agency (as, say, certain forms of utilitarianism do not). Because Nietzsche's two most common—and closely related—specific targets are, however, Christian and Kantian morality, the critique of the descriptive component of MPS figures prominently in Nietzsche's writing, and any account of the logic of his critique that omitted it would not do justice to his concerns.

Part I begins with the central questions about the metaphysics and epistemology of moral value. I argue that Nietzsche has no clear semantics of such judgments (a view to which I've converted notable skeptics; see Hussain 2013: 412), but I argue that he has, like most major figures in the Western tradition, a definite view about the metaphysics: there are no objective facts about what is morally right and wrong, good or bad. Nietzsche is a thorough-going anti-realist about *what ought to be done*, including, importantly, *his own judgements on that score*. (He is also a thorough-going anti-realist about *all* judgments of value, including, I argue judgments of epistemic value, a point to which I return in Chapter 4.) Chapters 1 and 2 develop Nietzsche's *explanatory* arguments for anti-realism and argue, on textual and philosophical grounds, against readings which take Nietzsche to think some particular evaluative perspective—perhaps connected to his elusive idea of the "will to power"—in fact undergirds his critical judgments about MPS. This aspect of his view—its global anti-realism about moral value—has vexed some contemporary commentators, who still maintain allegiance to the idea of some kind of "objective" vindication for their value judgments (for them, perhaps, God is not yet dead). I criticize this resistance in both the text and the footnotes, and return to it briefly in Chapter 4 where I consider the implications of Nietzsche's arguments for *all* judgments of value, not just moral value. In Chapter 4, I also try to situate the preceding claims in the context of Nietzsche's so-called (and much-discussed) doctrine of "perspectivism."

But the immediate question posed by Chapters 1 and 2 is: if moral value judgments are neither factual nor objective, then what is going on? What is the psychology of moral judgments? Nietzsche should be located within the familiar tradition of moral anti-realists who are also sentimentalists, like Hume and, in the German tradition, Herder[13]—that is, philosophers who think the best explanation of our moral judgments is in terms of our emotional or affective responses to states of affairs in the world, responses that are, themselves, explicable in terms of psychological facts about the judger. Of course, if our emotional judgments have *cognitive* content—if they are, in fact, epistemically sensitive to the putatively moral features of the world—then sentimentalism is compatible with moral realism (and, more precisely, knowledge of real moral facts). That is not, however, Nietzsche's view: Nietzsche understands our basic emotional or affective responses as brute artifacts of psychology and/or culture, though there is nothing in Nietzsche's view to rule out the possibility that more complicated judgments (e.g., about "guilt") might not involve a cognitive component added to the non-cognitive one (but on Nietzsche's view that cognitive component is systematically false). It is the burden of Chapter 3 to explain in a plausible way Nietzsche's views on this score.

If morality is not objective, if moral judgments are the causal product of non-cognitive affective responses to states of affairs—responses which are themselves explicable in psychological terms—then what to make of the other family of issues associated with moral psychology, namely, action, freedom, and responsibility? These are the subjects of Part II in this volume.

Chapter 5 gives a systematic overview of Nietzsche's picture of agency: his "hard incompatibilism" in contemporary lingo and his "fatalism" (in a sense to be explained), emphasizing his arguments that the feeling of "freely willing" an action is epiphenomenal, not evidence of the causal structure of action; and that action arises from mechanisms we do not at all understand introspectively. Chapter 6 asks then why Nietzsche still sometimes uses the language of "freedom" and what it means in his hands; I here also take issue with the views of various "moralizing" readers of his

[13] On Herder, in relation to Nietzsche's sentimentalism, see Forster (2017).

texts. Once again, careful attention to the texts reveals Nietzsche's deflationary and revisionist sense of "freedom," one that does not underwrite a conception of free will (and moral responsibility) that would be recognizable in either the Humean or Kantian strands of the modern philosophical tradition. For Nietzsche, the resolute naturalist, we are not free or morally responsible. I also here debunk Nietzsche's rhetoric of "self-creation"—a favorite slogan for existentialist and other "self-help" readings of Nietzsche—since it is swamped by his fatalism, his view that psychological and physiological facts about persons dramatically circumscribe what they can become and what they can value. Nietzsche is here closer to the Plato of the *Republic*, with its "Myth of the Metals," except that for Nietzsche it is not a myth, but a fact, that people differ fundamentally in psycho-physical type, though not along Plato's lines and with no reference, of course, to metals! As often happens in Nietzsche, talk of "self-creation"—like talk of "freedom" and "responsibility"—is presented in a highly revisionary and deflationary sense. Here I consider a resonance with the views of Spinoza, perhaps the only modern source for some of what Nietzsche says. Chapter 7, based on an essay co-authored with a leading figure in experimental philosophy and cognitive science, Joshua Knobe, looks at the empirical evidence in support of Nietzsche's conception of agency (as set out in the preceding chapters), and compares it with pictures of moral psychology in the Aristotelian and Kantian traditions: those latter views do not fare well in light of empirical evidence, unsurprisingly.

This book has exegetical aims, to be sure, but it is not an exercise in the "history of ideas." I believe Nietzsche is right (at least on topics about which one can be right or wrong), and certainly in his big picture, which is why it is worthwhile to set out his views in some detail. Among Nietzsche's views that seem to me plausible and correct are: his anti-realism about value, his sentimentalism, his skepticism about consciousness and rational agency, his fatalism, and his skepticism about the post-hoc rationalizations of moral philosophers. For reasons that will become clear, I do not take a position on whether Nietzsche is right that morality is dangerous to the most valuable kinds of human flourishing—though I do believe we should be worried by his challenge, as I am.

The aim of this volume, in short, is to articulate and defend moral psychology in a Nietzschean spirit. Because of this double aim I will often move from exposition to philosophical argument independent of the exposition. I thus hope the volume will be of interest to philosophers interested in the philosophical issues, even if not especially interested in Nietzsche.

PART I

Metaphysics and Epistemology of Value

1

Nietzsche's Anti-Realism about Value

The Explanatory Arguments

1. Introduction

Much of the popular image of Nietzsche, as scholars have long known, is remarkably wrong-headed and often silly, from the idea that he was the philosopher of the "superman,"[1] or the last metaphysical philosopher, who discovered that the essence of the world is really "will to power." These popular myths arose from an aggregation of superficial readings, mischief by Nietzsche's sister and others after his death, and the pernicious influence of ideologically motivated misreaders like Martin Heidegger, among other factors.

Yet one part of the more-or-less popular perception of Nietzsche turns out to be quite correct, while, ironically, it has been some scholars who have gone to extravagant lengths to resist the obvious, thereby providing unintended support for Nietzsche's quip that "Christian morality has been the Circe of all thinkers so far—they stood in her service" (EH IV:6). The obvious, if "terrible truth" as Nietzsche would say, is that there are no objective facts about values, including, most importantly, the values we associate with morality. Nietzsche's main arguments for this skeptical conclusion are *explanatory*, that is, they are arguments of the form that objective facts about value are no part of the best explanation of what we observe or experience. It is the task of this chapter to set out, and defend, Nietzsche's arguments for this conclusion.

Before we launch into the interpretation and argument, a few words about terminology and the conceptual landscape are necessary. In most of this chapter I will focus on one kind of value, namely, *moral* value and *moral* judgment, that is, claims and judgments about what ought to be done (or valued) because it is right, just, obligatory, maximizes goodness, and so on, and not simply because it reflects self-interest ("prudential value").

[1] The image of the Übermensch appears only in one work, *Thus Spoke Zarathustra*, in which Zarathustra is a parody of the Christ-figure teaching an anti-Christian "doctrine," as it were, including the idea of the superman. That rhetorical ploy drops out of Nietzsche's corpus thereafter, though he certainly thinks that there are "higher" and "lower" human beings, and his critique of morality is centrally concerned with the deleterious effects of morality on the flourishing of the higher human beings (Leiter 2015a: 92–100).

I will occasionally touch on non-moral value (e.g., aesthetic value, prudential value), and will have more to say about those kinds of value (and especially *epistemic* value) in Chapter 4.

Questions about the "objectivity" of morality and moral judgment are customarily located in the philosophical field of "metaethics," and while metaethics, since the early twentieth century, has advanced our ability to frame and debate these issues, it has also often blurred the line between two questions that—for purposes of interpreting thinkers prior to the linguistic turn of the twentieth century—ought to be kept separate. One question, the "metaphysical" question, might be put thus: Are there any mind-independent facts about morality? Are there any facts about what is morally right and wrong, good and bad, that obtain independent of anyone's judgments about them—now or even under ideal circumstances? I will refer to the metaphysical question, in short, as being whether there are any judgment-independent or mind-independent facts about moral value.[2]

In what follows, I should like to separate these "metaphysical" questions from what we may call the "semantic" question: what is the meaning of moral *language*? Is it, for example, primarily descriptive and fact-stating, or is it rather expressive of feelings or non-cognitive attitudes? Should moral language be interpreted truth-conditionally? Since G.E. Moore in the early twentieth century, philosophers have leaned toward answering both semantic *and* metaphysical questions, and, more significantly, toward framing the metaphysical questions in terms of the semantic one.[3]

What has resulted is a shift in Anglophone philosophical sensibility: to deal satisfactorily with metaethical problems has come to mean dealing with *both* the metaphysical and semantic issues. While this represents a philosophical development of some interest, as a guide to interpretive strategy for historical figures it invites contrivance and anachronism. For example, while it seems clear that Nietzsche has distinct views on the central metaphysical question about value, it seems equally apparent that there are inadequate textual resources for ascribing to him a satisfying answer to the semantic question. Elements of his view, for example, might suggest assimilation to what we would call non-cognitivism[4] and, in particular, expressivism, yet we do not really find

[2] The independence at stake here is *epistemic*: facts are metaphysically objective insofar as their existence and character does not depend on what anyone judges to be true about their existence and character, even under idealized epistemic circumstances. This kind of mind-independence is thus compatible with constructivist views according to which what is objectively valuable for an agent depends on the agent's attitudes, a view that has, recently, been attributed to Nietzsche in Silk (2015). I think this reading is implausible for reasons I will return to in the notes, below.

[3] This has not meant, of course, that one's semantics of ethical discourse had to track one's metaphysics of morality: consider an emotivist like A.J. Ayer as opposed to an error theorist like John Mackie. While the emotivist and the error theorist can answer many of the metaphysical questions in unison, they will disagree importantly over the semantics: while for the former the meaning of ethical terms is primarily expressive, for the latter ethical discourse is indeed declarative and assertoric (in keeping with its typical surface syntax), but is just systematically false. The twentieth-century innovation of framing metaphysical questions semantically has not, then, entailed a complete collapse of the distinction such that metaphysics *necessarily* dictates semantics or vice versa.

[4] For example, describing master and Christian morality as "opposite forms in the optics of value [*Werthe*]," Nietzsche goes on to assert that, as opposite "optical" forms, they "are... immune to reasons and

textual answers in Nietzsche to the full range of semantical problems an expressivist theory should encompass.[5] The reason for this should be obvious: while Nietzsche was among the first to recognize the extent to which linguistic and grammatical practices generate metaphysical assumptions and problems, he simply did not view metaphysical questions *themselves* as best framed as issues about the semantics of a given region of discourse (e.g., are the terms genuinely and successfully referential?).

All of this is prefatory to an important point about my approach throughout. While I shall frequently appropriate the language of twentieth-century metaethics in discussing Nietzsche's views, I ultimately interpret Nietzsche only as answering the *metaphysical* questions about value. Nietzsche, in my view, has no interesting *or* even precisely determinable semantics of evaluative discourse: there are simply not adequate grounds for "assigning" Nietzsche a view on such subtle matters as whether ethical language is primarily referential or expressive, when it clearly evinces aspects of both descriptive and prescriptive discourse.

None of this makes Nietzsche unique: most philosophers prior to the twentieth century did not have an interesting or determinable semantics of ethical discourse either (though the secondary literature of recent pedigree may sometimes suggest otherwise). It is also not an inexcusable failing: for surely it was the metaphysical questions that have animated the debate from the Sophists onward. And surely it is because of their stand on the metaphysical questions that we typically group philosophers like A.J. Ayer and John Mackie together as moral skeptics—their differences on the semantics notwithstanding.[6]

2. Nietzsche's Metaphysical Anti-Realism about Value

I want now to say a bit more about the nature of Nietzsche's denial of the objectivity of value. An obvious, indeed often explicit, target of Nietzsche's skepticism is *Platonism* about value. Plato himself, to be sure, does not think there is a *special* problem about the objectivity of value, since he thinks values are objective in the same way all Forms

refutations. One cannot refute Christianity; one cannot refute a disease of the eye... The concepts 'true' and 'untrue' have, as it seems to me, no meaning in optics" (CW Epilogue). This passage, however, is ambiguous. For the passage could mean that "true" and "false" are meaningless *not* because evaluative judgments are essentially non-cognitive, but rather because competing evaluative views are *immune* to the effects of reasoning. There may be rational grounds for thinking one view better than another, perhaps for thinking one true and the other false, but since reasoning has so little impact in this context, it is "meaningless" (in the sense of pointless) to raise issues of truth and falsity. For an effort to construe Nietzsche as a non-cognitivist, see Clark and Dudrick (2007), and for persuasive criticism of that effort, Hussain (2013: 405–8).

[5] For a contemporary discussion of how vexing those are, see Schroeder (2008).

[6] At times, though, the semantic questions have seemed to overshadow the metaphysical ones. Consider, for example, all the philosophical energy expended on the so-called Frege-Geach problems about giving an expressivist account of moral terms embedded in the antecedents of conditionals. Surely, though, anti-realism about value should not turn on such a fine-grained difficulty for non-cognitivist semantics; rather, if metaphysical considerations require anti-realism, then we should simply countenance some revision of ordinary linguistic practice. The point in this regard is well-made in Wright (1988: 31).

are.[7] A Form, says Plato, "is eternal, and neither comes into being nor perishes, neither waxes nor wanes" (*Symposium* 211a). In the *Phaedo*, he calls them "constant and invariable" (78d) while in *The Republic* he refers to them as "the very things themselves . . . ever remaining the same and unchanged" (479e). Forms are, in the words of *The Symposium*, "pure, clear, unmixed—not infected with human flesh and color, and a lot of other mortal nonsense" (211a).

Many of Nietzsche's skeptical-sounding passages involve denials of this kind of Platonism about value. So, for example, Zarathustra declares:

> Verily, men gave themselves all their good and evil. Verily, they did not take it, they did not find it, nor did it come to them as a voice from heaven. Only man placed values [*Werte*] *in* things to preserve himself—he alone created a meaning for things, a human meaning. Thus he calls himself 'man,' which means: the esteemer [*der Schätzende*].
>
> To esteem is to create [*Schätzen ist Schaffen*]: hear this, you creators! . . . Through esteeming alone is there value [*Wert*]: and without esteeming the nut of existence would be hollow . . . (Z I:15)

Similarly, writing in his own voice in *The Gay Science*, Nietzsche observes that, "Whatever has *value* in our world now does not have value in itself, according to its nature—nature is always value-less, but has been *given* value at some time, as a present—and it was *we* who gave and bestowed it" (GS 301).

It is fashionable for contemporary value realists in academic philosophy to deny they are Platonists, and, in one limited sense, most are not: they do not typically think of values as supra-sensible forms available to a kind of a priori intuition (or recollection). What most self-described value realists share with Plato, however, is the idea that what is *really* valuable or obligatory or right exists independently of what human beings judge to be really valuable or obligatory or right.[8] Even naturalistic value realists, who are happy to agree that "without esteeming, the nut of existence would be hollow"—as Peter Railton, for example, puts it: "In a universe without subjectivity [i.e., without creatures for whom things matter], there is no value either" (1986a: 18)—still think that what *actually* has value does not depend epistemically on human judgment, even if value presupposes the existence of those for whom things have value.

[7] I here confine attention to the theory of forms of the middle books.

[8] This is true even of a reading like that in Silk (2015), which suggests that Nietzsche is a constructivist in the precise sense of thinking there are facts about what an agent ought to do or value that depend on the agent's "evaluative attitudes," i.e., "attitude[s] that tend[] to motivate an agent when combined with her ordinary factual beliefs" (2015: 253). Normative facts on this account are still epistemically independent of what human beings judge to be the case, in the sense discussed earlier. What is puzzling about Silk's account is that it has no real textual support. Silk suggests that "Nietzsche regards some values as having genuine normative force" (2015: 249), i.e., values "that make legitimate claims on us and afford a critical, authoritative perspective on how to act, feel, and be" (2015: 249). But none of the passages Silk cites say anything of the kind: they are all passages in which Nietzsche makes evaluative judgments—no one disputes he does that!—and all are equally compatible with a metaethical view in which Nietzsche understands evaluative judgments to be caused by and to express non-cognitive attitudes. What is missing is some textual evidence that Nietzsche takes these evaluative judgments to be judgments about attitude-dependent facts, as Silk wants to claim.

Some recent self-described value realists—sensibility theorists like John McDowell and David Wiggins—have argued for a stronger constitutive relationship between human responses and objective facts about value, though they have had trouble explicating this in a way that does not involve vicious circularity (see Sosa 2001 for critical discussion). Passages like GS 301—"Whatever has *value* in our world now does not have value in itself, according to its nature—nature is always value-less, but has been *given* value at some time, as a present—and it was *we* who gave and bestowed it"—might, in isolation, appear suggestive of such a view, though in fact Nietzsche thinks only *some* people are really value creators. In GS 301, he singles out the "higher human beings," writers and "contemplative" ones as those who give the gift of value to things in the world, not through their constitutive responses but by persuasively appraising (or devaluing) particular people, attributes, and actions. Although (as we will see in Chapter 3) Nietzsche shares something with the sentimentalist tradition in moral philosophy deriving from Hume and Herder, his point in this context is different: his point is that it is the great creative geniuses who are responsible for "the whole eternally growing world of valuations, colors, accents, perspectives, scales, affirmations, and negations" (GS 301), who teach entire generations and epochs to feel differently than they had before. What results is a common *feeling* of the world as having a certain evaluative cast, a kind of skeptical and relativized version of the sensibility theories recently popular among apologists for morality.

In sum, most contemporary value theorists are still "Platonists," since they too are committed to a conception of value as mind- or judgment-independent, the same conception of value that is also central to the world's major religious traditions (though sometimes value is not independent of the mind of God, but it is certainly independent of human minds). It is this conception of value that Nietzsche rejects. Thus, by "anti-realism" about value I will mean precisely rejection of the Platonist view, while a "realist" about value thinks, with Plato, that there are mind-independent facts about value, even if the realist rejects the metaphysics of Forms, knowledge by recollection and other idiosyncratic parts of the Platonic philosophical picture.

A final word is needed here about the scope of Nietzsche's anti-realism about value. Some judgments of value are *epistemic*: for example, "this is what one ought to believe based on evidence" or "that theory is warranted." I want to bracket questions about epistemic value here, and will return to them in Chapter 4. For now, I want to focus only on and delineate further the differences between kinds of non-epistemic value, in order, in particular, to note a change in view from my earlier work.

In that earlier work (Leiter 2002: 45–7, 106–12), I had argued that Nietzsche could *not* be skeptical about the objectivity of *all* non-epistemic value judgments because he had to admit the objectivity of judgments of *prudential value*, that is, judgments about what is good or bad for a person (or judgments about what is in a person's self-interest). The reasons given then now seem to me mistaken, and in ways that bear on the argument here. Recall that Nietzsche's central objection to morality—or to what I call "morality in the pejorative sense" (hereafter MPS), to pick out that cluster of values that is the actual target of his critique—is that its cultural prevalence is inhospitable to the flourishing of the highest types of human beings, namely, creative geniuses like Goethe and Beethoven. Nietzsche argues for this conclusion on the basis of a speculative moral psychology that shows how agents who took seriously the norms of MPS would, in fact, be unable to realize the kinds of excellence we associate with geniuses like Goethe and Beethoven. If this is Nietzsche's argument, then it might seem that at the core of his critique of MPS is a judgment about *prudential* value (i.e., about what is *good* or *bad* for an agent), namely, the judgment that MPS is *bad for* certain persons because it is an obstacle to their flourishing. And if that judgment were not objectively true, then Nietzsche's critique of MPS might seem to have no force.

Commitment to the objectivity of prudential value is not, of course, an ambitious position. Railton, for example, dubs it "relationalism" (1986a) and suggests that we "think of [non-moral or prudential] goodness as akin to nutritiveness." Just as not all nutrients are good for all kinds of creatures, so too not everything is prudentially good for everyone: to use Railton's standard example, cow's milk is prudentially good for calves, but not for human babies. So, too, what is good for the herd, may be bad for the higher men, and vice versa. Many of Nietzsche's favorite Greek philosophers, the Sophists, already recognized the objectivity of judgments of relational value (Leiter 2002: 45–6), and that might also lend support to the interpretive hypothesis that Nietzsche accepts the same view. Indeed, as Railton notes, "realism with respect to non-moral [or what I am calling prudential] goodness... [is] a notion that perfect moral skeptics can admit" (1986b: 185). And Nietzsche is, indeed, a "perfect" moral skeptic, or so I shall argue, since he *clearly* holds that *moral* values (valuations of what is good or bad *simpliciter* or non-relationally) are not objective. So, for example, while the judgment MPS is bad for higher human beings might be objectively true, the judgment that MPS is disvaluable *simpliciter* or should be defeated *because* it is bad for higher human beings is not.

It now seems to me, however, that Nietzsche's position does not even require the objectivity of judgments of prudential value. It does, to be sure, have to be objectively true that MPS values prevent nascent Goethes from becoming Goethes, but that causal claim need entail no evaluative assessment about whether that is a good or bad outcome. Nietzsche presumably expects the readers "suited" to his insights to view this outcome as *bad for* Goethe, but all he needs for the force of his critique is the truth of the causal claim that MPS values have certain kinds of effects. That judgments of prudential value need not be objective is fortunate given the scope of the explanatory arguments for anti-realism about value that we now turn to consider.

3. Explanatory Arguments for Anti-Realism I: The Basic Argument

On the reading I will defend, Nietzsche is a value skeptic in the precise sense of affirming the *metaphysical* thesis that there do not exist any mind-independent or judgment-independent facts about value (I will often refer to this view as simply "skepticism about moral [or value] facts," "moral anti-realism," or "anti-realism about reasons"). From this it will, of course, follow that there is also no moral knowledge, but it is the argument for the metaphysical thesis that is crucial for Nietzsche. And Nietzsche's central argument is a version of familiar "best explanation" arguments for value anti-realism.

A word first about the idea of "inference to the best explanation." The "best" explanation of some phenomenon satisfies a variety of epistemic and pragmatic desiderata (cf. Quine and Ullian 1978), ones derived from the successful empirical sciences, which remain our paradigms of fruitful ways of explaining observable phenomena. These desiderata include: (1) simplicity (especially ontological simplicity), as opposed to *gratuitous* complexity (i.e., the gratuitous positing of entities that satisfy no other epistemic or pragmatic desiderata); (2) consilience, that is, the ability to show how seemingly disparate phenomena have common causes and thus are not really independent, but causally dependent on the same underlying facts; and (3) conservativism, that is, explaining phenomena in a way consistent with, and thus not unsettling, other beliefs about the world that have been well confirmed. This is a non-exhaustive list, to be sure, but it is on these that I will focus.

Consider an example: sitting at home, watching a movie on your computer, suddenly the computer goes off, as do all the lights in the house. What is the best explanation of this phenomenon? Here is one hypothesis: mischievous leprechauns have invaded the house, discovered the circuit breakers, and flipped them all simultaneously, cutting power to all electrical devices. This explanation does complicate our ontology: it posits leprechauns, beings who are capable of mounting mischievous attacks, for example. That would not be objectionable if, for example, there were other observable phenomena that were satisfactorily explained by such an expansion of our ontology: for example, finding little green hats in the backyard, or pots of gold at the end of rainbows, or, even better, the corpses of very small persons dressed in green. But absent that, this hypothesis would be quite radical: it would add to our ontology a class of little creatures (are they humans? they seem to have complex cooperative planning capacities!) that, heretofore, we had no reason to think existed.

Our first hypothesis, in short, is not a plausible candidate for the best explanation of the phenomenon. So let us turn to a second hypothesis: there has been an electrical power failure in the neighborhood. This hypothesis would win additional support from observable facts such as: (1) all items powered by electricity went off simultaneously; perhaps (2) lights and other electrically powered items went off in neighboring properties; and perhaps (3) there was a thunderstorm or an electrical explosion that would explain the sudden cessation of electricity to homes in the area. This explanation, assuming the observable evidence confirms it, would be simple (no new ontological entities), consilient (it would explain what happened in the house and in neighboring properties), and conservative (electricity, power outages, the role of storms in causing them, are all part of our familiar and well-established theory of how the world works).

Standard "best explanation" arguments for moral anti-realism focus on the fact of moral judgment, and claim that the best explanation of such judgments is not the objective moral features of the situation to which the judger putatively responds, but rather psychological and sociological factors that cause the agent to give expression to the particular moral judgment. In the version of this argument I have defended in earlier work (Leiter 2001), the central problem with explanations of our moral judgments that appeal to the existence of objective moral facts is that they fail to satisfy demands of consilience and simplicity. Moral explanations fail along the dimension of consilience because they posit facts—"moral" facts—that are too neatly tailored to the explanandum (they are, as I shall say, explanatorily "narrow"), and that do not effect the kind of unification of disparate phenomena we look for in successful explanations. They fail along the dimension of simplicity because they complicate our ontology without any corresponding gain in explanatory power or scope.[9] The latter claim is, of course, crucial to the anti-realist argument. For if it were true that *without* moral facts we would suffer some kind of explanatory loss, then moral explanations (and moral realism) would be in the same metaphysical boat as the postulates of any of the special sciences: physics cannot, after all, do the explanatory work of biology, which is why, by "best explanation" criteria, we can admit biological facts into our ontology.[10]

No a priori considerations can demonstrate that there will never be an explanatory loss from eliminating moral facts from our best account of the world. Two sorts of considerations, however, may make us skeptical of the realist's claim. First, outside the contemporary philosophical debate, we do not find scholars in other disciplines actually trying to do any explanatory work with moral facts. Philosophers might notice, for example, that while there are Marxist historians using broadly "economic" facts to explain historical events, there is no school of "Moral Historians" using moral facts to do any significant explanatory work. No thriving explanatory research program in any of the human sciences that I am aware of requires objective moral facts to explain observable phenomena; such explanations appear to be entirely an artifact of professional Anglophone philosophy.

A second ground for skepticism about moral explanations is more specific: namely, that the actual candidates proffered in the philosophical literature are, by and large, not

[9] Some moral realists claim that moral properties are just identical with or supervenient upon the non-moral natural properties that figure in the alternative explanations of moral judgments. But a claim of *identity or supervenience can not—in isolation—save moral realism against the explanatory argument*, for we must earn our right to such claims by both (a) vindicating the identity/supervenience thesis on non-explanatory grounds; and (b) vindicating the added theoretical complexity involved in these theses by demonstrating that they produce a gain in consilience or some cognate epistemic virtue (e.g., explanatory unification). I have argued (Leiter 2001) that they do not.

[10] More precisely, non-reductive moral realists want to defend moral explanations in a way akin to Jerry Fodor's famous defense of the autonomy of the special sciences (Fodor 1975): they want to claim that there are distinctive "groupings" and generalizations in moral explanations that can not be captured by a more "basic" explanatory scheme or science. Just as nothing in physics captures the distinctive categories and generalizations of economics and psychology, so too biology and psychology are supposed to miss the distinctive generalizations of moral theory.

very promising. Some moral explanations are just patently vacuous—think of Nicholas Sturgeon's well-known claim that if asked to *explain* Hitler's behavior, we might appeal to his moral depravity, which sounds more like a repetition of the question than an explanation—but even more ambitious moral explanations in the philosophical literature do not withstand scrutiny, as I have argued in detail elsewhere (see Leiter 2001).[11] Let us consider just two examples here.

David Brink claims that "moral explanans will generalize better than would explanans in terms of the lower-order facts that constitute these moral facts." (Brink 1989: 195). (By "moral explanans," he means using a moral category—e.g., an "unjust practice" to explain observable events, rather than simply appealing to the underlying non-moral facts picked out by the moral category [e.g., the social and economic facts about the practice deemed unjust].) Brink gives the example of explaining "political instability and social protest in [apartheid] South Africa" in terms of racial oppression (an unjust practice), rather than in terms of the particular social, economic and political conditions in *which it happens to be realized* in South Africa—since surely "there would still have been racial oppression and instability and protest under somewhat different" conditions (1989: 195). As a result, the "moral explanation"—appealing to the unjust practice of racial oppression—"will occupy a distinct and privileged explanatory role" (1989: 195).

But will it? Brink himself notes that "our interest in explanations is typically an interest in understanding past events or predicting future events" (1989: 194). During the heyday of the empiricist Covering Law Model of explanation during the 1940s and 1950s, there was supposed to be a strict symmetry between explanation and prediction, but Carl Hempel later relaxed this requirement as follows: "Any rationally acceptable answer to the question 'Why did X occur?' must offer information which shows that X was to be expected—if not definitely, as in the case of... explanation [by appeal to a covering law], then at least with reasonable probability" (1965: 369). Thus, to think we have understood the past event we must think that if we had known what we now take to explain that event we would have been able to predict its occurrence—at least with reasonable probability. We should, of course, be careful how stringent we make this demand, lest it start to label as pseudo-explanations seemingly sound and familiar explanations, like the sort found in history. Yet Brink's example cannot even satisfy a very weak requirement of predictability. Take the South Africa case: racial oppression existed *for decades* without the significant political unrest and social protest that finally marked the collapse of apartheid. So too with racial oppression in the American South, which existed for nearly a hundred years after the Civil War with only episodic and

[11] Peter Railton's work (e.g., 1986b) invokes a much richer form of historical explanation, but involves both a controversial reforming definition (itself defeasible on simplicity grounds) and a controversial set of Marxian theses about the mechanisms of historical change. But the crucial point in this context is that he does not rely on a Fodor-type strategy for defending moral realism: he thinks the reforming definitions of concepts like "moral rightness" earn their place in virtue of the fruitfulness of the theory in which they are embedded.

ineffectual resistance. From the standpoint of the historian, then, what exactly would be the "distinct and privileged explanatory role" of racial oppression? What predictions, if any, follow from knowing that a society is racially oppressive? Does it not seem, instead, that we would have to turn precisely to the particular lower-order social, economic, and political facts to really explain why social protest arose against racial oppression at the times it actually did? Indeed, we would look in vain for real historians explaining the end of American apartheid by reference to its mind-independent injustice.[12]

Brink's example faces a second, and even more important, difficulty: namely, that it seems sufficient for the explanation (such as it is) that people *believe* racial oppression to be unjust, regardless of whether it really is unjust. That is, it seems sufficient to "explain" the social protest against racial oppression in terms of the protesters' belief that racial oppression is unjust, without assuming that it really is unjust. To be entitled to the additional assumption that it really is unjust, we must know what explanatory gain is to be had by complicating our theory and ontology in this way.

Now we would have such an explanatory gain if (a) injustice produces certain regular effects (e.g., social instability, revolution, etc.) *independent* of what people believe about the justice of some socio-economic arrangement, *or* because of what people believe, where these beliefs themselves are best explained by the reality of injustice; and (b) the injustice is multiply realized in non-moral states of affairs. Both conditions are essential. Condition (a) guarantees that it is injustice itself, and not simply people's beliefs, that does the explanatory work. Condition (b) guarantees that the regularity at issue correlates with the moral fact of injustice itself, and not with some non-moral state of affairs to which injustice is (allegedly) reducible. For if injustice is multiply realized in various kinds of non-moral states of affairs, then only the fact of injustice will suffice for identifying the regularity, not the underlying social and economic facts in which injustice is realized. Of course, as in the case of water being H_2O, we might argue that even if injustice is not multiply realized, appreciating its micro-reduction base in some non-moral states of affairs permits the unification of what were thought to be disparate macro-phenomena, and thus the added theoretical and ontological complexity of the identity thesis at issue would still earn its place in our best picture of the world. But this is a fragile thesis: for this kind of reduction might be thought to eliminate, rather than vindicate, the macro-property, so everything would turn on the details of the proposed reduction.

Joshua Cohen's argument that "the injustice of slavery contributed to its demise" (1997: 94) seems to offer an account that would satisfy both (a) and (b). For Cohen

[12] In the case of the demise of segregation in America, the standard historical accounts emphasize three factors: (1) the migration of Southern blacks to the North (in the wake of the collapse of the Southern agricultural economy) which gave rise in the 1930s and 1940s to Congressional districts in which blacks had real political power; (2) the frustration of WWII black GIs who faced segregationist impediments to seizing GI Bill opportunities, and who, in conjunction with newly empowered black labor unionists, came to constitute much of the leadership of the civil rights movement at the local level; and, most importantly, (3) Cold War imperatives to do something about Jim Crow, which impeded efforts to win the hearts and minds of Africa and Asia.

explicitly rejects the view that "all that matters [in explaining the demise of slavery] ... are beliefs about injustice" rather than the injustice of slavery itself (1997: 124). For "the injustice of a social arrangement limits its viability" (1997: 93), and thus explains why such arrangements collapse or are overthrown. It is, of course, hardly controversial that slaves, like all people, have interests in "material well-being, autonomy, and dignity"—"fundamental interests" as Cohen calls them (1997: 116)—that are violated by the institution of slavery; nor should it be controversial that the fact that "slavery conflicts with the interests of slaves" contributes to "the limited viability of slavery" (1997: 94). What is crucial, as Cohen recognizes, is that the "injustice" of violating fundamental interests "conveys information relevant to explaining the demise of slavery that is not conveyed simply by noting that slavery conflicts with the interests of slaves" (1997: 94). But why think this is true? Why isn't appeal to the brute conflicts of interests—between slaves and masters—enough?

One possibility is that the moral convictions of some people (e.g., abolitionists) that slavery was unjust contributed causally to the demise of slavery *and* those moral convictions are, themselves, best explained "by the injustice of slavery" (1997: 123).[13] As Cohen writes:

> [P]art of the explanation for the moral belief [that slavery is unjust] is that slaves have interests in material well-being, autonomy, and dignity, and are recognized as having them; that slavery sharply conflicts with those interests, and is recognized as so conflicting; and that those interests are legitimate, and recognized as such. And why is this sequence of points not naturally captured by saying that people believe slavery to be unjust in part because it is unjust? (1997: 128–9)

The final and putatively rhetorical question, however, simply masks the fact that explanatory considerations are doing no work here. For even Thrasymachus and Callicles could agree that slaves have the "fundamental interests" Cohen ascribes to them, and that slavery "sharply conflicts with those interests," without agreeing that any of this has anything to do with injustice. That additional theoretical claim depends on the viability of Cohen's substantive account of justice—which, following John Rawls and T.M. Scanlon, is "based on an idealized notion of consensus—a free, reasonable, and informed agreement" (1997: 120)—that Thrasymachus and Callicles reject. We need, then, an independent argument—one having nothing to do with explanatory considerations—about why *this* is what justice *really* consists in.

What Cohen (and Brink) ultimately need to claim is that "injustice" identifies "features of the system" that "are a source of instability" (1997: 132). But they also need the claim that "injustice" is a way of classifying the causally relevant phenomena that identifies regularities we would miss if we only employed the classificatory schema of some underlying domain of facts (e.g., psycho-social facts about interests and their conflict).

[13] On this point, Cohen fudges, and says only that the moral convictions are "explained in part by the injustice of slavery" (1997: 123). But this would only suffice if it is shorthand for "the injustice of slavery is part of the *best* explanation for the moral convictions." It is not clear that this is what Cohen claims, or what he is entitled to claim.

Sustaining this latter claim would make the argument directly analogous to Jerry Fodor's famous argument (Fodor 1975) that the special sciences give us classificatory schema (and resultant causal regularities) that would be lost if we could avail ourselves only of physics. In the end, though, Cohen never gives us an argument for this claim—essentially, for (b) above. He writes, for example, that one could explain the demise of slavery,

> ...simply [by] stat[ing] the properties of slavery—the conflict between slavery and slave interests—...without taking a position on whether those properties indeed are what makes slavery unjust; in short...the fact that the properties *are* injustice-making is not itself a part of my argument. Still, they are, and can unobjectionably be presented via the moral classification. Moreover, that mode of presentation is morally important. For the world looks different if we think that injustice-making features limit the viability of systems that have them. (1997: 132)

This extraordinary passage, alas, confirms the worry that moral explanations are, as Cohen himself feared "simply collages of empirical rumination and reified hope, pasted together with rhetorical flourish" (1997: 93). For the only reason Cohen gives for employing the "moral" explanation—a classification, by the way, that is only "unobjectionable" to moral realists of the contractarian variety that Cohen favors—as distinct from the non-moral account of *the same causal features* is that when we talk the language of morality "the world looks different." That is no doubt true, but it hardly counts, on its face, as an epistemic virtue that a classificatory scheme makes things "look different." After all, someone who thought invisible spirits—angelic and diabolic—explain things that happen in the real world could claim as much: a world populated by good and evil spirits does, indeed, look different from a world divested of omnipotent, supernatural spirits.

So much by way of the first best-explanation argument for moral anti-realism.[14] Perhaps because philosophers have come to recognize that the explanatory argument for value realism is implausible, Anglophone philosophers have, more recently, taken to denying the relevance of explanatory power to value realism at all (e.g., Scanlon 2014). I will return to this topic in Chapter 4, but the shape of the dialectic should hardly be surprising to a Nietzschean: when we can no longer defend the objectivity of morality within a naturalistic worldview, we have to reject the strictures of such a view in favor of alternatives that permit our commitment to moral truths to remain firm. "Christian morality has been the Circe of all thinkers so far—they stood in her service" (EH IV:6).

[14] Late in his career, Hilary Putnam (2004) argued that attempts to show that value was "subjective" themselves depended on epistemic values, and so failed. It is, of course, true that the explanatory arguments for value anti-realism presuppose that "figuring in the best explanation of experience" is a reliable epistemic norm for identifying the objective ontology of the world, and in light of that epistemic norm, anti-realism about moral and many other kinds of value will be justified. That leaves open, of course, the status of epistemic values themselves, a topic to which we return in Chapter 4.

4. Explanatory Arguments for Value Anti-Realism II: The Explanation of Disagreement

Nietzsche, more than most philosophers, is alert to "the tremendous realm of tender value feelings and value distinctions that live, grow, reproduce, and are destroyed," which leads him to ridicule those philosophers who "wanted morality to be *grounded*" (BGE 186), which was simply "an erudite form of good faith in the dominant morality, a new way of *expressing* it" (BGE 186). Against this rationalization of local prejudice and custom—which still dominates "moral philosophy" to this day—Nietzsche complains that this kind of philosophy arises from ignorance "about peoples, ages, and histories" and a failure to "compar[e] many *different* moralities" (BGE 186). In this passage, he gestures at his primary arguments for anti-realism about morality: the best explanation for disagreement in moral experience and moral attitudes does not presuppose the existence of objective moral facts.

In his early work, Nietzsche emphasizes that moral judgment involves a kind of projective error. So, for example, in *Daybreak*, he notes that just as we now recognize that it was "an enormous error" "when man gave all things a sex" but still believed "not that he was playing, but that he had gained a profound insight," so, too, man "has ascribed to all that exists a connection with morality [*Moral*] and laid an *ethical significance* [*ethische Bedeutung*] on the world's back," which will "one day" be viewed as meaningful as talk about "the masculinity or femininity of the sun" (D 3). In *Human-All-Too-Human*, Nietzsche compares religious, moral and aesthetic judgment with astrology:

> It is probable that the objects of the religious, moral [*moralisch*] and aesthetic experiences [*Empfinden*] belong only to the surface of things, while man likes to believe that here at least he is in touch with the heart of the world [*das Herz der Welt*]; the reason he deludes himself is that these things produce in him such profound happiness and unhappiness, and thus he exhibits here the same pride as in the case of astrology. For astrology believes the heavenly stars revolve around the fate of man; the moral man [*moralische Mensch*], however, supposes that what he has essentially at heart must also constitute the essence [*Wesen*] and heart of things. (HAH 4)

Just as the astrologist thinks that there are astrological facts (about man's future) supervening on the astronomical facts about the stars—when, in fact, there are only the stars themselves, obeying their laws of motion—so too the "moral man" thinks his moral experiences are responsive to moral properties that are part of the essence of things, when, like the astrological facts, they are simply causal products of something else, namely our feelings. As Nietzsche puts it, moral judgments are "images" and "fantasies," the mere effects of psychological and physiological attributes of the people making those judgments, attributes of which they are largely unaware (D 119).

As I argued in Leiter (2015a: 120), these kinds of remarks do suggest a "best explanation" argument for anti-realism about moral value: the best explanation for our moral experiences is not that they pick out objective moral features of phenomena, but rather that they are caused by facts about our psychological make-up: for example, various feelings, such as *ressentiment* or what Sinhababu (2007) has dubbed "vengeful thinking" to describe the mechanism by which "slavish" types come to believe strength, nobility, and wealth constitute what is "evil." But the general form of explanation extends well beyond the appeal to *ressentiment* made famous in the *Genealogy*. A philosopher's morality simply bears "decisive witness to... the innermost drives of his nature" (BGE 6), meaning the latter explain the philosopher's moral commitments. More generally, "moralities are... merely a sign language of the affects" (BGE 187), a view we will return to in some detail in Chapter 3, but its import is that the affects *explain* an agent's moral judgments. Nietzsche makes the point even more explicitly in his first mature work: "Our moral judgments and evaluations are only images and fantasies based on [i.e., caused by] a physiological process unknown to us" (D 119). If the *best* explanation of our moral judgments appeals only to psychological or physiological facts about us, and need make no reference to objective moral facts, then we have reason to be skeptical about the existence of objective moral facts for the reasons given in the preceding section.

But Nietzsche mounts another kind of argument that appeals to a different kind of moral disagreement.[15] While he does, as we noted at the start of this section, chide moral philosophers for their ignorance "about peoples, ages, and histories" which results in a failure to "compar[e] many *different* moralities" (BGE 186), he also calls attention to a phenomenon that seems to me much more important, indeed, the single most important and embarrassing fact about the history of moral theorizing by philosophers over the last two millennia: namely, that after two thousand years, moral philosophers cannot agree on what we *really* ought to do![16] Perhaps many moral philosophers appear to agree that "it is wrong to break a promise," for example, but the question is: why is it wrong (and when is it permissible)? Here the philosophers disagree. Some think "the wrong-making feature of an action is that it fails to maximize utility" while others think "failing to keep a promise is an irrational act." With regard to such foundational questions, the history of moral philosophy is the history of intractable disagreement.

[15] Cf. Loeb (1998) for a contemporary version, which I will reference in what follows.

[16] Derek Parfit (2011a) is the most notable recent attempt to show otherwise, though (with the exception of Nietzsche) he really only canvasses the views of "friends of Derek," and tries to show that, in fact, they all agree. For pertinent doubts, see Schroeder (2011). Notable for our purposes is that Parfit shares Nietzsche's intuition that failure to converge on moral truths would undermine the purported objectivity of moral thought (2011b: 571), and he correctly recognizes the need to explain away his apparent disagreement with Nietzsche, "since he is the most influential and admired moral philosopher of the last two centuries" (571). His discussion of Nietzsche is problematic in several respects (see Janaway 2017 for critical discussion). More surprisingly, in discussing moral disagreement, Parfit dismisses disagreement about foundational questions out of hand, saying only that "we would expect there to be more disagreement about" this, and that it is enough that theories agree about "which acts are wrong" (2011b: 554). It is hard, though, to see how disagreement about *why* an act is wrong is not a very serious kind of *moral* disagreement, especially since such disagreements typically explain disagreements about other particular cases. See *infra* n. 24.

Is the criterion of right action the reasons for which it is performed or the set of consequences it brings about? If the former, is it a matter of the reasons being universalizable, or that they arise from respect for duty, or something else? If the latter, is it the utility it produces or the perfection it makes possible? If the former, is utility a matter of preference-satisfaction or preference-satisfaction under idealized circumstances—or is it, rather, unconnected to the preferences of agents, actual or idealized, but instead a matter of realizing the human essence or enjoying some "objective" goods? Perhaps a criterion of right action isn't even the issue, perhaps the issue is cultivating dispositions of character conducive to living a good life? Or perhaps the issue is whether *moral* reasons for keeping a promise should really outweigh egoistic or prudential reasons for doing so?[17] And here, of course, I have merely canvassed just *some* of the disagreements that plague Western academic moral theory, not even touching on non-Western traditions, or radical dissenters from the mainstream of academic moral theory, such as Nietzsche himself (though we will say more about the dissenters, below).

This persistent disagreement on foundational questions, of course, distinguishes moral theory from inquiry in the sciences and mathematics, not, perhaps, in kind, but certainly in degree. In the hard sciences and mathematics, intellectual discourse regularly transcends cultural and geographic boundaries and consensus emerges about at least *some* central propositions.[18] How to explain the failure of moral theory to achieve anything like this?

The best-explanation argument against moral realism that concerns us in this context will differ along three key dimensions from the more familiar kinds already discussed. First, what is at issue is not what we might call "raw" moral judgments—consider Gilbert Harman's famous flaming pussycat case (Harman 1977: 4–7), where someone witnesses young hoodlums dousing a cat and setting it on fire and reacts by judging the act morally wrong or reprehensible. Instead, our data points consist of philosophical theories about morality (and reasons for action more generally) that purport to explain and justify particular judgments.[19] Second, the explanatory question concerns not any particular philosophical theory, but rather the fact that there exist incompatible philosophical theories purporting to answer moral questions. And they are not simply

[17] Recall that the great English utilitarian Henry Sidgwick thought that there was an irresolvable duality of practical reason, with no decisive utilitarian argument against the egoistic view of reasons for action available.

[18] Justin Clarke-Doane has pressed on me the possibility that disagreement in mathematics is also deep and perhaps intractable; for some discussion see Clarke-Doane (2014). I am not sufficiently expert in the mathematics to properly evaluate this intriguing thesis, though it does seem in tension with all the sociological evidence about mathematics, i.e., the cross-cultural and apparently progressive convergence on a host of fundamental propositions of mathematics, including in set theory, one of Clarke-Doane's primary examples. See Jech (2002).

[19] There is another kind of fundamental disagreement about morality in particular, namely, about whether we should even aspire to such theories (think, e.g., of Philippa Foot or Bernard Williams). That is a kind of meta-foundational disagreement in my sense, since it is a disagreement about whether there exist theoretically articulable criteria for moral judgment. (Thanks to Sam Rickless for pressing me on this issue.)

incompatible philosophical theories: the disagreements of moral philosophers are amazingly intractable. Nowhere do we find lifelong Kantians suddenly (or even gradually) converting to Benthamite utilitarianism, or vice versa. So the "best explanation" argument asks: What is the best explanation for the fact that philosophical theories reach different and quite intractable conclusions? Nietzsche's skeptical answer will be that the best explanation is that the psychological needs of philosophers lead them to find compelling dialectical justifications for very different basic moral claims, and there are no objective moral facts or facts about reasons for acting to stand in the way of satisfying those psychological needs. (We will set out this position more systematically shortly.) Third, consilience and simplicity are again theoretical desiderata to be weighed in comparing explanations, but their interaction with moral realism is different: the claim at issue will be that skepticism about morality is part of a more consilient and simpler explanation for the existence of incompatible philosophical theories of morality than is the assumption that there are objective facts about fundamental moral propositions, but somehow competing philosophical theories of morality simply fail to converge upon them.

In short, what makes this explanatory argument from moral disagreement especially interesting is that, unlike most familiar varieties, it does not purport to exploit anthropological reports about the moral views of exotic cultures, or even garden-variety conflicting moral intuitions about concrete cases (such as abortion or the death penalty). Instead, Nietzsche locates disagreement at the heart of the most sophisticated moral philosophies of the West, among philosophers who very often share lots of beliefs and practices and who, especially, in the last century, often share many of the same judgments about concrete cases.[20] Yet what we find is that these philosophers remain locked in apparently intractable disagreement about the most important and fundamental issues about morality.[21]

[20] It is important to see that convergence on concrete cases (which is almost always *ceteris paribus*) does not defeat the argument. I suppose no one would think that Mussolini and Roosevelt really converge on the same moral truths just because they both agree about the concrete question that *normally* the trains *should* run on time. Moral philosophers—at least the conventional kind who subscribe to the propositions in question—are surely less far apart than Mussolini and Roosevelt, but that does not alter the fact that their *apparent* agreement on suitably general and hedged "concrete" moral propositions belies real disagreements, which come out as soon as we press on the concrete cases.

It is sometimes claimed that *all* moral philosophers agree that "Babies should not be tortured for fun," an ethical question for which, as far as I know, no one has ever sought an answer, just as no one has ever asked whether, "Monkeys ought not to talk with their mouth full at the table" or "It would be wrong for dogs to be knighted." Convergence on the answers to moral or etiquette questions no one asks may or may not be probative of anything. (Note that many moral philosophers also support the moral permissibility of late-stage abortions, even for discretionary, rather than health-related, reasons. At that point, it turns out that everything turns on what is meant by "babies," by "torture," and "for fun.") More generally, convergence, just like disagreements, demands explanation, and sometimes the best explanation of convergence will not involve realism about the underlying facts, as opposed to the influence of sociological or psychological factors.

[21] It may be useful to distinguish the argument at issue here from some related skeptical-soundi ng arguments based on the phenomenon of disagreement. One is "the so-called pessimistic induction on the

Let us now try to state this argument from disagreement for moral anti-realism more precisely.

First, if there were mind-independent moral facts, epistemically well-situated observers would probably converge upon them after two thousand years. Second, contemporary philosophers, as the beneficiaries of two thousand years of philosophy, are

history of science," as Philip Kitcher calls it (1993: 136) (or the skeptical meta-induction as Putnam earlier dubbed the same phenomenon). Here is Kitcher's statement of the skeptical position:

> Here one surveys the discarded theories of the past; points out that these were once accepted on the basis of the same kind of evidence that we now employ to support our own accepted theories, notes that those theories are, nevertheless, now regarded as false; and concludes that our own accepted theories are very probably false. (1993: 136)

This basic argumentative strategy might, indeed, seem to have some force against theories of morality. After all—so the argument would go—many earlier claims about morality were based on the same kinds of evidence about what is "intuitively obvious" that underlie contemporary Kantian and utilitarian theories. Yet we now regard intuitions about, for example, the obvious moral inferiority of certain classes of people as social or cultural or economic artifacts, not data on which we might base a moral theory. Is it not possible—especially with the often surprising results about diversity of intuitions being adduced by experimental philosophers?—that the intuitions undergirding our current moral theories will also turn out to seem equally unreliable, and so our moral theories false?

This strategy of skeptical argument is easily rebutted, however. To start, many of the racist and sexist claims of earlier moral theories were based *not* on intuitions, but on putatively empirical claims: Aristotle's views about "natural" slaves, for whom slavery was supposed to be in their non-moral interest, or Kant's disparaging remarks about Africans, depended on armchair psychological and sociological hypotheses that are not factually accurate. Indeed, the kind of response to the skeptical induction that Kitcher develops on behalf of the scientific realist would seem to help the moral realist as well. For Kitcher says that, in fact, "more and more of the posits of theoretical science endure within contemporary science" (1993: 136), and, indeed, that our earlier mistakes (which we now recognize as such) fall into a recognizable pattern, so that we can see where and why we are likely to have gone wrong in the past, and thus be more confident that we are not replicating those mistakes in our current theories.

So, too, the moral realist might claim that the mistakes made by earlier moral theorists also fall into a discernible pattern, typically consisting in failing to include within the moral community—the community of persons with moral standing—people who belonged there because of false assumptions about those persons that admit of straightforward historical, sociological, and economic explanations. Thus, on this story, what we learn from the history of failures in past moral theories is precisely that we should be especially skeptical about excluding some persons (or, not to prejudge the issue, some sentient creatures!) from the category of beings with moral standing. Of course, as everyone knows, the criteria of moral standing remain hotly contested, a fact to be exploited by the skeptical argument I will attribute to Nietzsche.

Now in the context of scientific realism, Kitcher wants to draw a stronger conclusion against the skeptic, namely, that we are actually entitled to a kind of "optimistic induction" from the fact that since every successor theory "appears closer to the truth than" the theory it displaced "from the perspective of our current theory," to the conclusion that "our theories will appear to our successors to be closer to the truth than our predecessors" (1993: 137). But the moral theorist can not avail himself of a similar "optimistic induction," and for a reason that will be important to the skeptical argument here: namely, that it is *not* the case that, for example, later *deontological* theories view earlier *utilitarian* theories as getting closer to the moral truth than their utilitarian ancestors, and vice versa.

More recently, there has been a lively debate among philosophers about the epistemological implications of disagreement among what are usually called "epistemic peers." What is standardly at issue in this literature is whether or not the fact of such disagreement should lead one to adjust the degree of credence an agent assigns to his own beliefs (see, e.g., Christensen [2007] and Kelly [2005] for contrasting views). By contrast, the skeptical argument at issue here aims for a *metaphysical* conclusion via an abductive inference: namely, that the fact of disagreement about X is *best explained* by there not being any objective fact of the matter about X. As I read it, the disagreement literature to date does not weigh the epistemic import of a successful abductive inference for this kind of skepticism.

epistemically well-situated observers. Third, contemporary philosophers have not converged upon mind-independent moral facts. Hence, from inference to the best explanation, we can conclude that there are no mind-independent moral facts.[22]

The proposed inference to the best explanation, in turn, requires the truth of four premises:

(1) Sentimentalism. Basic intuitive moral judgments (e.g., about the right-making or good-making features of situations or actions) are caused by basic emotional or affective responses.
(2) Non-cognitivism about affects. The affects involved in basic intuitive moral judgments have no cognitive component: they have no cognitively evaluable belief component, but rather a distinctive phenomenal feel.
(3) Philosophical arguments for what we morally ought to do (for moral facts) always involve a premise that depends on a basic intuitive moral judgment.
(4) Philosophers have not converged on our real reasons for acting.

Chapter 3 will set out arguments for the first and second premises. The fourth premise has been defended already. The third premise makes a claim about the logical structure of arguments for what we morally ought to do that seems hard to dispute: such arguments depend on a premise that appeals to what is supposed to be intuitively plausible. Now the "Kantian" loosely construed—that is, someone who thinks rational action itself, either as a matter of logic (e.g., arguably Kant or Alan Gewirth) or its constitutive character (e.g., Christine Korsgaard or David Velleman), supplies the crucial normative premise—will deny that intuition is at issue, as opposed to the demands of rationality or action. I shall simply record my view that these arguments are implausible, so much so

[22] This argument, of course, makes two key assumptions about epistemic access and epistemic capacities: first, it assumes that *if* there were objective facts about what we morally ought to do, such facts would be knowable in principle by epistemically well-situated agents; and second, it assumes that two thousand years of moral philosophy should have rendered us epistemically well-situated observers (if it has not, why not?).

An easy way for the moral realist to defeat the argument is to deny one or both of the epistemic assumptions. There are, of course, serious costs to doing so. If one denies the first assumption, and allows that objective moral facts can be wholly evidence-transcendent, even under ideal conditions, then one has to admit that we can never really know if we have made a genuine mistake about what we ought to do. One need not agree with Marx's Second Thesis on Feuerbach ("The dispute over the reality or non-reality of thinking which is isolated from practice is a purely scholastic question") to nonetheless agree that it is a high cost for the realist to allow that there are practical truths, but, alas, they remain beyond our ken.

If the realist denies the second assumption, then the realist must consign to irrelevance some (or perhaps all) of two thousand years of moral philosophy as epistemically inadequate to what we morally ought to do. But what could justify doing so? Is there some other method for discovering mind-independent moral facts? Holy texts, divine revelations, the words of prophets, the advice of poets appear to be as deeply in conflict as the views of moral philosophers, but even if they were not, there is so much other evidence that these sources are epistemically unreliable that they seem poor contenders as alternatives. If that is right, then this second realist response appears simply ad hoc.

With respect to the possible realist repudiation of the first assumption, we may also ask: what could justify it, beyond the desire to salvage moral realism? Put differently, we may ask whether there is an inference to the best explanation of intractable disagreement among moral philosophers that would include as a premise the existence of evidence-transcendent moral truths?

that Gewirth's has no defenders anymore, and Korsgaard's and Velleman's constitutivism will, one hopes, go the same way (see Enoch 2006). With apologies to members of this particular Kantian sect, I will say nothing further about these views.

Since philosophers develop arguments that depend on key intuitive premises, that are non-cognitive, but explicable in terms of facts about the psychology and sociology of those who make the judgments, it should hardly be surprising that their philosophical systems are locked in intractable conflict, since their arguments depend, both logically and causally, on views that are psycho-social artifacts that vary with person, time, and place. Bentham thinks it intuitively obvious that the experience of pain is the most morally salient fact; Kant (on certain readings) thinks it intuitively obvious that the motive for action is the most morally salient fact. What would an argument for either premise look like that did not already presuppose the intuition? In short, given these premises, the best explanation for the views philosophers defend are the psychological and sociological facts that explain their basic affects; mind-independent facts about our moral reasons for action are explanatorily otiose, i.e., we do not need them for the most simple and consilient explanation of the phenomenon.

5. Nietzsche on Disagreement

Let us now look at Nietzsche's version of the argument. The following passage is a natural place to start:

> It is a very remarkable moment: the Sophists verge upon the first *critique of morality* [*Moral*], the first *insight* into morality:—they juxtapose the multiplicity (the geographical relativity) of the moral value judgments [*Moralischen Werthurtheile*];—they let it be known that every morality [*Moral*] can be dialectically justified; i.e., they divine that all attempts to give reasons for morality [*Moral*] are necessarily *sophistical*—a proposition later proved on the grand scale by the ancient philosophers, from Plato onwards (down to Kant); —they postulate the first truth that a "morality-in-itself" [*eine Moral an sich*], a "good-in-itself" do not exist, that it is a swindle to talk of "truth" in this field. (WP :428; KSA 13:14[116])

This is a *Nachlass*[23] passage, but it has many analogues in the published corpus and is of a piece with a general picture Nietzsche has of the discursive pretensions of philosophers. Consider his derisive comment in *Beyond Good and Evil* about Kant's moral philosophy, which he describes as "[t]he... stiff and decorous Tartuffery of the old Kant, as he lures us on the dialectical bypaths that lead to his 'categorical imperative'—really lead astray and seduce" (BGE: 5). Kant's "Tartuffery" and Spinoza's "hocus-pocus of mathematical form" in his *Ethics* are simply, Nietzsche says, "the

[23] For those who are not Nietzsche scholars, the *Nachlass* refers to the voluminous notebook material that Nietzsche did not publish during his lifetime; much of it was plainly material he rejected, since he produced his books for publication by culling other material from these same notebooks. Some of that material was published after his death under the title *The Will to Power*, a project Nietzsche at one time entertained completing, and then abandoned.

subtle tricks [*feinen Tücken*] of old moralists and preachers of morals [*Moralisten und Moralprediger*]." As Nietzsche explains it:

> They all pose as if they had discovered and reached their real opinions through the self-development of a cold, pure, divinely unconcerned dialectic... while at bottom it is an assumption, a hunch, a kind of "inspiration"—most often a desire of the heart that has been filtered and made abstract—that they defend with reasons sought after the fact. They are all advocates who don't want to be called by that name, and for the most part even wily spokesman for their prejudices which they baptize "truths." (BGE 5)

Later in the same book, Nietzsche notes that moral philosophers "make one laugh" with their idea of "morality as science," their pursuit of "a rational foundation for morality," which "seen clearly in the light of day" is really only a "scholarly form of good *faith* in the dominant morality, a new way of *expressing* it." Pointing at Schopenhauer's attempt to supply a rational foundation for morality, Nietzsche says "we can draw our conclusions as to how scientific a 'science' could be when its ultimate masters still talk like children" (BGE 186). The real significance of the claims of moral philosophers is "what they tell us about those who make them" for they are "a sign-language of the affects" (BGE 187), betraying things about the psychological needs and condition of those who make them.[24]

How do these considerations, elliptical as some of them are, support a skeptical conclusion about the objective existence of moral facts or properties? Recall the passage with which we began this section: Nietzsche claims that the key insight of the Sophists into morality was that "every morality [*Moral*] can be dialectically justified; i.e., they divine that all attempts to give reasons for morality [*Moral*] are necessarily *sophistical*—a proposition later proved on the grand scale by the ancient philosophers, from Plato onwards (down to Kant)" (WP 428). The Sophists, on this account, advance two closely related claims: (1) that "every morality can be dialectically justified" and; (2) that "all attempts to give reasons for morality are necessarily *sophistical*," where "sophistical" is obviously meant to have the pejorative connotation that the *apparent* dialectical justification does not, in fact, secure the truth of the moral propositions so justified. The purported dialectical justification can fail in this way if either it is not a valid argument or some of the premises are false.[25] But, then, what is the force of the claim that "every morality can be dialectically justified"? It must obviously be that every morality can have the *appearance* of being dialectically justified, either because its logical invalidity is not apparent or, more likely in this instance, because its premises, while apparently acceptable, are not true.

[24] In fact, Nietzsche thinks this last point applies quite generally, not only to moral philosophers. He frequently describes (see, e.g., D I or GS 335) moral judgments as caused by certain *feelings*, learned through a combination of customary practices and parental influence, while the moral concepts and reasons people offer for these judgments are merely post-hoc (cf. D 34). I will return to this topic in detail in Chapter 3.

[25] Whether or not Nietzsche is thinking of this issue in Aristotelian terms is not clear, though it might seem the natural candidate point of reference for a classicist like Nietzsche, but I have found, in any case, the discussion in Smith (2007) helpful in framing the possibilities at issue.

Yet Nietzsche goes further when he asserts that the second claim—namely, that "all attempts to give reasons for morality are necessarily *sophistical*"—is established ("proved" [*beweisen*] he says) by the work of the philosophers from Plato through to Kant (though he would presumably add, as other passages make clear, Schopenhauer to the list of evidence). But in what sense do the moral philosophies of Plato, Aristotle, the Stoics, Hutcheson, Mill, Kant, and Schopenhauer et al. establish or "prove" that "all attempts to give reasons for morality are necessarily *sophistical*"? Nietzsche's thought must be that all these philosophers appear to provide "dialectical justifications" for moral propositions, but that all these justifications actually fail. But that still does not answer the question of how the *fact* of there being all these different moral philosophies *proves* that they are sophistical, i.e., that they do not, in fact, justify certain fundamental moral propositions?

The best explanation argument supporting moral anti-realism laid out at the end of the last section would supply Nietzsche an answer. Philosophers, even after two thousand years, fail to converge on the moral facts because the diverse psychological needs of persons (including philosophers) mean different philosophers find different intuitive premises in moral arguments plausible (since all such judgments about plausible moral premises are the causal product of affective responses, that vary with psychological constitution). That is the best explanation of the intractable philosophical disagreement we find, and it is an explanation in which the idea of un-cognized objective moral facts is explanatorily irrelevant.[26]

[26] Huddleston (2014: 329) points to one passage that seems in tension with the line of argument I have reconstructed here. He writes:

> In Book V of *The Gay Science*, Nietzsche derides as "childish" the argument made by those who "see the truth that among different nations moral valuations are *necessarily* different and then infer from this that *no* morality is at all binding [*einen Schluss auf Unverbindlichkeit aller Moral machen*]" (GS 345)

The actual meaning of the mistaken inference being criticized by Nietzsche is a bit more complex than this gloss on the passage suggests, however. First, the argument criticized in GS 345 is different than the argument at stake in WP 428 as I reconstruct it: for GS 345 involves appeal to differences in ordinary moral opinions "among different nations," while the whole interest of the WP 428 argument is that it depends on "expert" disagreement, that is, foundational disagreement about morality among major philosophers across the ages. Someone who thought the WP 428 abductive argument for moral skepticism was correct could agree that moral differences "among different nations" is poor evidence for moral skepticism.

Second, and more importantly, the context of this passage suggests that its subject is not the same as the subject of WP 428, namely, whether it is a "swindle to talk of 'truth'" when it comes to morality. The topic of GS 345 is the failure of most thinkers to really consider the problem of the *value* of morality. Nietzsche gives several examples of the failure to engage with this problem. One is to draw inferences about whether a morality is or is not "binding" from the fact that there is "some consensus of the nations, at least of tame nations, concerning certain principles of morals" (which is taken as evidence that "these principles must be unconditionally binding also for you and me") or the converse inference, already quoted. But a more "refined" mistake is to commit the genetic fallacy, to fail to realize that, "Even if a morality has grown out of an error, the realization of this fact would not as much as touch the problem of its value" (GS 345). I take it, then, that whether or not a morality ought to be treated as binding is the same as the "problem of its value," not the problem of its truth. It is clearly compatible with my reconstruction of the WP 428 argument that anti-realism about moral value has no bearing on the question which moralities are valuable. Only on the un-Nietzschean assumption that a true morality is necessarily valuable (an assumption Nietzsche obviously rejects), or the question-begging assumption that a morality Nietzsche judges to be valuable is therefore true, would we be able to assimilate the concern of GS 345 to that of WP 428 and the skeptical argument from disagreement defended in the text.

The alternative, "moral realist" explanation for the data—the data being the existence of intractable disagreement between incompatible philosophical theories about morality—is both less simple and less consilient. First, of course, it posits the existence of moral facts which, according to the more familiar best-explanation argument discussed earlier, are not part of the best explanation of other phenomena. Second, the moral realist must suppose that this class of explanatorily narrow *moral facts* are undetected by large numbers of philosophers who are otherwise deemed to be rational and epistemically informed. Third, the moral realist must explain why there is a failure of convergence among epistemically well-situated philosophers who are the beneficiaries of two thousand years of inquiry. We can agree with Peter Railton that we lack "canons of induction so powerful that experience would, in the limit, produce convergence on matters of fact among all epistemic agents, no matter what their starting points" (1986a: 6), and still note that there exists a remarkable cross-cultural consensus among theorists about fundamental physical laws, principles of chemistry, and biological explanations, as well as mathematical truths, while moral philosophers, to this very day, find no common ground on foundational principles even within the West, let alone cross-culturally. How can a moral realist explain this? Let us consider, now, some possibilities.

6. Objections to the Explanatory Arguments for Value Anti-Realism

Moral realists have developed a variety of "defusing explanations" (Doris and Plakias 2007: 311, 320–1; cf. Loeb 1998 for a useful survey and rebuttal of various strategies) to block the abductive inference from apparently intractable moral disagreement to skepticism about moral facts. Moral disagreement is, after all, an epistemic phenomenon, from which we propose to draw a metaphysical conclusion. The "defusing" explanations of moral disagreement propose to exploit that fact, by suggesting alternate epistemic explanations for the disagreement, explanations that are compatible with the existence of objective moral facts. We may summarize the "defusing" objections to the skeptical argument as follows: (1) moral disagreements about *concrete* cases are not really intractable, they merely reflect factual disagreements or ignorance, and thus belie agreement on *basic* moral principles; (2) even if moral disagreements *are* about basic moral principles, they are not really *intractable* but rather resolvable in principle; (3) even if there are real and intractable moral disagreements about foundational moral principles, these are best explained by cognitive defects or the fact that they occur under conditions that are not epistemically ideal: e.g., conditions of informational ignorance, irrationality or partiality; and (4) even if there are real and intractable moral disagreements about foundational moral principles that cannot be chalked up to cognitive defects or non-ideal epistemic conditions, they are still best explained in terms of differences in "background theory." Let us consider these in turn.

(1) Moral disagreements about concrete cases are not really intractable, they merely reflect factual disagreements or ignorance, and thus belie agreement on basic moral principles. Although this was an important worry in, for example, the responses of Boyd (1988) and Brink (1989) to Mackie's original version (1977) of the argument from moral disagreement, it is obviously irrelevant to Nietzsche's version of the argument for moral anti-realism, which appeals precisely to disagreement about foundational moral principles, as exemplified, for example, by the dispute between Kantians and utilitarians, among many others. So we may set this earlier defusing explanation to one side.

(2) Even if moral disagreements are about basic moral principles, they are not really intractable but rather are resolvable in principle. This has been the standard optimistic refrain from philosophers ever since "moral realism" was revived as a serious philosophical position in Anglophone philosophy in the 1980s. With respect to very particularized moral disagreements—e.g., about questions of economic or social policy—which often trade on obvious factual ignorance or disagreement about complicated empirical questions, this seems a plausible retort. But for over two hundred years, Kantians and utilitarians have been developing increasingly systematic versions of their respective positions. The Aristotelian tradition in moral philosophy has an even longer history. Utilitarians have become particularly adept at explaining how they can accommodate Kantian and Aristotelian intuitions about particular cases and issues, though in ways that are usually found to be systematically unpersuasive to the competing traditions and which, in any case, do nothing to dissolve the disagreement about the underlying moral criteria and categories. Philosophers in each tradition increasingly talk only to each other, without even trying to convince those in the other traditions.[27] And while there may well be "progress" within traditions—e.g., most utilitarians regard Mill as an improvement on Bentham—there does not appear to be any progress in moral theory, in the sense of a consensus that particular fundamental theories of right action and the good life are deemed better than their predecessors. What we find now are simply the competing traditions—Kantian, Humean, Millian, Aristotelian, Thomist, perhaps now even Nietzschean—which often view their competitors as unintelligible or morally obtuse, but don't have any actual arguments against the foundational principles of their competitors. There is, in short, no sign—I can think of *none*—that we are heading towards any epistemic *rapprochement* between these competing moral traditions. So why exactly are we supposed to be optimistic?

As grounds for optimism, many philosophers appeal to the thought (due to Derek Parfit) that secular "moral theory" is a young field, so of course it has not made much progress. This strikes me as implausible for several reasons. First, most fields with factual subject matters have usually managed to make progress, as measured by convergence among researchers, over the course of a century—and especially the last century, with the rise of research universities. Moral theory is, again, the odd man out, when

[27] Parfit is the lone, and unsuccessful, exception.

compared to physics, chemistry, biology, or mathematics. Even psychology, the most epistemically robust of the "human" sciences, managed to make progress: e.g., the repudiation of behaviorism, and the cognitive turn in psychology in just the last fifty years. Second, Spinoza, Hume, Mill, and Sidgwick (among many others) may not have advertised their secularism, but the idea that their moral theories are for that reason discontinuous with the work of the past hundred years does obvious intellectual violence to the chains of influence of ideas and arguments. Third, and relatedly, so-called "secular" moral theory regularly conceives itself in relation to a history that stretches back in time (sometimes back to the Greeks)—contrast that with the relative youth of modern physics!—so that it becomes unclear why the bogeyman of the deity was supposed to have constituted the insuperable obstacle weighing down intellectual progress. Most contemporary deontologists may be atheists, for example, but it is not obvious that their atheism enabled them to make stunning intellectual progress beyond Kant.[28]

If there is a reason for optimism, it will have to be sought in the next argument.

(3) Even if there are real and intractable moral disagreements about foundational moral principles, these are best explained by cognitive defects or the fact that they occur under conditions that are not epistemically ideal: e.g., conditions of informational ignorance, irrationality or partiality. This is, again, a familiar move in the metaethical literature responding to the argument from moral disagreement, but one must appreciate how strange it is in response to the Nietzschean argument appealing to disagreement among moral philosophers across millennia. Are we really to believe that hyper-rational and reflective moral philosophers, whose lives, in most cases, are devoted to systematic reflection on philosophical questions, many of whom (historically) were independently wealthy (or indifferent to material success) and so immune to crass considerations of livelihood and material self-interest, and most of whom, in the modern era, spend professional careers refining their positions, and have been doing so as a professional class in university settings for well over a century—are we really supposed to believe that they have reached no substantial agreement on any basic moral principles because of ignorance, irrationality, or partiality?[29]

Ignorance seems especially easy to dismiss as a relevant consideration. As Don Loeb puts the point: "It seems very unlikely that the continued existence of [the] debate

[28] Alastair Norcross suggests to me that the real problem is that ethics requires reliance on "intuitions," and our intuitions are still strongly tainted by our religious traditions. That seems a more plausible point, though it is unclear what criteria we are going to appeal to in order to sort the "tainted" from "untainted" intuitions. As Nietzsche would be the first to point out, the utilitarian obsession with sentience and suffering is, itself, indebted to Christianity—an ironic fact, given the centrality of the wrongness of suffering to Parfit's own moral philosophy (e.g., 2011b: 565 ff.).

[29] The irony here is that Nietzsche himself does deny that philosophers, at least great ones, are impartial—as he puts it, they are "all advocates who don't want to be called by that name" and "wily spokesman for their prejudices which they baptize 'truths'" (BGE 5). If moral philosophers were to cede this point to Nietzsche, then, of course, they would have forfeited their claim to justified moral knowledge.

[between Kantians and utilitarians] hinges upon disagreement over the non-moral facts" (1998: 290). What non-moral facts exactly bear on the question, for example, whether respect for the dignity of persons or maximization of utility is the criterion of rightness?

Nietzsche, in fact, presents a fine armchair test case for any thesis about moral disagreement, since he so clearly repudiates "the egalitarian premise of all contemporary moral and political theory—the premise, in one form or another, of the equal worth and dignity of each person" (Leiter 2002: 290). For Nietzsche is not only quite prepared, like any consequentialist, to sacrifice the well-being of some for others; he often seems ready to sacrifice the well-being of *the majority* for the sake of the flourishing of his favored examples of human excellence like Goethe (Leiter 2002: 113–36)—a view, that is, I presume, uncongenial to the vast majority of academic moral theorists. Here, then, is a stark philosophical challenge for moral realists: "defuse" Nietzsche's disagreement by reference to a cognitive defect of some kind: e.g., a failure to appreciate non-moral facts or norms of rationality.[30] This is, of course, just a version of Hume's famous challenge to explain the offense to reason in preferring the destruction of the world to a thumb prick, though in Nietzsche's case the options are more troubling because of the greater resonance they are likely to have to cosmopolitan moral philosophers: after all, if it were really true, as Nietzsche believes, that a culture suffused with moral norms of equality would prevent the developments of Goethes and Beethovens, how exactly is it irrational to prefer an inegalitarian culture that makes human excellence possible?[31]

But we may put Nietzsche to one side. Obviously, the standard-issue academic Anglophone philosopher thinks it intuitively obvious that "suffering is bad" or that "humans are possessed of dignity which precludes harming them" or some other familiar formulation. Someone part of the Homeric world—or maybe, in recent years, the Mafia?—would find these purportedly intuitively obvious claims bizarre. Suffering is essential to glory and honor, it is not objectionable but welcome.[32] Loyalty and the ability to exact revenge are far more important than suffering, and individuals can be harmed when honor, glory, or revenge demands it. It is not simply that all of human history reveals the powerful role of this competing set of norms, but that there is no refutation of commitment to them that does not presuppose a premise involving a

[30] I realize that "Kantians" from Kant to Gewirth to Korsgaard purport to have arguments showing such positions to be irrational, but the voluminous literature attacking their positions, perhaps, encourages the skeptical thought that something has gone awry.

[31] One might observe, of course, that most philosophers do accept the egalitarian premise, but they interpret it in ways that yield very divergent conclusions. And even the fact that they converge on this point admits of anti-realist explanations, as I argue in Leiter (2013b).

[32] Someone might object that even those committed to the view that suffering is bad and that inflicting suffering is wrong can allow that those are defeasible normative considerations, and so in fact the Homeric hero is not disagreeing. That could be true if there were evidence that the Homeric hero's "practical reasoning" worked this way: but, first, Homeric heroes don't engage in much practical reasoning (at least not as Homer presents them), and second, there is no indication that Homeric heroes are committed to the wrongness of suffering being a normative consideration that needs to be defeated.

different "intuitive" affective commitment. These norms can be coherently formulated and applied and they play, as much as we observers might regret it, an enormous role in human affairs.

Most academics have a profound affective identification with the intuitions at the foundation of both the Kantian and utilitarian traditions (I find myself moved by some aspects of both, but given the triumph of the "slave revolt in morality" as Nietzsche calls it, that should be expected).[33] Glory, honor, revenge, and loyalty lack academic defenders, but that is not to be regretted, since those normative ideals thrive and structure lives without academic philosophers writing in support. But calling attention to them indicates the diversity of views about what we really ought to do that have gripped human minds.[34]

To be sure, the moral realist might retort that the appeal of glory or revenge as a reason for acting is vulnerable to being explained away, perhaps along precisely the lines the realist David Enoch has proposed:

> Many moral matters are complex, and not at all straightforward; people are the victims of any number of cognitive shortcomings... and so that some may be more likely to make moral mistakes than others; many find it hard—or do not want—to sympathize and imagine what it is like to occupy a different position in the relevant interaction, and different people are sensitive to the feelings of others to different degrees; we let our interests influence our beliefs (moral and otherwise); we are subject to the manipulation of others, and so to the distorting effects also of their self-interests.... (Enoch 2009: 25–6)

Remember the question is what we *really* ought to do, and "moral" reasons for action as conceived within a particular parochial tradition might well yield to other considerations, as Sidgwick, Foot, and Williams recognized (albeit in different ways). But to evaluate Enoch's alternative explanation, let us take as an example Odysseus, who is celebrated by Homer for his talents at deception and his capacity to exact revenge. Odysseus, recall, returns after his long journey to find suitors in his home trying to seduce his faithful wife Penelope. Disguised as a beggar, Odysseus is the only one strong enough to string his old bow (the challenge put to the suitors by Penelope), at which point he slaughters the other suitors in revenge.

Has Odysseus made a mistake about what he really ought to do? Did he fail to "sympathize and imagine what it is like to occupy a different position in the interaction"? Let us grant that this is, in fact, a legitimate demand on his practical reasoning, though it looks dangerously close to assuming, without argument, that possibly self-regarding reasons (like honor) are out of bounds. But it is easy enough to imagine that Odysseus would reason in a loosely "Kantian" fashion as follows: "Were I to be found out trying

[33] I put to one side Aristotle and the neo-Aristotelians with their fanciful assumptions about what it means to be human: they have the distinct advantage of not regarding empirical evidence from the natural and human sciences of what humans are actually like as having any bearing on their ideas.

[34] For more recent empirical evidence of the remarkable cultural and economic diversity of ordinary moral opinion, see Awad et al. (2018).

to seduce another man's wife during his absence, he would be right to slaughter me." Was Odysseus insufficiently "sensitive to the feelings of others"? Again, let us grant that this consideration is even relevant to what he really ought to do. Has he really failed to be "sensitive to the feelings of others"? The feelings of others are, presumably on any view about how we ought to act, a defeasible consideration: it no doubt hurt Donald Trump's feelings that residents of London flew a giant balloon of a "Baby Donald" over the city during his recent visit to the country, yet his feelings were not a serious reason for the protesters not to do that. Even if Odysseus does not give much weight at all to the no-doubt strong preference of the suitors not to be slaughtered, this does not mean he gave it no weight: Odysseus surely knows his suitors would prefer not to be victims of his revenge. Yet he could reason, without error, as follows: "to try to marry a man's faithful wife while he is away engaged in an arduous life-and-death struggle for a worthy cause is an offense to honor and decency, and anyone who embarks on such a path has forfeited his claim to have his wish to live respected."

Of course, that reasoning would be in error *if* one granted a premise like "inflicting death on others for the sake of revenge is always wrong" or, alternatively, "inflicting death on others to avenge their wrongful actions is always wrong." But Odysseus accepts neither premise, not because either is false, but because the psychology and sociology of his own upbringing leaves him with no affective inclination toward accepting these premises such that they should influence his practical reasoning.[35] Odysseus disagrees with these reasons for acting that seem decisive to we moderns because his psychology and sociology are different, not because there is an objective reason for him not to slaughter the suitors of Penelope—or, for that matter, an objective reason for him to slaughter them.

A realist might protest that the *best* explanation of why we judge Odysseus mistaken about the moral facts of the situation is precisely that we are sensitive to the infliction of death on sentient beings for trivial reasons, and that any action with that attribute is a token instance of "moral wrongness": yes, we were brought up to be sensitive to that, but in being so raised, we were raised to be sensitive to actual moral wrongdoing! Now in order not to beg the question we have to ask whether the thesis that "moral wrongdoing" is identical with or supervenient upon, among other things, inflicting death on sentient beings for revenge, would be part of the best explanation of the Odysseus/contemporary dispute? The anti-realist explanation, recall, appeals to psychological and sociological facts, and their historical, cultural, and temporal variation; the realist explanation presumably does not deny any of those facts *but then adds a further fact*, namely, that killing for revenge is a case of objective moral wrongness. Does that additional metaphysical thesis, which certainly makes our ontology less simple, make the explanation more consilient? *What else does it help us explain*? I have already

[35] As noted, above *supra* n. 32, I do not think Odysseus actually engages in "practical reasoning," rather than acting instinctively. But this is a separate issue: for skepticism about the efficacy of practical reason, see Chapter 5.

argued both earlier in this chapter and elsewhere (Leiter 2001) that such an assumption has no consilience benefits at all. Is it a methodologically conservative assumption? It would be if our best-going theory of the world already required that there be objective moral facts, but I have already argued at length against that assumption. The moral realism add-on to the explanation is explanatorily otiose.

Yet surely it is possible that some heretofore unrecognized cognitive deficiencies of academic moral philosophy of the past 250 years explain the failure of even a modicum of consensus on foundational moral principles to emerge. Indeed, perhaps the lack of progress in moral philosophy is proof precisely of the epistemically defective condition of the discourse to date![36] Nothing in the argument so far rules out that possibility, but why in the world suppose this is the correct explanation for the state of affairs we find? Certainly no moral philosophers of the past two centuries would want to admit to such cognitive frailties, nor is it the case that we have any non-question-begging account of what exactly those deficiencies might have been. As between the two explanatory hypotheses—one based on skepticism about objective moral facts and reasons and one based on its denial—there is surely an enormous burden of proof for the proponent of the latter to explain the nature and character of the epistemic failings that have blocked access to the moral facts.

(4) Even if there are real and intractable moral disagreements about foundational moral principles that can not be chalked up to cognitive defects or non-ideal epistemic conditions, they are still best explained in terms of differences in "background theory." This "defusing explanation" was developed originally against arguments from moral disagreement appealing to very particular moral judgments. Against the familiar fact that people's moral intuitions about particular problems are often quite different, it is easy to reply, as Loeb puts it, that since "*all* observation is theory laden . . . theoretical considerations will play a role in moral observations, just as they do in any others," and thus "differences of belief among moral reasoners should be expected because the same information will be observed differently depending on what background theories are present" (1998: 288).

The skeptical argument from moral disagreement among systematic moral philosophies, as Loeb himself discusses, presents two discrete challenges to this defusing explanation. First, it is quite possible for Kantians and utilitarians to agree about the right action in particular cases, while disagreeing about the reasons the action is right, reflecting their disagreement about fundamental moral facts. In these cases, the disagreement we are trying to explain is *precisely* the disagreement in the "background theory," and it is the surprising resilience of such disagreements, so the skeptic argues,

[36] David Enoch suggests to me (personal communication) that perhaps philosophical tools are not the right way of achieving knowledge of moral truths. The alternatives—e.g., reading the Bible or intuition—are notoriously unreliable epistemic methods, however, that generate even more disagreement than the traditional discursive methods of philosophy. In any case, Parfittian optimism about secular, rational moral philosophy has been the default position for philosophers, which is why it is important to make it the target here.

that calls out for skepticism about moral facts. Second, where the disagreement about particular cases stems from differing background theories that hardly defuses an argument from skepticism appealing to intractable differences about background theories. As Doris and Plakias remark, in considering a more extreme case: "if our disagreement with the Nazis about the merits of genocide is a function of a disagreement about the plausibility of constructing our world in terms of pan-Aryan destiny, does it look more superficial for that?" (2007: 321). Of course, in the Nazi case, we might think the Nazi background theory vulnerable on other grounds (e.g., of factual error or partiality), but, as we have already noted, it is not at all obvious how a disagreement informed by differing moral theories—say, Kantian and utilitarian—is in any way defused by noting that the disputants disagree not only about the particular case, but about the foundational moral propositions which bear on the evaluation of the case.[37]

7. Has the Argument Proved Too Much?

I want to conclude the objections to the anti-realist argument from disagreement by considering three final worries: one *interpretive*—about saddling Nietzsche with the kind of moral skepticism at issue here—and two *philosophical*, pertaining to whether the argument sketched above has proved too much and, relatedly, whether it is self-referentially defeating. I will respond to the latter philosophical objections from a Nietzschean point of view as well.

On the interpretive question, it seems to me that nothing has misled readers more often about Nietzsche's metaethical view than the volume of his rhetoric: he writes (so the argument goes) *as if* there really is a fact of the matter about his judgments about the value of human greatness and the disvalue of Christianity and the herd and the rabble. In fact, however, Nietzsche's notorious rhetorical excesses make even more sense on the anti-realist picture. For if Nietzsche is a moral anti-realist committed to the polemical project of disabusing certain readers of their "false consciousness" about morality—their false belief that it is good *for them*—then he has every reason to use all available rhetorical devices—some rational and some non-rational—to achieve that end.[38] Indeed, recognizing that ours is a world without any objective moral facts, Nietzsche has a special reason to write most of the time *as if* his own (subjective)

[37] A more promising suggestion would be to appeal to differing background theories of rationality. This raises several issues, however. First, it is unlikely that such disagreements suffice to defuse all moral disagreements (not all utilitarians, for example, are committed only to instrumental theories of rationality). Second, one can worry that in some cases the disagreements about rationality really constitute part of the foundational moral disagreement, rather than standing apart from it as a free-standing bit of the background theory—that certainly seems to be Nietzsche's view of Kant's talk of "practical reason," for example.

[38] This is not inconsistent with the empirical finding that "high cognition" individuals find cognitive rather than emotional appeals more persuasive *when it comes to factual claims that are either true or false* (Haddock et al. 2008); but as we will see in Chapter 3, allegiance to morality is affective, not cognitive, and with respect to these affective attachment, while there can be room for appeals to "cognition" or factual claims, affective rhetoric is also crucial. (Thanks to Manuel Vargas for raising this issue with me.)

judgments of value were something other than matters of evaluative taste: for if they can claim a kind of epistemic and practical authority to which they are not really entitled, then they are more likely to influence belief and action, at least among readers who view truth as practically important (as Nietzsche supposes all his readers will: see GM III). Yet Nietzsche himself sometimes does admit the "terrible truth" about the subjective character of his evaluative judgments—as when he says that, "What is now decisive against Christianity is our taste [*Geschmack*], no longer our reasons" (GS 132) and when he describes the "revaluation of Christian values" as an "attempt, undertaken with every means" to bring "the *counter*-values [*die Gegen-Werte*]...to victory" (A 61)—not the "true" values or the "objectively correct" ones, but simply the *opposite* ones, the ones that appeal to a very different taste.

That brings us to the final philosophical objections to the line of skeptical argument explored here. The first is an objection that, no doubt, has already occurred to all readers who have gotten this far. Is not the apparently intractable disagreement among moral philosophers regarding foundational questions mirrored in many other parts of philosophy? Are not metaphysicians and epistemologists also locked in intractable disagreements of their own? Think of debates between internalists and externalists in epistemology, or between presentists and four-dimensionalists in the philosophy of time. If disagreement among moral philosophers supports an abductive inference to denying the existence of moral facts, what, if anything, blocks that inference in all these other cases?

Some recent writers (such as Bloomfield [2004] and Shafer-Landau [2005]) think this kind of "companions in guilt" consideration counts in favor of moral realism, notwithstanding the disagreement among moral philosophers. It is not entirely clear why they rule out, however, the other quite natural conclusion. Nietzsche, as far as I can see, has no reason to resist it, since he believes that, as an explanatory matter, the moral commitments of the philosopher—at least the great philosopher—are primary when it comes to his metaphysics and epistemology. Nietzsche writes:

> I have gradually come to realize what every great philosophy so far has been: namely the personal confession of its author and a kind of involuntary and unconscious memoir; in short, that the moral (or immoral) intentions in every philosophy constitute the true living seed from which the whole plant has always grown. In fact, to explain how the strangest metaphysical claims of a philosopher really come about, it is always good (and wise) to begin by asking: at what morality does it (does *he*—) aim? (BGE 6)[39]

[39] Nietzsche's thesis was explicitly about the "great philosophers"—like Kant and Spinoza—and not those "philosophical laborers" and "scholars" who possess "some small, independent clockwork that, once well wound, works on vigorously *without* any essential participation from all the other drives of the scholar" (BGE 6). Many professional philosophers may, indeed, be laboring away at problems in a "disinterested" way. Still, as the recent survey by David Bourget and David Chalmers (see http://philpapers.org/surveys/results.pl) brought out, there are striking, and surely not accidental, correlations between philosophical views across different areas: e.g., theism and moral realism and libertarianism about free will. Even the "philosophical laborers" are not wholly disinterested inquirers!

Since, for Nietzsche, the "morality" at which the philosopher aims is to be explained in terms of his psychological needs and drives, and since these differ among philosophers, it will be unsurprising that there are a diversity of moral views, and philosophical systems purportedly justifying them—and it will be equally unsurprising that this same diversity, and intractability, spills over into metaphysical and epistemological systems, since they are just parasitic on the moral aims of the philosophers. Nietzsche, at least, then has good reason to bite the skeptical bullet about much philosophical disagreement.

Of course, we would need to think carefully about individual cases of philosophical disagreement, since not all of them, in all branches of philosophy, are as intractable or as foundational as they are in moral philosophy. Some philosophical disagreements can, in fact, be defused fairly easily. Thus, to take an example from one of my other specialties, the debate in legal philosophy between natural law theorists and legal positivists about the nature of law has both an element of tractability (natural law theorists like John Finnis have, in fact, conceded most of the claims that actually matter to legal positivism as a theory of law[40]) and admits, in the intractable parts, of defusing by reference to the transparent and dogmatic religious commitments of the natural law theorists on the remaining issues they refuse to cede. In sum, the skeptical argument from disagreement among philosophers may have implications beyond moral philosophy, but what precisely they are will have to be decided on a case-by-case basis.

That still leaves a slightly different version of the worry that the argument "proves too much." For surely most philosophers will *not* conclude from the fact of disagreement among moral philosophers about the fundamental criteria of moral rightness and goodness that there is no *fact* of the matter about these questions, as I claim Nietzsche does. But why not think that this meta-disagreement itself warrants a skeptical inference, i.e., there is no fact about whether we should infer moral skepticism from the fact of disagreement about fundamental principles among moral philosophers, since philosophers have intractable disagreements about what inferences the fact of disagreement supports?

Again, however, we need to be careful about the data points and the abductive inferences they warrant. The question is always what is the *best explanation* for the disagreement in question, *given its character and scope*. The "meta-disagreement"—about whether disagreement in foundational moral theory really warrants skepticism about moral facts—is, itself, of extremely recent vintage, barely discussed in the literature.[41] Even if my reconstruction of the Nietzschean argument and the challenge in

[40] See, e.g., Leiter (2007b: 162–4, including n. 42).

[41] A simple version of the argument featured at the start of MacIntyre (1981), but was largely neglected in subsequent scholarly discussion by academic moral philosophers. Nearly four decades of moral philosophy later, the skeptical case is even stronger.

Loeb (1998), for example, succeed in making the issue a topic of debate,[42] and even if, after some critical discussion, the meta-disagreement continues to persist, that still would not support the meta-skeptical conclusion that there is no fact of the matter about whether or not disagreement in foundational moral theory supports skepticism about moral facts. For before we are entitled to that conclusion, we would have to ask what the best explanation for the meta-disagreement really is. Surely one possibility—surely the most likely possibility?—is that those who are professionally invested in normative moral theory as a serious, cognitive discipline—rather than seeing it, as Marxists or Nietzscheans might, as a series of elaborate post-hoc rationalizations for the emotional attachments and psychological needs of certain types of people (bourgeois academics, heirs to the "slave revolt in morals")—will resist, with any dialectical tricks at their disposal, the possibility that their entire livelihood is predicated on the existence of ethnographically bounded sociological and psychological artifacts, whose interest is on a par with etiquette manuals, not a contribution to knowledge. Nothing in the argument here establishes that conclusion, but nor is there any reason to think it would not be the correct one in the face of meta-disagreement about the import of fundamental disagreement in moral philosophy. In any case, we can hardly see why Nietzsche would resist such a conclusion. I would not either: philosophers need to face up to the possibility that much of their activity, and its seemingly intractable disputation, is due to the fact that it is an intellectual activity without any real cognitive content.

[42] Obviously, Pyrrhonian skeptics have mounted challenges of this form for a very long time, but they are not specific to ethics and they do not offer them to support an abductive inference to a metaphysical conclusion, as Loeb and I do. Jessica Berry (2011) argues that Nietzsche's point is, in fact, the Pyrrhonian one—namely, to elicit a suspension of belief—though I think this is hard to square with his rhetoric. I am also skeptical that "the passages in which Nietzsche does embrace caution, *ephexis*, and suspicion... far and away outnumber those in which he sounds adamant and dogmatic" about the non-existence of moral facts (Berry 2011: 190). She offers her alternative, Pyrrhonian, reading of the disagreement passages in Nietzsche at (2011: 184–208).

2

Nietzsche's Metaethics

Against the Privilege Readings

1. The Problem of the Revaluation

Everyone knows that Nietzsche proposed a revaluation of values, that is, a new assessment of the value of our "moral" values (what is now commonly denominated in the scholarly literature as "morality in the pejorative sense" or "MPS" [following Leiter 2002: 74–80]).[1] By MPS values, he means some motley assortment of normative views familiar from Judeo-Christian cultural traditions and their philosophical formulations by deontological and utilitarian theorists like Kant and Bentham (see Leiter 2015a: 61–4). Nietzsche held that MPS values were not conducive to the flourishing of human excellence, and it was by reference to *this* fact that he proposed to assess their value.[2] Even if one rejects, however, this specific formulation of the grounds on which the revaluation proceeds, one may still agree that the enterprise of assessing the value of certain other values (call them the "revalued values") invites the following metaethical question: what status—metaphysical, epistemological—do the values used to undertake this revaluation (the "assessing values") enjoy? More specifically, one might want to ask questions like: Are the assessing valuations true and the revalued valuations false? Are the assessing valuations justified (in some sense to be specified) while the revalued valuations are not? Are there reasons for everyone to accept the assessing values rather than the revalued values?

What animates these sorts of questions is a worry about Nietzsche's revaluation that might be summed up more simply as follows: in offering a revaluation of MPS is Nietzsche doing anything more than giving his idiosyncratic opinion from his idiosyncratic evaluative perspective? Is there anything about Nietzsche's evaluation that ought to command the attention and assent of others? In short, is there any sense in which Nietzsche's evaluative perspective can claim some epistemic *privilege*—being "correct," being better justified—over its target? If Nietzsche is, as I argued in Chapter 1, an anti-realist about value, then these questions seem especially urgent.

[1] See the discussion in the Introduction, Section 4.

[2] See, e.g., Foot (1973: 162): "It is, then, for the sake of 'the higher' man that the values of Christian morality must be abandoned, and it is from this perspective that the revaluation of values takes place." I defend a version of Foot's view in Leiter (2002: 144–6).

A number of Nietzsche commentators have offered an affirmative answer to the last question. I will call these sorts of answers the "Privilege Readings" of Nietzsche's metaethics. Writers who defend the Privilege Reading all hold that Nietzsche's evaluative standpoint in undertaking the revaluation enjoys some *epistemic privilege* over its target *in the sense that it is objectively correct or, at least, better justified.* Defenders of the Privilege Reading differ, however, on precisely what the source of the privilege is supposed to be. I shall discuss two main possibilities. The first is what I will call the "Realist" reading of Nietzsche's metaethics, which locates the source of the privilege in there being objective (i.e., mind-independent) facts about value, somehow related to Nietzsche's idea that life is will to power. The second is Philippa Foot's non-realist interpretation, which locates the source of the privilege in the interpersonal appeal of Nietzsche's evaluative perspective. In this chapter, I argue that neither interpretation succeeds. Such a conclusion fits better with the explanatory arguments for anti-realism about value developed in Chapter 1, and would imply that Nietzsche's own evaluative position is neither objectively true nor even better justified than its target.

I proceed as follows: in Section 2, I survey various types of Privilege Readings of Nietzsche's metaethics; in Section 3, I argue at length against the most common version of the Realist variety; in Section 4, I argue (more briefly) against Foot's version of a non-Realist Privilege Reading.

2. The Privilege Readings: Realism

According to the Privilege Readings of Nietzsche's metaethics, Nietzsche holds that his own evaluative standpoint is either objectively "correct" or better justified than its target. I will class Privilege Readings as coming in two main varieties: Realist and Privilege Non-Realist (P-Non-Realist).[3] Realist readings of Nietzsche's metaethics hold that he thinks there are *objective* evaluative facts, in the sense that facts about *what ought to be done* or *what is really valuable* are mind-independent (i.e., epistemically independent of anyone's judgment about what ought to be done or what is really valuable, even under ideal epistemic conditions). Realist readings view "power [as] the fundamental value or standard that Nietzsche uses for the purposes of assessing the values of morality" (Hussain 2011: 147), though how exactly it plays that role admits of varying interpretations; I return to a central one, below. By contrast, the P-Non-Realist accepts that there are no objective evaluative facts in the preceding sense, but locates the privilege of Nietzsche's own evaluative judgments in the fact that enjoy wide

[3] Constitutivism, one of the current fads in Anglophone moral philosophy, holds that objective normative standards can be derived from the nature of human agency: to be an agent is to be committed, in some sense, to normative standards of action. Surprisingly, one recent commentator has suggested this might have been Nietzsche's view (Katsafanas 2013a). I discuss some of the textual problems for this view in the notes, below. For general doubts about constitutivism as a philosophical position, see Enoch (2006, 2010); and for doubts about Katsafanas' version, Huddleston (2017) and Robertson (2017) are, together, devastating.

interpersonal appeal or acceptance. I return to the latter in the next section; here I consider the Realist reading.

According to the Realist, Nietzsche holds that only power *really* has value and that power is an objective, natural property that some states of affairs, persons, and acts possess or lack in varying degrees. Nietzsche's evaluative perspective is privileged, in turn, because it involves the assessment of (1) prudential value (value *for* an agent) in terms of degree of power, and (2) non-prudential value in terms of maximization of prudential value (i.e., maximization of power).

A minor cautionary note about terminology is in order at the start. Naturalistically-minded realists typically hold that value itself is a natural property, not simply that what has value (i.e., power) is a natural property (a view which could have been palatable to the arch-anti-naturalist G.E. Moore). For reasons already noted in Chapter 1, there is no clear textual basis for assigning Nietzsche a view on this particular question: some texts suggest property-identification, some do not. What is clear is that the secondary literature defending this Privilege Reading conventionally presents Nietzsche's view as "naturalistic," and it is in fact "naturalistic" in one familiar sense. In the nineteenth century especially, naturalists were simply those who denied that there were any supernatural properties or entities. In the theory of value, then, one might plausibly think of Nietzsche as being a kind of naturalist in the sense of resisting religious and quasi-religious theories that view goodness as supervening on non-natural or supernatural properties;[4] as against this, Nietzsche claims that goodness *at least* supervenes on a (putatively) natural property, namely power.

Now we can state more precisely what is at stake in the Realist reading of Nietzsche's metaethics. One could agree that Nietzsche employs "power" (in some sense) as an evaluative standard, but still disagree with the Realist that it is an *objective fact* that power is what is ("really") valuable—for example, power might just be what Nietzsche happens to think is valuable.[5] So, too, one could agree that Nietzsche evaluates persons and states of affairs in terms of their degree of power but could still disagree that power is itself an objective natural property—for example, one might think that Nietzsche's evaluative use of "power" is extremely plastic and subjective. In both cases, these interpretive positions seem to me the correct ones, that do justice to the texts and fit with Nietzsche's explanatory arguments for value anti-realism discussed in Chapter 1. So what justifies going beyond them with a Realist reading? And do these arguments succeed?

Although versions of the Realist construal of Nietzsche have been defended by many commentators who address Nietzsche's metaethics, I will concentrate on the

[4] Another possible target for Nietzsche is Plato, who holds that value supervenes on the associated Form of the predicate picking out the property. (Of course, on Plato's view, this is true of all predicates, as discussed in Chapter 1.)

[5] Katsafanas (2013a, 2016) trades extensively on conflating these two possibilities: he adduces evidence that Nietzsche thinks power is what is valuable, and slides from that to the claim that Nietzsche thinks it is *really*, *objectively* valuable, but that is simply a non-sequitur on the evidence.

(representative) version articulated in the work of the American scholar Richard Schacht.[6] On Schacht's account of the revaluation, Nietzsche:

> ...is proposing to evaluate [moral values] by reference to a standard of valuation independent of them, from a perspective which transcends them. And the sort of "value" of which he speaks when viewing them from this perspective is one which he considers, in contrast to them, to have a kind of validity which they lack...For this perspective is a privileged one, which an understanding of the fundamental character of life and the world serves to define and establish.
>
> (Schacht 1983: 348–9)

More precisely, Nietzsche's account of "the fundamental character of life and the world" *as will to power* is supposed to "ground" his own evaluative standpoint. As Nietzsche writes (in a passage Schacht quotes): "assuming that life itself is the will to power," then "there is nothing to life that has value, except the degree of power" (WP 55). Nietzsche's revaluation of values, then, assesses MPS values on the basis of their "degree of power," something which constitutes an "objective measure of value" (WP 674). Hence the privilege of his view: it embraces as an evaluative standard the only thing in life that (in fact) has value (namely power), and employs this "objective measure of value" in the revaluation (e.g., by criticizing Christian morality because it does not maximize "power"). It is in this respect that Nietzsche's conception of value, according to Schacht, is supposed to be "naturalistic" (Schacht 1983: 398–9).

There are two interrelated grounds for rejecting this Realist reading: philosophical and textual. Philosophically, it attributes to Nietzsche an argument of dubious merit. Textually, it depends on attributing to him both a view he does not seem to hold and an argument found only in texts of questionable canonical status. These considerations reinforce each other: views supported by bad arguments, based on views that Nietzsche does not seem to hold, and that are found only in texts of questionable canonical status, probably should not be attributed to Nietzsche. As an interpretive principle, this ought to be uncontroversial. I now turn to the task of showing that the most influential construal of Nietzsche's metaethics—the Realist reading—violates this interpretive principle.

2.1 The Millian Model

Construing Nietzsche as a Realist about value commits him to an implausible philosophical view, moreover one that he does not even seem to hold. To see why this is so,

[6] Schacht (1983: 348–9, 398–9). For related accounts, see Morgan (1941: 118 ff.); Kaufmann (1974: 199–200)); Wilcox (1974: 194–9); Hunt (1991: Chapter 7). While some type of Privilege Reading has been the majority view in the Anglo-American Nietzsche literature, the "popular" view of Nietzsche has actually been—at least on this issue—closer to the truth. For example, Alasdair MacIntyre's Nietzsche (1981) though at times crudely drawn and oversimplified, is essentially the real Nietzsche as far as his metaethics goes; see especially MacIntyre (1981: 107, 111) ("the power of Nietzsche's position depends upon the truth of one central thesis: that all rational vindications of morality manifestly fail and that *therefore* belief in the tenets of morality needs to be explained in terms of a set of rationalisations which conceal the fundamentally non-rational phenomena of the will").

we require a more precise statement of the Realist argument. We may have such a statement if we construe Nietzsche on what I will call the "Millian Model."

What I have in mind is John Stuart Mill's well-known and oft-criticized "proof" of the principle of utility:

> The only proof capable of being given that an object is visible is that people actually see it. The only proof that a sound is audible is that people hear it; and so of the other sources of our experience. In like manner, I apprehend, the sole evidence it is possible to produce that anything is desirable is that people do actually desire it. (Mill 1979 [1861]: 34)

Thus: to show that something is visible, show that it is seen; to show that something is audible, show that it is heard; analogously,

(P) To show that something is desirable (i.e., valuable), show that it is desired.

Millian hedonism holds that only happiness or pleasure is intrinsically desirable or valuable ("Prescriptive Hedonism"). Let us call "Value Nihilism"[7] the view that there is nothing that has value or is valuable (or desirable). To get Prescriptive Hedonism from (P), then, simply add 'Descriptive Hedonism'—the thesis that people do in fact intrinsically desire *only* pleasure as an end. If (P) is valid, Descriptive Hedonism true, and Value Nihilism false, then the truth of Prescriptive Hedonism follows.

(P), of course, is not valid, and this has been the basis for much criticism of Mill's proof. But before seeing why this is so (and whether a modification cannot save the argument), note that the same type of argument seems to capture what the Realist construal of Nietzsche has in mind. That is, to get the Realist Nietzschean conclusion that what is valuable is power, take (P) and plug in a strong form of Nietzsche's descriptive doctrine of the will to power—the doctrine, roughly, that all persons intrinsically "desire" only power. If (P) is valid, Value Nihilism false, and the descriptive doctrine of the will to power is true, then the normative conclusion about power seems to follow.[8]

[7] I introduce "Value Nihilism" here as a term of art to mark a presupposition of the argument some interpreters would attribute to Nietzsche. The idea of Value Nihilism has some relationship to what Nietzsche sometimes means by nihilism, especially in the *Nachlass*, but in that regard it describes a view that involves a mistaken supposition about the kind of foundations value could possibly have. But that is not my concern here.

[8] There is a vigorous and insightful attack on the analogy between Nietzsche's doctrine of will to power and psychological hedonism in Chapter 1 of Richardson (1996). Richardson identifies three initially striking disanalogies between Nietzsche's notion of will to power and the hedonist's notion of pleasure. First, will to power, for Nietzsche, characterizes drives (e.g., the sex drive), and only applies to persons derivatively (insofar as persons are conglomerations of drives that stand in a certain hierarchical relation to one another); by contrast, pleasure for the hedonist describes a motive or drive *of persons*. Second, power, for Nietzsche, is not a state with a distinctive qualitative feel; rather power, claims Richardson, consists in "growth" or "enhancement" of a particular drive with its own preexisting ends. By contrast, the hedonist is supposed to be committed to the idea of pleasure or happiness as a distinct qualitative state, present on all occasions of pleasure (mental or physical). Third, and relatedly, power is not a *static* end-state: if power consists in growth in a drive, then "power" is not a state one aims to be in. By contrast, pleasure for the hedonist is a distinctive state one desires to be in, and that one aims for (hence the famous paradox of hedonism described by Sidgwick). Does Richardson's perceptive analysis undermine the strategy of the argument in the text? I think not, and for two broad reasons.

Note, however, that the Millian Model argument as formulated so far would show only that power is what is non-morally valuable or good for an agent—what I called earlier *prudential* value. But as we have already seen, it is part of Nietzsche's metaethics, on the Realist reading, that power (more precisely, maximization of power) is what is also non-prudentially valuable. Commentators are less clear (as is Mill himself) on what the argument is supposed to be for this conclusion about non-prudential value.

Take, for example, the following passage from the *Nachlass*, about which Schacht makes much: "There is nothing to life that has value, except the degree of power—assuming that life itself is the will to power" (WP 55). On the Millian Model, this becomes an argument for what is *valuable for* persons. But Schacht wants to read it more broadly as follows:

> Human life, for Nietzsche, is ultimately a part of a kind of vast game... [which] is, so to speak, the only game in town.
>
> ...The nature of the game, he holds, establishes a standard for the evaluation of everything falling within its compass. The availability of this standard places evaluation on footing that is as firm as that on which the comprehension of life and the world stands. (Schacht 1983: 398)

What the *argument* here is supposed to be is obscure,[9] though, again, the truth of the strong form of the descriptive doctrine of the will to power is supposed to do some work. We can, however, at least say this: if the Millian Model argument for prudential value or non-moral goodness does *not* work, then that provides a very strong (if defeasible) reason for supposing that there is no further argument for the related account of non-prudential value as consisting in maximization of power. I now propose to show that the Millian Model argument, in the precise form described above, fails, both philosophically and textually.

First, as a purely textual matter (and as Richardson himself notes), Nietzsche explicitly invites the analogy with psychological hedonism, suggesting at times that power is a better explanation than pleasure for various phenomena, and describing will to power in terms evocative of psychological hedonism (cf. WP 434, 1023). Moreover, as Maudemarie Clark has observed, Nietzsche's earliest discussions of will to power, and even very late ones in GM, are psychological in character, concerned with the desire for a feeling of power as the best explanation of human behavior (Clark 1990: 208–12). Richardson's analysis is really most applicable to some of the discussions of will to power in the *Nachlass*—though, admittedly, it at least resonates with *some* material in the published work as well.

Second, and more importantly, even if Richardson were right on all three points, this would not vitiate the point of pursuing the analogy. For all we need for purposes of the Millian analogy is the claim that there exists an essential and omnipresent tendency of human behavior, whether that tendency is toward pleasure or power. Though Richardson argues—generally quite persuasively—that will to power characterizes "drives" first-and-foremost, he himself notes that our and Nietzsche's primary interest is in persons as conglomerations of drives; thus will to power ultimately (or derivatively) explains human behavior by identifying the end towards which it is directed. The character of that end will not matter for the course of the argument—it does not even matter, for example, that it is not a "state" or static condition. All that matters is that human behavior be *telic*, something Richardson claims is central to Nietzsche's notion of will to power.

[9] It is evocative of constitutivism in ethics discussed *supra* n. 3, though Schacht himself does not pursue the constitutivist reading.

The first problem is that (P) is not valid. While from the fact that X is heard, it follows that X is audible, it does not follow from that fact that X is desired that X is desirable *in the sense necessary for the argument*. For while "audible" can be fairly rendered as "can be heard," "desirable," in the context of Prescriptive Hedonism, means "*ought* to be desired" (not "can be" or "is" desired). Thus, while it follows that:

If X is heard, then X can be heard ("is audible"),

it does not follow that,

If X is desired, then X ought to be desired ("is desirable").

Yet in claiming that pleasure or power are valuable, Mill and the Realist Nietzsche are advancing a normative thesis. The truth of this normative thesis, however, simply does not follow from the corresponding descriptive thesis.

Many, of course, have thought this too facile a response: surely a philosophical intelligence like Mill's could not fall prey to such a simple mistake. Supplement the argument, then, by adding an 'Internalist Constraint' (IC), one that many philosophers have found plausible in the theory of value:

(IC) Something cannot be valuable for a person unless the person is capable of caring about (desiring) it.

The (IC) is motivated by the thought that it cannot be right to say that "X is valuable" for someone when X is alien to anything a person cares about or *could* care about: any plausible notion of value, the (IC) supposes, must have some strong connection to a person's existing (or potential) motivational set.

How does the (IC) help? Recall (P):

(P) To show that something is desirable (i.e., valuable) show that it is desired.

Now the (IC) puts a constraint on what things can, in fact, be desirable or valuable: namely, only those things that agents can, in fact, care about or desire. This suggests that we might reformulate (P) as follows:

(P') To show that something is desirable (i.e., valuable), show that it is or can be desired.

(P') now is simply a different formulation of the (IC): if we accept the (IC) then we should accept (P'). But what happens, then, if we grant the truth of Descriptive Hedonism: namely, that only pleasure is, in fact, desired. In that case, it would now follow that only pleasure is desirable (ought to be desired) (assuming, again, that Value Nihilism is false). That is, since something ought to be desired only if it can be desired (internalism), then if only X *can* be desired, then only X ought to be desired (assuming that Value Nihilism is false).

Will this argument rescue the Realist reading of Nietzsche? Two obstacles remain. The first, and perhaps less serious one, is that we must have some reason for accepting the (IC)—or, more modestly, some reason for thinking Nietzsche accepts it. It is not clear, however, that there are adequate textual grounds for saying where Nietzsche stands on this question. Since the (IC) does, however, seem to be presupposed by the Nietzschean remarks from the *Nachlass* that support Realism—in the sense that such remarks do not constitute a good argument without the (IC)—let us grant that Nietzsche accepts the (IC), and let us simply put aside the contentious issue of whether we ought to accept the (IC) as a general philosophical matter.

A second difficulty will still remain: namely, that the argument for Realism still depends on the truth of the relevant descriptive thesis, in Nietzsche's case, the doctrine of the will to power. This presents two problems. First, in the works Nietzsche chose to publish, it seems clear that he did not, in fact, accept the doctrine in the strong form required for the Realist argument (namely, that it is only power that persons ever aim for or desire). Second, it is simply not a plausible doctrine in its strong form.

For the Millian Model argument for Realism to work in its new form (that is, supplemented with the (IC)) it must be the case that that which *ought* to be desired ("is valuable") is the only thing that is, in fact, desired. Since the Realist Nietzschean conclusion is that only power is valuable, power must be the only thing that is, in fact, desired (assuming, again, that *something* is valuable, i.e., that Value Nihilism is false). Many, of course, have thought that Nietzsche held precisely this view, and he sometimes makes remarks suggestive of such a view.[10] However, he says other things which are flatly inconsistent with the stronger remarks which might suggest that the latter are hyperbolic or rhetorical over-reaching; for example:

> Life itself is to my mind the instinct for growth, for durability, for an accumulation of forces, for *power*: where the will to power is lacking there is decline. It is my contention that all the supreme values of mankind *lack* this will... (A 6)

But if all actions manifested this *will*, then this *will* could never be found lacking. Yet Nietzsche thinks it can be lacking, which means he must countenance the possibility that not everyone aims for ("desires") power. This passage is not atypical. In the immediately preceding work he claims that the "effects" of liberal institutions are "known well enough: they undermine the will to power" (TI IX:38). But if the strong reading were correct, then the agents making up liberal institutions would themselves be expressing will to power in, somehow, "undermin[ing]" it. And in the immediately subsequent work (his last), Nietzsche refers to "the terrible *aspects* of reality (in affects, in desires, in the will to power)..." (EH IV:4), which certainly sounds as if will to power is simply one among various characteristics of reality—*alongside* affects and desires,

[10] Zarathustra states that, "Where I found the living, there I found will to power" (Z II:12); Nietzsche refers to "the will to power which is the will of life" (GS 349); he says "the really fundamental instinct of life... aims at *the expansion of power*" (GS 349); "life simply *is* will to power," meaning a striving "to grow, spread, seize, become predominant" (BGE 259); he refers to his "theory that in all events a *will to power* is operating" (GM II:12); he claims that "[a] living thing seeks above all to *discharge* its strength—life itself is *will to power*" (BGE 13). Note that some of these passages suggest that will to power is but one among other motives or tendencies, just the strongest one, but not the only one.

rather than the essential core of them all. (Young [2010: 546] adduces similar passages from elsewhere in the corpus.)

Three other general textual considerations count against attributing the strong doctrine of the will to power to Nietzsche. First, if, as the defenders of the strong doctrine believe, "his fundamental principle is the '*will to power*,'"[11] then it is hard to understand why he says almost nothing about will to power—and nothing *at all* to suggest it is his "fundamental principle"—in the two major self-reflective moments in the Nietzschean corpus: his last major work, *Ecce Homo*, where he reviews and assesses his life and writings, including specifically all his prior books (EH III); and the series of new prefaces he wrote for *The Birth of Tragedy*, *Human, All Too Human*, *Dawn*, and *The Gay Science* in 1886, in which he revisits his major themes. That this putative "fundamental principle" merits no discussion on either occasion strongly suggests that its role in Nietzsche's thought has been greatly overstated.[12]

Second, the single most famous passage on will to power in the Nietzschean corpus is the concluding section (1067) of *The Will to Power*, where he affirms that, "*This world is the will to power—and nothing besides*! And you yourselves are also this will to power—and nothing besides!" Although a favorite of commentators for many years,[13] the passage has been conclusively discredited by the leading scholar of the *Nachlass*, the late Mazzino Montinari. Montinari has shown that Nietzsche had, in fact, discarded the passage by the Spring of 1887 (1982: 103–4)! It was, as Montinari notes, made

[11] Jaspers (1965: 287). For similar views, see Müller-Lauter (1971) and Heidegger (1982).

[12] Katsafanas (2013a), whose reading depends centrally on an implausibly strong form of the doctrine of will to power (all action aims at power), suggests that failure to mention will to power in the 1886 prefaces is not surprising since "will to power is first introduced in *Zarathustra* itself" (2013a: 250), while the 1886 prefaces were added to pre-*Zarathustra* books. But Katsafanas goes on to admit in a footnote that "some of Nietzsche's 1886 prefaces discuss later developments in his thought" (2013a: 251 n. 15), without explaining why one they conspicuously do not discuss is will to power. This is all the more notable in the case of *The Gay Science*, since the fifth book, added at the same time as the new prefaces, does mention will to power once (GS 349). With respect to *Ecce Homo*, Katsafanas notes that the phrase will to power occurs "four times" (2013a: 251), but neglects to mention that none of these references pertain to the strong psychological form of the doctrine on which his reading depends. Indeed, the reference in EH IV:4, discussed above in the text, makes clear that "will to power" is one of the "terrible aspects of reality" that stands alongside other affects and desires. Similarly, in EH III:W(1), Nietzsche merely ridicules the Germans for their willingness to embrace "'faith' as well as scientific manners, 'Christian love' as well as anti-Semitism, the will to power (to the *Reich*) as well as the [Gospel of the humble]." In short, the occasional references to "will to power" are irrelevant to the doctrine Katsafanas wants to attribute to Nietzsche. (Katsafanas [2013a:251] also inflates his count of references to will to power by including passages that do not mention "will to power" at all but mention what he deems "cognates." But the sheer capaciousness of what Katsafanas would count as "power" is evidence, precisely, for the anti-realist reading: power functions mostly as a term of endorsement for Nietzsche, not as a term that picks out mind-independent properties or features of persons or states of affairs.)

Katsafanas also argues that if, as I claim, "one of Nietzsche's concerns is the rejection of a certain conception of free will" (2013a: 251), the fact that it is only discussed four times in EH would not show "that Nietzsche abandons or considers unimportant his critique of free will" (2013a: 251). But this would be a relevant observation *only if* I had claimed that the critique of free will was the organizing theme of Nietzsche's philosophical work, which of course I did not claim. The problem for Katsafanas is that he alleges that the strong doctrine of will to power is the organizing theme of Nietzsche's corpus, and yet it merits no defense or even mention as such in *Ecce Homo*.

[13] We even find John Richardson invoking the passage early on in (1996: 8).

part of the Köselitz-Forster compilation of *The Will to Power* (the basis for the English-language edition by Kaufmann and Hollingdale) notwithstanding 'Nietzsche's literary intentions' (1982: 104).

Third, Maudemarie Clark has argued that Nietzsche could not have accepted the *strong* doctrine of the will to power given the putative argument he gives for it. Clark points out that the *only argument* for the strong doctrine of the will to power in Nietzsche's published works—in Section 36 of *Beyond Good and Evil*—is cast in the conditional form: if we accept certain initial hypotheses, then, Nietzsche thinks, the strong doctrine of the will to power follows. But one of the antecedents of this conditional is the "causality of the will," and Clark points out, obviously correctly, that Nietzsche clearly *rejects* such causality elsewhere in his work (for further discussion, see Chapter 5). Therefore, this section can not constitute an argument for the strong doctrine of the will to power that Nietzsche, himself, would actually accept! Rather than embracing the strong doctrine, Clark argues that Nietzsche is, somewhat ironically, illustrating the very flaw of philosophers he warns against in the surrounding passages: namely, their tendency to propound theories of the essence of reality that are just projections of their own evaluative commitments (Clark 1990: 212–27). (Note, too, that Montinari claims [1982: 104] that the one surviving relic of Section 1067 of *The Will to Power* in the published works is precisely the ironic Section 36 of *Beyond Good and Evil*, though Montinari fails to note how utterly different it is.) Even if Clark's ingenious reconstruction is questionable at points, its central conclusion—that Nietzsche does not accept the strong doctrine of the will to power—wins support from the other considerations already adduced.

But what, then, does Nietzsche believe about will to power? As Kaufmann and Clark, among others, have noted, Nietzsche's doctrine of will to power in its original deployment and most of its later development is *psychological* in character: the will to power is posited as the best psychological explanation for a wide variety of human behaviors.[14] As Nietzsche puts it in a famous (and central) passage from the *Genealogy*, "Every animal—even the dumb philosopher—strives instinctively for the optimal conditions... in which it can experience its maximum feeling of power" (GM III:7). Here the idiom is explicitly psychological—"striving," "feeling"—but as the preceding passages and considerations make clear, Nietzsche could not have believed that striving for a feeling of power was the exclusive explanation for all human behavior. To the extent he sometimes seems to embrace this stronger claim, we must simply take Nietzsche to have overstated his case—something which his penchant for hyperbolic rhetoric and polemics often leads him to do.[15]

[14] Cf. Kaufmann (1974), Chapter 6; Clark (1990: 209–12). Even Richardson concedes (1996) that the primary interest of the will to power doctrine—for Nietzsche and for us—is in its application to human beings.

[15] The other explanation for these passages is, of course, Clark's: namely, that in these passages he is not making a descriptive claim, but rather being ironic, alerting us to the fact that he is really just affirming his evaluative perspective, according to which power is a good thing.

If the preceding argument is correct, that would actually be fortunate, since it simply would not be plausible that will to power is the exclusive explanation for all human behavior, and any philosophical doctrine based on such a view would be of dubious merit.[16] Do I manifest the will to power by showing up to teach my classes? By holding my office hours? Do I express a desire for power when I shop for groceries? Buy furniture for the house? Cook dinner? Surely the list of ordinary activities and actions that do not seem helpfully explained by reference to a fundamental drive for (or tendency towards) power could go on and on.

Someone might object, of course, that what the Nietzschean Realist claims—on the Millian Model—is that power is *the only end that could be intrinsically desirable*, so that the real question is what intrinsic ends are a person's various ordinary activities and actions means towards. I shop in order to eat: but why do I eat? In order to have energy and strength (might we say *power*?) to pursue my real interests and goals? What, then, moves me towards my real interests and goals? Could it be a desire for power of some sort? And, if so, of *what sort* precisely? One worry that haunts Realist readings is that "power" becomes so capacious a notion that it simply denominates every end of action.[17]

Note, again, though, that the Realist must claim that it is *always* going to be the will to power that provides the unifying explanation for these particular desires and actions. But is that really plausible? Perhaps the best reason for being skeptical about the strong descriptive doctrine of the will to power is the attractiveness of a clear competitor doctrine: namely, Descriptive Hedonism, that is, the view that people only desire pleasure as an end-in-itself. From Mill to Freud to innumerable students in introductory ethics classes, this doctrine—or its variants—has had a strong intuitive appeal. While Nietzsche sometimes suggested that pleasure was a mere epiphenomenon of the feeling of power,[18] it is hardly obvious that the issue should be decided in his favor. In any event, surely it is quite plausible that in at least *some* cases it is pleasure, not power, that we are after. But admitting that possibility undermines the strong descriptive doctrine of the will to power, for it means that things beside power can, in fact, be desired.[19]

[16] Katsafanas (2013a, 2016) bites this bullet. For philosophical doubts, see the critique in Huddleston (2017).

[17] Notice that this worry obtains even if the global explanatory hypothesis about will to power is shifted to the nonconscious level, i.e., it is what explains all our unconscious desires. Once again, there is no scenario in which such a hypothesis could be warranted as the best explanation for what we observe about people.

[18] The topic is usefully discussed in Chapter 9 of Kaufmann (1974).

[19] Recently, a more philosophically sophisticated reader of Nietzsche than Schacht has tried to come to the defense of something like Schacht's interpretation. Nadeem Hussain (2011) admits, as I have argued in the text, that Nietzsche does not accept a "strong form of the [descriptive] doctrine of will to power" (2011: 149), but suggests the right way to understand the argument is in terms of a claim about "what is essential to life," namely, "a tendency towards expansion, growth, domination, overcoming of resistances, increasing strength, and so on" (2011: 153). He locates this way of thinking in "a kind of naturalism about values that was quite widespread among late nineteenth-century thinkers" (159), though he traces it to Bentham, and offers up Marxist historical determinism as an example (160–1). (That latter example seems inapt, since it turns on an equally implausible doctrine, namely, the teleological conception of history, which we now know to be false.) In the end, Hussain admits that this alternative does not yield "a valid argument... that

In sum: even if we grant internalism, the argument for Nietzschean Realism will still be a bad one because the descriptive thesis on which it depends is not a thesis Nietzsche accepts and is simply not plausible in the form required by the argument.[20] Since, as a matter of interpretive charity, we ought not to attribute bad arguments to philosophers unless we have to, the badness of the Realist argument constitutes the first (defeasible) reason for not construing Nietzsche as a Realist.

2.2 The textual pedigree of the Millian Model argument

Nietzsche only makes the remarks that seem to suggest the Millian Model argument in passages from the *Nachlass*, work that Nietzsche never published during his lifetime.[21] Thus, even if one thought that Nietzsche really held the strong descriptive doctrine of the will to power in his published works, it is still the case that he only uses this doctrine to argue for the normative conclusion in *Nachlass* material.

Important doubts have been raised about the canonical status of the *Nachlass* material (e.g., Hollingdale [1985]: 166–72, 182–6; Montinari [1982]; Magnus [1988]: 222–32, 234 n. 18). It appears that Nietzsche wanted some, perhaps much, of this material destroyed, and it was only the intervention of others, independent of Nietzsche, that resulted in the material being saved for posterity. More recently, Julian Young (2010: 539–42) has confirmed and documented Nietzsche's abandonment of a project organized under the rubric *Will to Power* in favor of one organized around the idea of a *Revaluation of All Values*. Commentators committed to the centrality of "will to power" to Nietzsche's thought have tried to resist this evidence. Paul Katsafanas, for example, has admitted that "if Nietzsche consigned so many of his writings on will to power to the wastebasket, he can hardly have regarded those notes as important," but then

would show how [this] fact [about life's tendency]...does indeed entail...that we should value power" (2011: 162), thus leaving his clever alternative in the same dialectical trouble as Schacht's.

[20] There is an additional hurdle for the Realist which I have not touched upon here: namely, the claim that "degree of power" is somehow an "objective measure of value" (WP 674). Here, again, I think there is considerable room for skepticism about what this could possibly mean (should we think power quantifiable?); but since there are other substantial reasons for rejecting the Realist construal, I shall not belabor this point here.

[21] There are also some remarks in books he published (or intended to publish) that might be misconstrued as Realism. For example, Nietzsche writes: "What is good? Everything that heightens the feeling of power in man, the will to power, power itself" (A 2). But in the context, it is clear that this is not a proposal for a definition (reforming or otherwise) of "good" but rather simply an endorsement: power is what is good, while, as he says in the next sentence, "[e]verything that is born of weakness" is "bad" (A, 2).

Similarly, John Wilcox points to the "Note" at the end of GM, I—where Nietzsche calls for "physiologists and doctors" to get involved in the study "of the *value* of existing valuations"—as evidence that Nietzsche recognized the need for scientific help in his Realist construal of value as power (Wilcox 1974: 200–1). Yet this passage concludes, "*All* the sciences have from now on to prepare the way for the future task of the philosopher: this task understood as the solution of the *problem of value*, the determination of the *order of rank among values*." Now as Wilcox himself earlier notes (1974: 41), the *philosophers* are precisely the ones who "*create values*," who "*are commanders and legislators*" (BGE 211). Thus, what Nietzsche must be calling for is for scientific illumination of the effect of particular values on different types of persons (do they contribute, as Nietzsche puts it in the Note, to "the preservation of the greatest number" or to "producing a stronger type"), as an aid to the philosopher's creative work. But the values themselves are creations; the "physiologists and doctors" simply help the philosopher understand the effects of different sorts of values.

claimed that this "story is apocryphal" (2013a: 248), relying only on one Anglophone scholar who says Nietzsche was only discarding the "*page proofs* of *Twilight of the Idols*" (2013a: 248). It appears, however, Katsafanas did not consult the original German source for the story, namely, Carl Albrecht Bernoulli's *Franz Overbeck und Friedrich Nietzsche: Eine Freundschaft* (1908) (which is unreferenced in Katsafanas' discussion). Bernoulli, a student of Nietzsche's friend and former colleague Overbeck, does indeed report that when Nietzsche left his flat in Sils Maria in September of 1888, he instructed his landlord Herr Durisch to "burn" his papers and notebooks, though the landlord disregarded the instructions (1908: 301).[22] Nietzsche left for Turin a couple of weeks later, and suffered his final mental collapse in early January of 1889. Bernoulli does not specify the exact contents of the voluminous material Nietzsche asked to be destroyed, but Young claims (though without a cited source) that "many" of the "693 fragments" that Nietzsche's sister put into the posthumous *Will to Power* "had in fact been consigned to Nietzsche's wastepaper basket in Sils, from which, for unknown reasons, Durisch retrieved them" (Young 2010: 628 n. 9; but see my n. 22 for a much lower estimate). So at least some of what we have in the book known as *The Will to Power*—including its concluding section (as noted earlier)—represents work Nietzsche had rejected, and, more importantly, other *Nachlass* material was also intended as refuse. This is hardly surprising, given that Nietzsche's practice throughout his productive life was to cull the books he published from material in his notebooks—he was passing over and leaving material behind in the notebooks all the time.

The preceding considerations suggest that a view ought not to be attributed to Nietzsche *solely* on the basis of its articulation in Nietzsche's unpublished notebooks, and that is a view that, indeed, most scholars now accept. But this is precisely what the defender of the Realist construal of Nietzsche must do in order to saddle Nietzsche with the Millian Model argument, for *that* argument appears *only* in *Nachlass* material. Instead of pursuing this textually suspect course, we might, in the spirit of interpretive charity, simply surmise that Nietzsche recognized the untenability of the Millian Model argument and that this is why the explicit textual support for the Realist construal of Nietzsche is found only in material Nietzsche never published.

In sum, the Realist construal of Nietzsche faces five hurdles quite apart from how it could fit with his explanatory arguments for anti-realism: (1) internalism must be a justifiable constraint in the theory of value; (2) Value Nihilism must be false;

[22] Thanks to William Leiter for help both deciphering and translating the Bernoulli manuscript. It is unclear what Bernoulli's source for this claim is; he does mention later in the same discussion a short essay by one Fritz Kögel in *Das Magazin für Literatur* (1893), pp. 702–4, but this article only recounts Kögel's discovery of a draft of the foreword to TI in the papers Nietzsche left behind in Sils, which suggests Bernoulli must have some other source for his very different claim—perhaps Overbeck himself? Matt Meyer points out to me that Nietzsche's sister, Elisabeth, recounted a similar story to Bernoulli's in her 1907 book *Das Nietzsche-Archiv, seine Freunde und seine Feinde*, 25–8, but claims only that of the material left behind in Sils, very little of it made its way into *The Will to Power*. (She does admit that there was a lot of material left behind in Sils, presumably material now in the *Nachlass*.) Interestingly, Elizabeth reports (21) other incidents in which Nietzsche asked that unused material be burned, so this may have been a standing practice of his!

(3) Nietzsche must hold the strong descriptive doctrine of the will to power; (4) this descriptive doctrine, in its strong form, must be compelling; and (5) we must have reason for attributing an argument to Nietzsche that he only makes in texts of questionable canonical status. I have suggested that while the Realist may surmount (1) and (2), (3) through (5) will prove more intractable and, moreover, that they will mutually reinforce their intractability: that is, by reasonable interpretive scruples, it seems we ought not to attribute Realism to Nietzsche when it presupposes an implausible view (the strong doctrine of the will to power) that he does not seem to hold, and when his arguments for its Realist implications appear only in the *Nachlass*. I conclude, then, that we ought to reject the Realist construal as an adequate account of Nietzsche's metaethical position.

3. Nietzsche as P-Non-Realist

Although Philippa Foot is less explicit about the Privilege issue than defenders of Realist readings, the gist of her discussion is clearly to show that Nietzsche is doing something more than simply expressing his idiosyncratic view, a view that admits of no interpersonal justification. While agreeing that Nietzsche's intention is, in part, "to present us with a clash of interests—the good of the strong against that of the weak," Foot adds that "this is not all he wants to suggest" (1973: 162). Noting that Nietzsche "seems to want to say that anyone who is strong, independent, and so on—anyone who fits his description of the higher type of man—is one who *has value* in himself" (1973:163), Foot goes on to explicate this notion of "value" as follows:

> [I]t does make sense to say that *we value* strong and exceptional individuals.... We do find patterns of reaction to exceptional men that would allow us to see here a valuing rather similar to valuing on aesthetic grounds.... I am thinking of the interest and admiration which is the common attitude to remarkable men of exceptional independence of mind and strength of will.... [Nietzsche] is appealing to our tendency to *admire* certain individuals whom we see as powerful and splendid.... [There is] a similarity between the way we attribute *value* (aesthetic value) to art objects and the *value* that Nietzsche attributes to a certain kind of man, both resting on a set of common reactions.... (1973: 163)

Foot is presupposing here a general picture of Nietzsche's critique similar to the one first noted in Section 4 of the Introduction, defended in Leiter (2002), and presupposed throughout this volume: that is, Nietzsche's criticism of morality is that it thwarts the development of great individuals or (as Nietzsche calls them) "higher men." What is significant here is that Foot's view is also an example of a non-realist Privilege Reading. Nietzsche, on this picture, does not claim that his evaluative perspective is objectively correct or better justified; he simply claims that it enjoys a certain sort of interpersonal appeal, owing to our "common attitude to remarkable men," "our tendency to *admire* certain individuals," to find them aesthetically appealing. There may be no fact-of-the-matter as to whether higher men are or are not *really* valuable, but Nietzsche's evaluative standpoint is privileged by virtue of its appeal to all of us. We're all interested, it seems, in the flourishing of higher men.

What is right about this picture is that Nietzsche sometimes seems to conceive of the appeal of higher men in "aesthetic" terms. For example, Nietzsche does say that whether to prefer the cultivation of higher or lower men is "at bottom a question of taste and aesthetics" (WP 353) and he suggests that evaluating a man in terms of "how much he costs, or what harm he does" is as inappropriate as "apprais[ing] a work of art according to the effects it produces" (WP 878).[23] Yet, as an interpretive claim about Nietzsche, Foot's account is ultimately untenable.

This follows from what we may call Nietzsche's "Callicleanism," after Plato's Callicles in the *Gorgias*. It has now become something of a commonplace for commentators to note that Nietzsche did *not* accept one sort of Calliclean view: the view that "anyone who is to live aright should suffer his appetites to grow to the greatest extent and not check them" (*Gorgias*, 419e).[24] To the contrary, Nietzsche never tires of calling attention to the value of self-restraint and self-denial, especially for productive creative work (e.g., BGE 188). Yet the genuine need to correct this one (and at one time, widespread) misperception about Nietzsche's relation to Callicles has obscured a more important respect in which Nietzsche's view *is* Calliclean: namely, in its embrace of the Calliclean doctrine that the inferior employ morality to make "slaves of those who are naturally better" (*Gorgias*, 491e–492a), that "the weaker folk, the majority... frame the laws [and, we might add, the morals] for their own advantage' in order to "frighten [the strong] by saying that to overreach others is shameful and evil" (*Gorgias*, 483b-d). In short, Callicles' view is that morality is simply the prudence of the weak who, unable to do what the strong can do, opt instead to put the actions of the strong under the ban of morality. This, in fact, is Nietzsche's view as well (cf. Leiter 1997: 279).

[23] Note, of course, that these are both *Nachlass* passages; I do not know of any comparably explicit passage in the published work.

[24] See, e.g., Nehamas (1985: 202–3); Foot (1991: 19). The mistaken view of Nietzsche's relation to Callicles is usually attributed to E.R. Dodds (1959). This is actually unfair, since Dodds' treatment is much better than that. For example, Dodds only remarks in passing on a possible affinity between Nietzsche and Calliclean hedonism (1959: 390); the bulk of Dodds' discussion focuses on the very affinities I emphasize in the text (1959: 389–90). Dodds even concludes by saying—again quite rightly—that, "Callicles... would certainly not have understood [Nietzschean] concepts like 'sublimation' and 'self-transcendence,' while Nietzsche would have rejected with contempt the crude hedonism of Callicles" (*Gorgias*, 494a) (1959: 391). A much better example of the crude misreading of Nietzsche's relation to Callicles is W.K.C. Guthrie's account of Callicles as holding that "the strong man should live to the utmost of his powers and give free play to his desires" and his abrupt conclusion that Nietzsche "was blood-brother to Callicles." (Guthrie 1971: 106–107). Guthrie's dismissive reference here is a fine example of how otherwise impeccable scholarly standards collapse in the vicinity of Nietzsche. Here again, though, Dodds strikes the right note, when he suggests that what Nietzsche admired was Callicles' "realism," his "saying plainly what others think but do not care to say" (1959: 389). That suggests that in Guthrie's tripartite division of "Sophistic" themes—upholders of human convention (e.g., Protagoras), realists (e.g., Thucydides), upholders of nature (e.g., Callicles [not a Sophist], Antiphon)—Nietzsche is closer to the second group rather than the third. Indeed, as a more careful review of Nietzsche's texts would demonstrate, Thucydides and Sophistic realism figure centrally in Nietzsche's picture of the Sophistic culture that he admires (see D 168; TI X:2; WP 429). See Leiter (2002: 47–53).

For example, in the *Genealogy*, Nietzsche describes slave morality as simply "the prudence [*Klugheit*] of the lowest order" (GM I:13), and he comments that:

> When the oppressed, downtrodden, violated exhort one another with the vengeful cunning of impotence: "let us be different from the evil, namely good! And he is good who does not do violence, who harms nobody, who does not attack, who does not requite...."—this listened to coolly and impartially really amounts to no more than: "we weak ones are, after all, weak; it would be good if we did nothing *for which we are not strong enough*." ...

We hear echoes of the same Calliclean view when Nietzsche observes that "everything that elevates an individual above the herd and intimidates the neighbor is...called *evil*" (BGE 201); when he suggests that "[m]oral judgments and condemnations constitute the favorite revenge of the spiritually limited against those less limited" (BGE 219); finally, when he claims that the "chief means" by which the "weak and mediocre...weaken and pull down the stronger" is "the moral judgment" (WP 345).[25]

What obstacle, then, does Nietzsche's Callicleanism present for the P-Non-Realist like Foot? Recall that Foot wanted to resist the view that in his revaluation Nietzsche simply "present[s] us with a clash of interests—the good of the strong against that of the weak" (1973: 162); instead, Foot suggests that Nietzsche is appealing to a "common" tendency to admire higher men, men who would otherwise be thwarted by the reign of moral values. But Nietzsche's Callicleanism suggests something a bit different: namely, that it may be part of the very appeal of morality that it *does* thwart the flourishing of higher men. Of course, it cannot be quite that simple, since Nietzsche does not think that the *ressentiment* that drove the slave revolt in morals is part of the psychological motivation of everyone who, today, embraces slave moralities (Leiter 2015a: 139–41). Indeed, as he is at pains to emphasize (e.g., BGE 260), normative traces of master and slave morality coexist in both cultures and individuals: even today, in a moral culture suffused with egalitarianism, pity, sensitivity towards suffering and so on, we still admire excellence, strength, resoluteness, decisive action (think only of the popular culture's fascination with Mafiosi and other strongmen). Might this be enough for the core of Foot's point?

Problems, however, remain. Even if Nietzsche does not think every adherent of morality today is in the grips of *ressentiment*, he is explicit that morality *even today* has characteristics that reflect its origins. Recall some of the remarks just noted, e.g., that "everything that elevates an individual above the herd and intimidates the neighbor is...called *evil*" (BGE 201) or that "[m]oral judgments and condemnations constitute the favorite revenge of the spiritually limited against those less limited" (BGE 219). Even if higher men are sometimes still admirable in the eyes of the base and low, it is hard to see how Nietzsche's evaluative perspective—that it is an *objection* to morality that it thwarts the high, while advancing the interests of the low and base—could enjoy

[25] I should add that this similarity between Nietzsche's view and Callicles' is surely not mere coincidence. Nietzsche was trained in classical philology, knew the texts of the Presocratics and the Sophists thoroughly, and unquestionably thought better of them than he did of Socrates and Plato.

a privilege in virtue of this shared admiration. On the Calliclean picture, there is a fundamental hostility between the high and low, the strong and the weak, one which will not be bridged by inviting the low to admire the high, or the weak, the strong. "The well-being of the majority and the well-being of the few are opposite viewpoints of value," Nietzsche says in the "Note" at the end of the first essay of the *Genealogy*. And in Nietzsche's revaluation, we might add, never the twain shall meet.[26]

Foot's aim, to be sure, is not purely exegetical: she wants to make sense of Nietzsche in a way that makes his position attractive. Nonetheless, we should—at least for exegetical purposes—separate the question "What was Nietzsche's view?" from the question "What view—with at least *some* textual pedigree—would we prefer that he held?" If I am right that neither the Realist nor Foot's non-realist Privilege Readings are plausible interpretations of Nietzsche's metaethical position, then we are left with two possibilities: either some other plausible Realist interpretation of Nietzsche's metaethics has yet to be constructed on the basis of Nietzsche's texts or the Privilege Readings of Nietzsche's metaethics are simply wrong: Nietzsche's own evaluative perspective in undertaking the revaluation does not, in fact, enjoy any metaphysical or epistemic privilege over its target. At bottom, Nietzsche has nothing to say to those readers who don't share his evaluative tastes. That conclusion, of course, is precisely what we should expect if the argument of Chapter 1 is correct, namely, that Nietzsche is an anti-realist about value, including his own.

Although this may seem initially surprising, such a conclusion actually makes sense of a puzzling feature of his work, one worth remarking on by way of conclusion. The feature is this: Nietzsche is quite concerned to *circumscribe* his audience, to disinvite most readers from going further. As he puts it most simply at the beginning of *The Antichrist*: "This book belongs to the very few." In particular, Nietzsche's ideal reader is marked by "Reverence for oneself" (A Pref)—one of the defining traits, he tells us elsewhere, of the "noble" person (BGE 287). Similarly, in his autobiography Nietzsche says regarding "the air of my writings" that "[o]ne must be made for it" (EH Pref:3). He claims, too, that, "Ultimately, nobody can get more out of things, including books, than he already knows" (EH III:1; cf. BGE 87). And in a related vein, he says that, "Nobody is free to have ears for Zarathustra" (EH Pref:4), presumably because "Zarathustra experiences himself as the *supreme type of all beings*" (EH Z:6). Elsewhere he remarks that, "Today's ears resist...our truths "(BGE 202). And he recognizes that, "Our highest insights must—and should—sound like follies and sometimes like crimes when they are heard without permission by those who are not predisposed

[26] This is not to deny, however, that, as Nietzsche puts it, "in all the higher and more mixed cultures there also appear attempts at mediation between these two moralities [master and slave moralities], and yet more often the interpenetration and mutual misunderstanding of both, and at times they occur directly alongside each other—even in the same human being, within a *single* soul" (BGE 260). That there are (clearly failed) *attempts* [*Versuche*] at mediation or that both viewpoints can exist in one soul does not, of course, show that there is an evaluative standpoint from which one could successfully mediate and reconcile the normative claims of the opposing moralities.

and predestined for them" (BGE 30). In another work, finally, he gives perhaps his fullest exposition of this theme:

> It is not by any means necessarily an objection to a book when anyone finds it impossible to understand: perhaps that was part of the author's intention—he did not want to be understood by just "anybody." All those of noble spirit and taste [*Geschmack*] select their audience when they wish to communicate; and choosing that, one at the same time erects barriers against "the others." All the more subtle laws of any style have their origin at this point: they at the same time keep away, create a distance, forbid "entrance," understanding, as said above—while they open the ears of those whose ears are related to ours. (GS 381)

Now if we assume that Nietzsche does not believe his own evaluative perspective enjoys any privilege over the morality he revalues, then it would, indeed, make sense for Nietzsche to want to circumscribe his audience to those who share his evaluative taste: to those for whom no justification would be required, those who are simply "made for it," "those whose ears are related to ours," who are "predisposed and predestined" for Nietzsche's insights. For such an audience, one's values require no epistemic privilege to nonetheless carry the weight they must carry for Nietzsche's critique of morality.

3

Moralities are a *Sign-Language of the Affects*

Since, for Nietzsche, there are no mind-independent facts about value, what really happens when we render judgments about value? This is not a question about what the semantic content of those judgments are, for reasons already discussed in Chapter 1. The question is: what psychological process is operative given that that there are no cognizable facts about the world to which evaluative judgment could be responsive or which they could represent?

Nietzsche, I argue, should be located within the familiar tradition of moral anti-realists who are also sentimentalists, like Hume and, in the German tradition, Herder—that is, philosophers who think the best explanation of our moral judgments is in terms of our emotional or affective responses to states of affairs in the world, responses that are, themselves, explicable in terms of psychological facts about the judger. Of course, if our emotional responses had *cognitive* content—if they were, in fact, epistemically sensitive to the putatively moral features of the world—then sentimentalism would be compatible with moral realism (more precisely, with knowledge of objective moral facts). That is not, however, Nietzsche's view: Nietzsche understands our *basic* emotional or affective responses as brute artifacts of our psychological constitution, though there is nothing in Nietzsche's view to rule out the possibility that more complicated feelings (e.g., "guilt") might involve a cognitive component added to the non-cognitive one, even if that is explanatorily otiose (I return to this topic, below). It is the burden of this chapter to explain—and, in part, defend—Nietzsche's views on this score.

Moral judgments, on Nietzsche's view, arise from the interaction of two kinds of affective responses: first, a "basic affect" of inclination towards or aversion from certain acts (or states of affairs), and then a further affective response (the "meta-affect") to that basic affect (that is, sometimes we can be either inclined towards or averted from our basic affects). Affects, for Nietzsche, are essentially conative, constituting motivations and influencing actions (and judgments). (In this regard, Nietzsche does not have a general account of the emotions, since he is only interest in the conative affects.) I argue that we should read Nietzsche as treating basic affects as *non-cognitive,* that is, as identifiable solely by how they feel to the subject who experiences the affect. By contrast, I suggest that meta-affects (I focus on guilt and shame) probably incorporate a *cognitive* component like belief.[1] After showing how this account of moral judgment comports with the reading of Nietzsche's moral philosophy I have defended in prior works (Leiter 2002, 2015a) and presuppose throughout this volume, I conclude by adducing philosophical and empirical psychological reasons for thinking that Nietzsche's account of moral judgment is correct.

1. Sign-Languages and Symptoms

The title of this chapter comes from BGE 187, though the theme in question—that moralities are "a sign-language of the affects"—is a pervasive one in Nietzsche's work throughout the 1880s and central to his moral psychology, as we have already seen in Chapter 1's discussion of his explanatory argument for value anti-realism. In *Daybreak*, recall, he declares that "our moral judgments and evaluations... are only images and fantasies based on a physiological process unknown to us" (D 119). Later in the same book, he writes that "there is nothing good, nothing beautiful, nothing sublime, nothing evil in itself, but that there are states of the soul in which we impose such words upon things external to and within us" (D 210). In *The Gay Science*, he suggests that, "Answers to the question about the *value* of existence may always be considered first of all as the symptoms of certain bodies" (GS Pref: 2). Again, in *Beyond Good and Evil*, he tells us that a philosopher's "morality" simply bears "decisive witness to... the innermost drives of his nature" (BGE 6). In the *Genealogy*, Nietzsche famously claims that "our... values... grow from us with the same inevitability as fruits borne on the tree" (GM Pref: 2). In *Twilight of the Idols*, Nietzsche remarks that "[J]udgments of value... have value only as symptoms" (TI II:2). And in a *Nachlass* note of 1885–86, he says "Moral judgments [are] symptoms and sign languages which betray the process of physiological prosperity or failure" (WP: 258).

Nietzsche has two main metaphors for describing moralities or systems of value—that of *sign-language* (*Zeichensprache*) and of *symptom* [*Symptome*]—and two main idioms in which to explain the referent of the sign-language or cause of the symptom, one psychological involving affects (*Affekten*), feelings (*Gefühle*), or drives (*Triebe*), and the other physiological. The physiological idiom is undoubtedly important to Nietzsche, influenced as he was by the German Materialist movement in Germany in the mid-nineteenth century and his extensive readings in the biological sciences (cf. Leiter 2002: 63–71; Emden 2014), but it seems equally clear that, apart from calling attention to the possibility of physiological explanations for evaluative orientations,

[1] We know that the four uncontroversially universal basic emotions—happiness, sadness, fear, and anger (Ekman and Friesen 1989)—have distinctive physiological, anatomical, neural, and behavioral signatures, and in some cases track bodily changes (see, e.g., LeDoux 1998; Prinz 2007; Prinz and Nichols 2010). This does not show that they are necessarily non-cognitive, though some have argued that we can so construe some of them (e.g., Prinz 2007: 51–68). Nietzsche can be agnostic about many of these issues, since the affects of *inclination* and *aversion* are what are crucially at issue for him.

Nietzsche makes no real intellectual contribution to this kind of explanation.[2] Like Freud, Nietzsche thinks that some class of mental phenomena are physically explicable, though, unlike Freud, he was fairly explicit in rejecting any type-identity of mental and physical states of the person (Leiter 2002: 24–5). But Nietzsche is like Freud in another respect, namely, that the explanatory idiom in which he does most of his work is a *psychological* one, and it is on that idiom we shall focus here.

What could it mean to diagnose particular evaluative judgments, or whole systems of value, as a "sign-language" or "symptom"? The idea of a "symptom" presents the more straightforward case. Consider: my *sore throat* is the symptom of a *viral infection*. That means: the symptom (the soreness of the throat) is *caused by* the virus. So if moral judgments are *symptoms* of certain psychological states that means those states are *causes* of the moral judgments. Of course, the relationship is not *simply* causal: rather the symptoms count as *evidence* for their cause, because they reveal something about the psychological states that give rise to them.

Sign-languages are, it seems, a bit different. A sign-language is some system of symbols or signs that have semantic content, that is, have some *meaning* in virtue of *representing* something else.[3] If I raise just my pointer and middle finger, that *means* either peace or victory. The referent of a sign with representational content need not, however, be the cause of that content, though there is certainly one familiar, contemporary view of semantic content in which that would be the case. But like a symptom, the sign does stand in some kind of meaningful inferential relation with its referent (or cause): in both cases, the referent, or cause, is expressed by the symptom or sign. Since Nietzsche uses the metaphors of "symptom" and "sign-language" interchangeably, and since there is no evidence he had a well-developed semantic view, it is natural to understand them the same way. Thus, in what follows, I will assume that the claim that a morality is a "symptom" or "sign-language" of X means that X is the *cause* of the morality (or the cause of some person making a particular evaluative or moral judgment) and, moreover, it is a cause whose existence can be (defeasibly) inferred from the symptom or sign.[4]

What, then, of the psychological causes on offer? Nietzsche refers primarily to just three: affects, feelings, and drives.[5] I take *affects* and *feelings* to refer usually to the

[2] He acknowledges as much in the "Note" at the end of GM I when he calls for a prize to encourage physiologists and doctors to study the effects of different values on persons. See the critical discussion of Emden (2014), in this regard, in Leiter (2017).

[3] There are non-representationalist views of semantic content (think Robert Brandom or Huw Price, for example), but there is no reason, of course, to think Nietzsche had such a view in mind, or, indeed, that he had loyalty to any particular theory of meaning. It is thus best to interpret his remarks in the most natural, "ordinary-language" way that still allows us to make sense of his terminology.

[4] I will thus assume that to the extent a symptom or sign *expresses* a meaning, it does so in virtue of how it is caused by the underlying item of which it is a sign or symptom.

[5] What then of "desire," which might also seem to be a motivationally effective state? Note that the German *Trieb* can mean either "drive" or "desire," and while Nietzsche will occasionally speak, for example, of a *Wunsch* (wish or desire), he seems to assimilate desires either to *drives* or to certain kinds of *affects*.

same kind of mental state for Nietzsche,[6] while I will construe drives, following Katsafanas (2013b), as *dispositions to have affective responses under certain conditions* (so, e.g., the sex drive is the disposition to become sexually aroused under particular conditions). We will consider each of these in turn, before taking up the reasons for thinking that, suitably construed, moralities *really are* symptomatic of our affects.[7]

2. Feelings and Affects

In *Daybreak*, Nietzsche's first mature work, "moral feelings" (*Moralische Gefühle*) are said to be inculcated when "children observe in adults inclinations for and aversions to certain actions and, as born apes, *imitate* these inclinations [*Neigungen*] and aversions [*Abneigungen*]; in later life they find themselves full of these acquired and well-exercised affects [*Affekten*] and consider it only decent to try to account for and justify them" (D 34). We may bracket for the moment the astute concluding observation—about the impulse to supply post-hoc rationalizations for evaluative judgments produced by a non-rational mechanism—in order to focus for now on what this passage tells us about Nietzsche's conception of affects and moral judgment.

Moral feelings or affects, in the passage under consideration, are equated with "inclinations for and aversions to certain actions," or, more precisely, with the mental state, whatever it is, that motivates one to perform certain actions or avoid certain other actions.[8] Nietzsche's ontology of the mind thus includes (unsurprisingly) mental states that are conative, in the sense that they produce what I will call henceforth *motivational oomph* (or *push*), that is, they incline towards or avert away from certain acts, even if they are not ultimately successful in producing action. In this respect, Nietzsche's usage is quite intelligible to us: we often assume that *affects* or *feelings* are characterized, in part, by their ability to produce *motivational oomph*, and, indeed, the fact that they do so is one of the main points thought to count in favor of meta-ethical views that understand moral judgments to involve the expression of feelings (a point to which we will return).

It is equally a part of ordinary usage to take feelings to have another crucial characteristic: namely, that they are phenomenologically distinctive. There is something *it feels like* to be inclined to stop the child from sticking his hand in the fire, and there is something *it feels like* to be inclined to avoid killing a child. A *non-cognitivist* view of affects claims that they can be fully individuated by their distinctive phenomenal feel;

[6] There are occasional exceptions, e.g., BGE 19, but these are somewhat anomalous.

[7] Of course, many different things might be symptomatic of our affects: e.g., our facial expressions, our behaviors. Nietzsche thinks, however, that moralities reveal things about our affects and drives that are especially important and which we would not otherwise recognize *unless* we interpreted moral judgments as expressive of affects. This will become clearer in the discussion that follows, below.

[8] There is a certain affinity here to aspects of Stoic moral psychology, with which Nietzsche, as a classicist, was certainly familiar, though he rejects the ultimately rationalist elements of the Stoic view. Brennan (2003) is a useful overview. The relationship between Nietzsche's view and that of the Stoics requires independent treatment.

a cognitivist view denies that, claiming, instead, that to individuate the affect one also needs to consider some aspect of its *cognitive* (i.e., truth-evaluable) content, such as a belief.[9] Cognitivist views of emotions, notoriously, are forced to deny that human

[9] The most ambitious attempt to read Nietzsche as holding a cognitivst view of the emotions is Poellner (2012). Poellner argues, plausibly, that Nietzsche employs an "*aestheticist* style of evaluation" (2012: 57), but argues, less plausibly, that this mode of valuation warrants a cognitivist and realist interpretation. Poellner cites (2012: 58) as an example Nietzsche's appraisal of Wagner's *Meistersinger*, which I quote in part:

> Now it seems archaic, now strange, acid and too young, it is as arbitrary as it is pompous-traditional, it is not infrequently puckish, still more often rough and uncouth—it has fire and spirit and at the same time the loose yellow skin of fruits which ripen too late. It flows broad and full: and suddenly a moment of inexplicable hesitation...an oppression producing dreams, almost a nightmare—but already the old stream of well-being, of happiness old and new, *very* much including the well-being of the artist himself. (BGE 240)

On Poellner's rendering, Nietzsche's evaluation of the music "concern[s] mostly its *expressive properties*" (2012: 60), that is, properties that express actual or possible mental states. Nietzsche's response to the music, Poellner says, is "more adequately characterized as a direct (non-inferential) experience, a perception, of certain sensory phenomena *as suitable* or appropriate for the expression of certain mental states" (2012: 59). Notice that the claim that the experience is one of certain phenomena "as suitable or appropriate" for expressing mental states is added by Poellner; nothing in the passage, as far as I can see, requires it. Undoubtedly, Nietzsche describes his experience of the music as expressing these properties: but where is the experience of *suitability* or *appropriateness*? It can not simply be that Nietzsche so describes the music, since that is equally compatible with denying the claim about *suitability*.

Poellner wants to import a kind of aesthetic realism (of a surprisingly Kantian kind) into his reading of Nietzsche. Poellner says, plausibly (and consistent with Nietzsche's view, I believe), that in an aesthetic experience the "awareness of certain phenomenal properties of the object...includes or motivates an affective response to the object" (2012: 61). To this, Poellner adds, without additional textual evidence from Nietzsche, that "an aesthetic experience presents its object as having an autonomous value" (2012: 61). "Autonomous" is, however, ambiguous, and Poellner's gloss on it may not be inconsistent with Nietzsche's writing: "The affective component of the experience is motivated by what the phenomenal object *itself* is, not by what it may be instrumentally good for" (2012: 61). None of this yet gets us the surprising idea that the aesthetic experience of the object represents it as "suitable" or "appropriate" for expressing the mental states it expresses. Bear in mind that Nietzsche clearly views aesthetic experience and pleasure as on a continuum with sexual experience and pleasure (see, e.g., GM III: 6 & 9; TI "What I Owe to the Ancients": 4). That a man finds a naked woman sexually arousing does not mean that he is committed to believing that naked women *ought* to command such a response, nor does it mean that his pleasurable arousal is only a matter of the instrumental value of naked women. We need clear textual evidence that Nietzsche thinks aesthetic experience is different.

Poellner's thesis that for Nietzsche the "grounds" of "ethical" value judgments "are ultimately located in experiences which are aesthetic" (62) is an attractive one, but what renders Poellner's view distinctive, and to my mind less plausible, is what he says about aesthetic value. On the one hand, as we have seen, Poellner views aesthetic experiences as *affective*, but he has a very particular (and, in my view, un-Nietzschean) *cognitivist* view of affects:

> [A]ffective experiences are essentially intentional or *representational*.... Affective experience represents these objects under *value aspects*; grief represents an event as sad (in a specific way), indignation as unjust or immoral, disgust represents its object as nauseous, sexual desire as physically attractive, "aesthetic" contemplative pleasure as beautiful or perhaps harmonious... [Thus] in saying that some affects represent putative features of objects, we are saying that, being intentional, they have conditions of success. My grief or horror or fear may turn out to have been misplaced, inappropriate, to have *mis*represented the object. (2012: 63, 64)

In his radical cognitivism about the emotions, Poellner has, I believe, gone beyond anything that Nietzsche's texts would warrant. We can agree, for example, that affective experiences have intentional objects (if I'm *afraid*, I'm [typically] afraid *of* something!), without agreeing that such experiences "represent[]

infants can have emotions, since they lack the concepts necessary for having truth-evaluable judgments (cf. Deigh 1994). That infants cannot have emotions might seem a *reductio* of the cognitivist position, at least to anyone who has ever cared for an infant. Cognitivist views of emotions (that equate them with judgments or beliefs) also have difficulty with irrational affects—e.g., phobias—since often those in their grips believe (judge) that it is irrational to be afraid of the objects in question (heights, flying, open spaces) yet still experience the feeling. A large body of psychological research shows that, as Jesse Prinz puts it, many "emotions can arise without judgment, thoughts, or other cognitive mediators" (2007: 57). While it may be doubtful that qualitative feel can distinguish all emotional states (Prinz's example is differentiating "anger" from "indignation" [2007: 52]), that is not necessarily pertinent to Nietzsche's concerns. For Nietzsche locates the *affective* source of moral judgment, in the first instance, in fairly basic or simple mental states of *inclination* and *aversion*, and it seems quite plausible that there is something it feels like to be *inclined towards* X or *averted away from* Y, even if the relevant *qualia* might be thought inadequate to pick out all conceptual nuances we might want to apply to such cases.[10] Yet when I find Nazi treatment of the Jews morally abhorrent, an intense *aversion* seems the right description of my feeling; and when I find myself filled with emotion watching Martin Luther King, Jr. face down racists in Chicago, *inclination* towards him seems key to the feeling I have. Moral philosophers, who spend too much time in their studies parsing their theoretically-informed feelings, often miss the absolutely crucial affective feelings, namely, that they are *for* and *against*.[11] It is likely, of course, that many of our conceptually nuanced distinctions between, say, *anger* and *indignation* are explanatorily otiose with respect to the *motivational oomph* associated with the feeling in question. I think that is the case, though there are some crucial exceptions, as the moral emotion of "guilt," discussed below, will suggest.

these objects under *value aspects*": the death of a loved one may cause my grief—an affect which has as its object his death—but that does not mean my feeling "represents" his death "as sad": it just means that I feel sad *about* his death. But Poellner needs a stronger claim, since he wants to say that my emotions, "in being intentional...have conditions of success" (2012: 64), that is, my grief could be false, because the death is not, in fact, sad. Poellner asserts that the "bodily sensations" of fear, for example, are caused by the representation of what is fearful, rather than being the cause of the feeling (2012: 64), but this is empirically false (Prinz 2007: 56–60). Poellner sometimes cites Peter Goldie, but Goldie warned us, correctly, against stripping the *feeling* out of emotions, even if they have intentional objects (he proposed instead a primitive mental state, "feeling towards," to capture what is at stake). In sum, I do not see the textual evidence for ascribing this view to Nietzsche, nor do I think it represents the most promising view of emotions.

[10] In this regard, I take the account of basic affects here to be consistent with the claim that Nietzsche takes "self-conscious" mental states to be epiphenomenal (Riccardi 2015: 225; Riccardi 2017), a topic to which I return in Chapter 5. Basic affects are not linguistically articulated, they are more like the phenomenal "feels" that, on any plausible view can be conscious without being linguistically articulated.

[11] As we will see in Chapter 5, Nietzsche is, correctly, skeptical that we can *really* correctly describe introspectively our mental states, though we can presumably detect the feeling of *inclination* and *aversion*. But philosophers tend to spend considerable time parsing culturally specific artifacts that they imagine to be their actual feelings, and for Nietzsche, those are explanatorily irrelevant.

Perhaps more pertinent is the other problem that is supposed to afflict non-cognitivist views of feelings or affects, namely, how to account for our propensity to think emotional responses can be assessed as warranted or not (cf. Prinz 2007: 60ff.). Even in infants, of course, emotional responses have causal triggers: the infant *sees* a scary monster and reacts by crying in fear. The infant's *fear* has an *intentional content*: it is *about* something, namely, the scary monster. We might believe the infant is wrong to be afraid (i.e., what the infant sees is not dangerous, since it is only make-believe), but that does not change the fact that the infant experiences upset and fear. I believe that a child is about to stick his hand in the flame, and so I *feel inclined* to stop him. "Feel inclined" understates the character of the feeling, of course: *I feel I must* stop him. But the fact that there is a causal relationship between a mental state with cognitive content and an affective response, does not show that to *identify* the affect one must understand it to be constituted, in whole or even in part, by a *cognitive* component. We need to account for the *intentionality* of emotions, to be sure, but that does not mean we have to identify emotions with *judgments* or, more generally, with propositional attitudes like belief and desire. It might suffice to introduce a kind of explanatorily primitive mental state, as Peter Goldie (2002: 19) famously proposes, like "feeling towards," one that capture both the *intentionality* of emotional states *and* their distinctive qualitative character.

So feeling inclined to do X or averse to doing Y can have a distinctive phenomenal character, even if the causal trigger for the feeling is a false belief of the agent with the distinctive feeling. When we criticize the resulting emotion, perhaps, then, we are making a different normative judgment, something like: a correct belief about the facts ought not cause such an affective response. Consider: the infant falsely experiences (without any conceptual content) the family dog as a danger, and so bursts into tears. We think the infant is *mistaken*, because we know that the family dog is not dangerous. But we do not criticize the infant for having an unwarranted affective response, rather we console the infant. Why? Perhaps because we do not think the infant is *epistemically responsible* for its false cognition of the family dog as dangerous. But when I react with anger to a perceived slight by the store clerk that, in reality, was nothing of the kind, I can be criticized not because anger is anything other than non-cognitive, and not because my "belief that I've been slighted" is a causal trigger for my anger, but because I am epistemically culpable for having a false belief, one that produces unhappy consequences (my anger, a fight with the clerk at the store, an unpleasant scene, etc.).

Yet it seems I can also be criticized for responding with anger even when my belief was correct, i.e., when the store clerk *really was* rude. How can that criticism make sense if the cognitive belief is just a causal trigger for an evaluative/affective response that has no cognitive content? The obvious answer is that such judgments are, themselves, the expression of other non-cognitive attitudes or feelings, such as an inclination towards non-aggressive responses to insults or an aversion to aggressive ones (we might call the latter the "Christian attitude"). Of course, if we view such criticism as making a cognitive, rather than non-cognitive, claim, then we will be forced towards an error-theoretic interpretation of such judgments (that is, we will have to interpret all such judgments as false). But on the general Nietzschean view, it is surely natural to treat such normative criticisms as, themselves, yet more expressions of affects or feelings.[12]

I belabor these points because I want to argue that Nietzsche's view of the basic affects or feelings is fundamentally *non-cognitivist*: he thinks our basic affects of inclination and aversion are marked by a distinctive conscious, qualitative feel.[13] And he thinks such qualitatively distinctive *feels* are the causal root of our moral judgments, even if those fully articulated judgments are influenced by other factors, to which we will turn momentarily. Given that Nietzsche focuses mainly on *inclination* and *aversion towards* as the crucial affective states, the claim that they can be individuated in non-cognitive terms is especially plausible. But we can now also see how the social practice of assessing such feelings as warranted or unwarranted can be compatible with the non-cognitive character of the feeling: to deem them warranted or unwarranted is either (1) to render an epistemic judgment about the cognitive judgment that is the causal trigger for the non-cognitive state, or (2) to express a meta-affect (i.e., an affect *about* an affect) about someone else's affective response to a causal trigger.

3. Drives

The other key element of Nietzsche's ontology of the mind, for purposes of explaining motivation and action, is the notion of a *drive*, which, following Katsafanas (2013b; cf. Richardson 2004: 34–9 for a related account), we will treat as a *disposition to have a particular affective response under certain circumstances*. Thus, for example, the sex drive would be a disposition to become sexually aroused in the presence of an attractive member of the opposite or same sex.[14] These affective orientations also structure how the world appears to us evaluatively: they influence, for example, "perceptual salience," the features of a situation that come to the fore for the agent (because the drive focuses attention on them) (Cf. D 119. Humeans also have a similar view: see, e.g., Sinhababu [2009: 469–70], discussing the "attention-direction" aspect of desire.) Katsafanas (2013b) argues that Nietzschean drives share two features of drives on the Freudian view (unsurprisingly given Freud's interest in Nietzsche). First, drives have a kind of constancy that particular desires do not. The music you desired to listen to in your twenties may no longer appeal in your forties; but the hunger drive keeps coming

[12] As I argued in Chapter 1, I actually think we should resist ascribing any *semantic* view to Nietzsche, so the claims in this paragraph should, strictly speaking, be treated as *explanatory* of moral judgment, rather than as part of a semantics of moral judgment.

[13] Note that while Nietzsche often claims that our drives are *unknown*, but operative unconsciously, he never makes such a claim about affects. More importantly, there is no reason to think the "feel" of affects requires linguistic articulation. I return to these issues in Chapter 5.

[14] The discharge of that drive would then involve acting on the sexual arousal or urge, but the drive can manifest itself in an affective response, even when it is not satisfied.

back whether you are twenty or forty. Second, drives do not depend on an external stimulus to be aroused. External stimuli can give rise to a desire to eat or to have sex, to be sure, but those same desires can simply arise in the absence of any stimuli. It is particularly useful to distinguish, as Freud does, between the *Ziel* (aim) of the drive (e.g., sex, eating) and the *Objekt* of the drive (e.g., this woman, this bit of food). Insofar as a drive is aroused not by an external stimulus, it will then seek out an object for its realization—and in so doing impose a "valuation" on the object.

The relationship between drives and affects is nicely illustrated by this passage from *Daybreak*:

> The same drive evolves into the painful feeling of *cowardice* under the impress of the reproach custom has imposed upon this drive; or into the pleasant feeling of *humility* if it happens that a custom such as the Christian has taken it to its heart and called it *good*. That is to say, it is attended by either a good or a bad conscience! In it itself it has, *like every drive*, neither this moral character nor any moral character at all, nor even a definite attendant sensation of pleasure or displeasure: it acquires all this, as its second nature, only when it enters into relations with drives already baptized good or evil or is noted as a quality of beings the people has already evaluated and determined in a moral sense... (D 38)

In the particular example on offer from Nietzsche, the same *drive* is said to have the potential to give rise to two different moral feelings, that of *cowardice* (which has an unpleasant valence) or *humility* (a pleasant valence), depending on the cultural context. The drive in question must be something like, *a disposition to avoid offending dangerous enemies*, which, if experienced by a Homeric Greek would then give rise to feelings of self-contempt for being a coward and, if experienced by a Christian, would be experienced as the admirable virtue of humility. Cultures, partly through the mechanisms of parental inculcation already noted (as well as concurrent social pressures), teach individuals to have particular affective responses to the very same drive. Notice, however, that we now have two layers of affects here: first, there is the affect of *aversion towards offending dangerous enemies* which is produced by the drive itself, but *then* there is the distinctively *moral affect* of feeling ashamed (as the Homeric Greek does) or proud (as the Christian does) of that affective response. The *moral affect*, then, is more complicated than what I have so far called "the basic affect" of inclination or aversion. The *feeling of being a coward*, on this account, represents the combination of a *feeling of aversion towards offending a dangerous enemy*, conjoined with a meta-feeling of contempt or disgust for having that original feeling. The meta-feeling is, at bottom, a feeling of aversion away from the basic affect, though perhaps to individuate it correctly we will need to add some kind of *belief* about why that basic feeling of aversion is contemptible: e.g., the belief that Homeric men slay their offending enemies, rather than cower before them. Perhaps this is also what Nietzsche is getting at when he writes: "[B]ehind feelings there stand judgments [*Urtheile*] and evaluations [*Werthschätzungen*] which we inherit in the form of feelings (inclinations, aversions). The inspiration born of a feeling is the grandchild of a judgment—and often of a false judgment!" (D 35).

So, for example, the Christian judges that a good person *chooses* to display humility, a trait admirable in the eyes of God, and thus when the Christian experiences the basic affect of aversion towards offending a dangerous enemy, he then experiences the meta-affect of a positive inclination or valence towards that basic affect: he is proud of his humility. The Christian then inculcates those same affective responses in his children, so that their feelings of inclination and aversion are traceable back to a false judgment, i.e., the judgment that there is a God who thinks humility a virtuous trait, as well as the false belief that the "humility" of the Christian is a free choice, rather than a reaction he cannot avoid having.[15] As Nietzsche observes, "we are all irrational" in that we "still draw the conclusions of judgments we consider false, of teachings in which we no longer believe—our feelings make us do it" (D 99), a claim well-supported by the recent empirical literature on "moral dumbfounding," which finds that people will often remain attached to a moral judgment, even when all their reasons for it are defeated (cf. Haidt 2001). (We return to this issue at the end of the chapter.)

If to individuate the meta-affect correctly, we need to take account of the cognitive judgment that informs it, then our picture would be complicated somewhat: we would have non-cognitivism about basic affects, and a cognitivist view about meta-affects. On the other hand, it might suffice for causal explanation of behavior to individuate only the meta-affect of aversion or inclination towards the basic affect. In other words, what might matter for explaining the behavior of the Homeric Greek afflicted with the basic affect of aversion towards giving offense to dangerous enemies is that he feels a motivational push *against* acting on that basic affect, i.e., he feels aversion towards his basic aversion towards offending dangerous enemies. His cognitive beliefs may be causal triggers for the meta-affect, but we need only understand the meta-affect to understand his behavior. But is that right? When the Homeric agent judges his aversion towards offending a stronger enemy as "cowardice," and feels "shame" or "guilt" about it, that judgment is a symptom of his basic affect of aversion towards offending dangerous enemies and his meta-affect of aversion towards the basic affect. But is it really explanatorily idle whether or not that meta-affect is one of "guilt" or "shame"?

Take a slightly different Greek example that suggests what the meta-affect is may not be explanatorily idle. Recall that Oedipus, upon realizing he has killed his father and married his mother, gouges out his eyes, because he is overwhelmed with *shame* and so does not want to look into anyone's eyes again (shame being crucially tied to *being seen* in the shameful condition). Of course, Oedipus did not freely and intentionally choose to kill his father and marry his mother, so his overriding moral emotion is not one of

[15] Recall GM I:13: "When out of the vengeful cunning of powerlessness the oppressed, downtrodden, violated say to themselves: 'let us be different from the evil ones, namely good! And good is what everyone is who does not do violence, who injures no one, who doesn't attack, who doesn't retaliate, who leaves vengeance to God, who keeps himself concealed, as we do, who avoids all evil, and in general demands very little of life, like us, the patient, humble, righteous'—it means, when listened to coldly, and without prejudice, actually nothing more than: 'we weak ones are simply weak; it is good if we do nothing *for which we are not strong enough*.'"

guilt—but what if it were? Eliminating the possibility of human eye contact would not relieve the pain of *guilt*, since guilt, as usually construed, does not require an observer. The agent who experiences the meta-aversion (of "guilt") to the basic aversion of not marrying one's mother or killing one's father would believe he was *responsible* for having done this and thus blameworthy for his lapse of judgment. But, of course, Oedipus doesn't believe any of that, since he did not freely do what he did, he was fated to do so, which is why his meta-aversion is that of shame rather than guilt. So his meta-affective aversion towards his aversion towards killing his father and marrying his mother is of a particular kind: it is *ashamed aversion*, which can be blunted by eye-gouging, rather than *guilty aversion*, which could not be. It thus seems that *sometimes* the distinctively moral emotion is constituted in part by a particular cognitive content (for example, the one—whatever it is precisely—that separates shame from guilt), and so Nietzsche cannot be a thorough-going non-cognitivist about the affects underlying moral judgment, even if he is a non-cognitivist about the basic affects.

That conclusion would, however, explain why Nietzsche holds out the hope that attacking the falsity of the judgments that are the "grandparents" of the meta-affects could make a difference: "We have to *learn to think differently* [*umzulernen*]—in order at least, perhaps very late on, to attain even more: *to feel differently* [*umzufühlen*]" (D 103). To be sure, it could be that correcting such mistaken judgments could make a difference to even non-cognitive affects, insofar as those judgments *happen to be* causally connected to the affects. But if such judgments are partly constitutive of the meta-affects, then the attack on the truth of the metaphysical presuppositions about agency (such as free will) that I have argued elsewhere (2002: 87–101; 2015a: 69–81) is a key part of Nietzsche's critique of morality would be especially relevant.

None of the preceding considerations undermine my basic thesis, however: namely, that for Nietzsche, moral judgments are produced by affective responses. The complication we have noted is that drives give rise to feelings of inclination or aversion, but *not* to all moral affects, some of the latter arising from the influence of culture (e.g., Homeric Greece vs. Christian) which yield meta-affective responses to the basic affects of inclination and aversion. Moral judgments are *still* symptoms of the affects, but the affects sometimes have two different sources: there is the affect of inclination or aversion towards particular actions or things or persons in the world, and then there are affective responses to those basic affects—where the latter are largely inculcated by the local culture and *perhaps* individuated by their cognitive content. The latter observation also explains why Nietzsche expresses the optimistic view that revising our beliefs might actually lead to a revision of our feelings, i.e., those meta-affects or meta-feelings whose object is partly individuated by the cognitive judgment in question.

Someone might object, of course, that if moral judgments are indeed symptoms of *affects*, but some of these affects (the meta- ones) are either contingently or perhaps constitutively (in the case of, say, guilt vs. shame) tied to beliefs, then moral judgments are not *only* the causal products of affective responses: they do depend on what people *believe*, not simply how they *feel*. That might suggest that Nietzsche's view of moral judgment would have to be tempered to say that moralities are symptoms of *affects, but not only affects*. I actually think Nietzsche has available a more ambitious response, since he also seems to hold the view that what I will henceforth call "belief fixation"—that is, the doxastic state in which an agent *takes a belief seriously enough that he will act on it*—is itself dependent on affective investment in the belief (think, e.g., of his explanation of how a desire to punish motivates belief in free will). I will return to this issue in Chapter 4. For purposes of this chapter, it will suffice if the reader is persuaded that moralities are symptomatic of affects, even if in some cases, they are symptomatic of affects *plus certain beliefs*.

A different kind of question also needs to be raised about Nietzsche's picture of moral psychology: namely, why should we think drives exist in the first place? In many passages, after all, Nietzsche notes how ignorant persons are about the drives that constitute them: "However far a man may go in self-knowledge, nothing however can be more incomplete than his image of the totality of *drives* which constitute his being," as he puts it in *Daybreak* (119). Since drives, unlike basic affects, are not identified directly by their conscious, qualitative feel, the grounds for positing their presence must amount to something like an inference to the best explanation of observable behavior and conscious feelings. Yet Nietzsche is notoriously promiscuous with his ontology of drives; in *Daybreak* alone he refers to "the drive to restfulness, or the fear of disgrace and other evil consequences" (D 109); the hunger drive (D 119); "moral... drives" (D 119); "our drive to tenderness or humorousness or adventurousness or... our desire [*Verlangen*] for music and mountains" (D 119); "the drive to praise or blame" (D 140); the drive to feel sorrow or sadness (when triggered by music) (D 142); and "the drive to attachment and care for others (the 'sympathetic affection')" (D 143). On top of that, Nietzsche also claims that drives vary in their degree of *strength* or *vehemence* (*Heftigkeit*) (D 109)—that is, how badly they need to be satisfied—and that this quality of drives is important to their role in explaining moral judgment and action (cf. D 119).

How are we to appraise Nietzsche's promiscuous ontology of drives? There is not even the pretense of demonstrating the explanatory need for some of the drives he posits, many of which are on a par with Moliere's doctor's explanation that opium makes one sleep because of its dormitive power! It is worth bearing in mind, however, that the interest of Nietzsche's hypothesis about the role of drives in moral judgment does *not* depend on any specific hypothesis about particular drives; it turns, rather, on the correctness of the basic model of the mind. We may view some of the specific claims simply as "placeholders" for a more adequate psychology, and it is reasonable to think some of the specific drives Nietzsche posits are explanatorily otiose and would drop out of a more systematic account.[16]

[16] My thinking here was influenced by discussion with Roger Eichorn.

4. Is it True That Moralities Are Just a Sign-Language of the Affects?

We have now given a systematic exposition of Nietzsche's idea that moral judgments are symptoms or sign-languages of the affects, in the sense that moral judgments are caused by affects and meta-affects, which are the joint product of nature and culture, as it were. This is, I have argued, Nietzsche's view, but the more pressing philosophical question is: why should we accept it?

The idea that moral judgments are caused by affective responses has three kinds of evidence in its favor: first, sincere moral judgments—not the lip-service to morality that is the stuff of so much public life—are typically motivationally effective (i.e., even if they do not result in action they produce what we earlier called *motivational oomph*); second, it is a view of moral judgments compatible with the most plausible metaphysics of morality, namely, anti-realism (the view that there are no objective moral facts), a view Nietzsche himself endorses as we saw in Chapter 1; and third, it squares best with existing empirical research on the psychology of moral judgment and moral disagreement. The latter two considerations are not decisive, of course, since it might turn out that Nietzsche held false views, if it happened that moral realism were true or that empirical psychology gave us a different account of moral judgment and disagreement. But if there is good textual evidence that Nietzsche held a view that also seems to be true, then that seems an additional reason of interpretive charity to ascribe it to him. Let us take these considerations up in turn.

First: sincere moral judgments motivate action or, at least, produce motivational oomph. If I genuinely judge that X is morally wrong or Y is morally right, I feel motivated, respectively, to prevent X or bring about Y, even if I fail to do either—cowardice, weakness of will, timidity and so on may all intervene to prevent people from acting on their moral judgments. But what is striking is that those who sincerely affirm a moral judgment at least feel a motivational tug in its direction. That fact has long been thought to be one of the strongest reasons in favor of anti-realist views of moral judgment. More precisely, it has been thought to count in favor of *non-cognitivist* views of moral judgments, according to which such judgments are caused by motivationally effective mental states, such as desires and feelings, rather than mental states like belief that only represent aspects of the world. Nietzsche, as I argued in Chapter 1, does not have a considered view about the semantics of moral judgment, but we can prescind from the semantics[17] and still recognize that the thesis that moral judgments are a "sign-language" of the affects is primarily a causal, psychological hypothesis. As a result, the considerations just adduced that count in favor of non-cognitivist semantics will also count in favor of Nietzsche's actual hypothesis. For if agents making sincere moral judgments are motivated to act in accordance with those judgments (whether or

[17] See Chapter 1, Section 1.

not they follow through on the motivation), then it counts in favor of any hypothesis about the causes of moral judgments that it should explain why such judgments produce motivational oomph. But the hypothesis that moral judgments are caused by affective responses is precisely that kind of hypothesis, since everyone agrees that affective or emotional responses put causal pressure on action. So the first reason to believe that moral judgments really are just "sign-languages of the affects" is that it explains why moral judgments are associated with motivation, namely, that they arise from feeling inclined to or averted from certain actions, even if the maker of the judgment does not actually act upon those feelings.

Second: any acceptable view of moral judgment ought to be consistent with a plausible account of the metaphysical status of moral facts, and any plausible view of moral judgment ascribed to Nietzsche should, in particular, be compatible with his own view about the metaphysical status of moral facts. I argued in Chapters 1 and 2 that Nietzsche's metaphysical view, following the pre-Socratics, is clear: there are no objective or mind-independent facts about what is morally right and wrong. Nature is, as he says in *The Gay Science*, "always value-less, but has been given value at some time, as a present—and it was we who gave and bestowed it." Such a metaphysical picture fits neatly with the idea that our judgments about moral value are not responsive to the pre-existing evaluative features of the world, but rather caused by non-cognitive affective states of the judger.[18]

Recall again some of the evidence adduced in Chapter 1. Early on in his first mature work, *Daybreak*, Nietzsche compares the way "man has ascribed to all that exists a connection with morality [*Moral*] and laid an *ethical significance* [*ethische Bedeutung*] on the world's back" to the earlier, and now discredited, "belief in the masculinity or femininity of the sun" (D 3). Later, in Book II of the same work (D 100), he compares the way "wise and noble men still believe in the 'moral significance [*sittliche Bedeutung*] of existence' " to the way they previously "believed in the music of the spheres," which is "no longer... audible to them." (The switch to *sittliche Bedeutung* probably reflects the fact that the theme of the "morality of custom [*Sitte*]"—i.e., *Sittlichkeit*—was introduced in Book I.) Passages like these invite both a metaphysical and an epistemological interpretation (I put aside the possible semantic reading, for the reasons already given). On the *metaphysical* reading, Nietzsche is saying that *there do not exist objective moral properties in the world*, just as there do not exist gendered properties of the sun, or musical properties of the heavenly bodies. To be sure, at one time, humans "perceived" the sun and the heavenly bodies as having gendered and musical properties, but those entities did not really (objectively) have them. Nietzsche's view thus seems to be a kind of *projectivism*, in particular, an instance of what Peter Kail (in discussing

[18] I concede it is possible someone might claim that affective responses are epistemically reliable ways of tracking the truth about what morality requires. That is plainly not Nietzsche's own view, and, given the overwhelming evidence of the ways in which emotional responses are epistemically unreliable in so many other contexts, it would be surprising, indeed, were they to turn out to be epistemically superior in this domain.

Hume) calls *explanatory projection* according to which "some feature of our mentality explains how the world appears to us." In a case of *explanatory projection*, "The thinker is not responsive to the world in a way whereby their beliefs, concepts and experience reflect their object. In a slogan: explanatory projection is non-detective [or non-detecting] explanation" (Kail 2007: xxix–xxx.)[19] On the *epistemological* interpretation, which I think Nietzsche probably also intends, our purported *knowledge* of objective moral facts is an illusion, an unsurprising upshot of the metaphysical reading. As Nietzsche puts it, once again in *Daybreak* (D:2): "it is a prejudice of the learned that *we now know better* than any other age . . . what is good and evil."

Third and finally: Nietzsche's view that moralities are a sign-language of the affects in something like the sense I have articulated here fits well with the empirical evidence about moral judgment and motivation. We should acknowledge, of course, that the evidence is ambiguous, but it certainly tends in the Nietzschean direction. Recall, for example, Nietzsche's claim, discussed earlier, that "moral feelings" (*Moralische Gefühle*) are inculcated when "children observe in adults inclinations for and aversions to certain actions and, as born apes, *imitate* these inclinations [*Neighungen*] and aversions [*Abneighungen*]; in later life they find themselves full of these acquired and well-exercised affects [*Affekten*] and consider it only decent to try to account for and justify them" (D 34). That point fits nicely with Jonathan Haidt's famous work on the "social intuitionist" model of moral judgment (Haidt 2001) according to which in most ordinary situations, moral judgments are produced by emotional or affective responses, the reasons adduced in their support being post-hoc: they do not explain the judgment, as evidenced by the resilience of the judgment even in the face of the defeat of the proffered reasons. Haidt, himself, is somewhat confused about the import of these empirical findings, for, contrary to Haidt, they state no dispute with a philosophical rationalist about moral judgment like Kant, since Kant is not committed to *either* the claim that most people actually arrive at their moral judgments through the exercise of practical reason *or* that most people arrive at moral judgments that can be justified, even after the fact, by the correct exercise of practical reason. The Kantian rationalist is committed, I take it, only to the claim that rational agents can, in principle, revise their moral judgments in light of practical reason, but nothing in Haidt's research rules out that possibility—indeed, he acknowledges that sometimes reasoning can result in a revision of moral judgments. But Nietzsche needs for his purposes only the descriptive thesis—that affective or emotional responses ordinarily determine moral judgment—since he has independent arguments for skepticism about practical reason against the moral rationalist like Kant that do not depend on the actual causal process by which people ordinarily arrive at moral judgments (see Chapter 1, Section 3 and Chapter 5, Sections 5 and 6).

[19] The contrast is with what Kail calls "feature projection," which he also finds in Hume, and which is central to the Freudian concept of projection: "In features projection, features of our mentality become represented as features of some other object (I project my hate in thinking that someone else hates me)."

Recent empirical work on moral psychology also lends support to Nietzsche's view of moral judgments as sign-languages of the affects. As a recent literature survey notes, individuals "with selective deficits in emotional processing" due to disease or injury to the brain render different moral judgments about hypothetical situation like the Trolley cases, than most emotionally normal subjects to hypothetical situations (Cushman et al. 2010: 53–4), suggesting that the affective responses are causes of the moral judgments. Psychologist and philosopher Joshua Greene (2007) has argued that emotional responses loom larger in deontological than consequentialist moral judgments, the latter demanding more "controlled cognition" (Cushman et al. 2010: 54), but in more recent work even Greene has acknowledged that "affect supplies the primary motivation to view harm as a bad thing" in the first place, so that even utilitarian reasoning has "an affective basis" (Cushman et al. 2010: 62).[20]

In a recent review of the empirical literature, Timothy Schroeder, Adina Roskies, and Shaun Nichols found that the view they dub "sentimentalism"—namely, the view that "the emotions typically play a key causal role in motivating moral behavior" (Schroeder et al. 2010: 77)—is well-supported by the "evidence from psychology and neuroscience" (Schroeder et al. 2010: 98), and that while "motivation derived [exclusively] from higher cognitive centers independently of desire is possible... the only known model of it is pathological" involving Tourette syndrome (Schroeder et al. 2010: 94). Such empirical findings do not rule out the possibility that moral judgments are not causal products of the affects, of course, but they suggest that the evidential burden must be borne by views that deny that causal role to affective responses.

Nietzsche's account of moral judgments as sign-languages of the affects seems, in short, to have the empirical evidence on its side, and this is not the first time a Nietzschean hypothesis has turned out to win support from subsequent empirical psychology, as we will see in Chapters 5 and 7. Of course, this raises a question that we first broached in the Introduction. Any reader of Nietzsche knows that he is not primarily concerned to report the findings of psychological "research" or to establish, through conventional methods of argumentation and the mustering of evidence, the truth of particular empirical hypotheses. His work is suffused with psychological and empirical claims, to be sure, but his aims are always much more polemical and practical: to transform the consciousness of at least some readers about the morality they take for granted, and thus, at the same time, to change their affective orientation towards their lives. Nietzsche's psychological claims are always subservient to these rhetorical aims, but this does not alter the fact that Nietzsche makes psychological claims, ones that admit of empirical study and confirmation, and many of which may, as recent research suggests, be true. But, how one might wonder, could Nietzsche have

[20] More precisely, "affect supplies the primary motivation to regard harm as bad. Once this primary motivation is supplied, reasoning proceeds in a currency-like manner [currency emotions are designed to participate in the process of practical reasoning]" (Cushman et al. 2010: 63). "[A]larm-bell emotions are designed to circumvent reasoning" (Cushman et al. 2010: 62) and, arguably, this is "the origin of the welfare principle" (93).

been so right about so much of moral psychology without employing the methods of contemporary empirical psychology? This is an important question in this volume, given that my interest in Nietzsche is not motivated by antiquarian concerns.

We already addressed this issue in Section 3 of the Introduction, but we may add one additional observation here. We must remember that the best account of the psychology of human agency, moral and otherwise, is on a clear continuum with ordinary "folk" psychological explanations of behavior, in a way that contemporary physical science is *not* derivable from "folk" physics, that is, from the ordinary categories we use to make sense of our observations about the physical world around us. Atoms, molecules, and invisible forces do not play an obvious role in my observation that if I drop the sofa on my toe, it will hurt, but contemporary empirical psychology avails itself of basically the same ontology—beliefs, desires, traits, bodily movements—that are the very stuff of unsystematic folk psychology. For a genius like Nietzsche, speculation drawing on his own observations and that of other psychologically astute historical figures from Thucydides to Schopenhauer, as well as his lively interest in contemporary psychological research, was sufficient to make his speculative psychology fruitful and often remarkably accurate: with unsystematic data and methods he could nonetheless arrive at hypotheses—including the hypothesis that moral judgments are sign-languages of the affects—that turn out to be supported by the more systematic data and methods the scientific study of human beings relies on today.

4

Anti-Realism, Value, Perspectivism

1. Introduction: The Scope of Value Anti-Realism

The ascription of moral anti-realism to Nietzsche, the view defended in the preceding chapters, is complicated by the fact that he does not appear to make the mistake of some twentieth-century anti-realists, like A.J. Ayer and Charles Stevenson, who simply assume that the metaphysical status of moral norms is different in kind from the status of epistemic norms. After all, as we have already seen, it is nature "that is value-less," and *all* value (*Werthe*) is "bestowed" by (at least some select) humans onto this value-free nature (GS 301). But judgments about what we *ought* to believe in light of the evidence also depend on *values*—"epistemic norms" is the current term of art—and it is hard to see why those values should be exempt from Nietzschean anti-realism. All putative knowing is, after all, as Nietzsche argues in the famous *Genealogy* passage on perspectivism (GM III:12), animated by *affects* (or interests), but if the basic ones are—as I claimed in Chapter 3—non-cognitive, then it is hard to see how they could be deemed epistemically reliable or special. The point is even more explicit in the late discussion of perspectivism in *The Gay Science* (in Book V, added in 1886), when Nietzsche says that "we 'know' (or believe or imagine) exactly as much as is *useful* to the interests of the human herd, to the species: and even what is here called 'usefulness' is finally also just a belief, an imaginary construct..." (GS 354). These passages are important, in this context, not because they express doubts about truth or its existence, but because their target is explicitly *epistemic*, suggesting that norms of epistemic warrant answer to interests and affects that, themselves, have no independent standing as reliable trackers of the truth.

The conjunction of an apparent global anti-realism about value and specifically moral anti-realism can appear perplexing, and has confused some Anglophone philosophers.[1] On the one hand, Nietzsche seems to deny the metaphysical objectivity of values on the basis of broadly naturalistic considerations (as argued in Chapters 1 and 2), considerations that themselves presuppose certain epistemic norms, the norms

[1] See Hilary Putnam (2004).

in virtue of which we deem nature to have the non-moral characteristics it has. Yet Nietzsche seems to have no reason to exempt epistemic values from his value skepticism. How then to understand his position? There is no reason, in my view, to think Nietzsche had a clear handle on this philosophical issue. Like a lot of intellectuals self-taught in philosophy,[2] he sometimes made a mess of certain philosophical problems, especially those related to knowledge and truth. Yet the problem his meta-normative skepticism presents is one that has become familiar in the second-half of the twentieth century, one that figures in the work of W.V.O. Quine and (in a rather different way) John McDowell, among other leading philosophers of recent decades. I propose in this chapter a resolution that may or may not have been one Nietzsche had in mind, but which makes good philosophical sense of his position (and, indeed, seems to me a sensible position).

I begin with a consideration of what Nietzsche actually says about perspectivism, then turn to objections to the kind of naturalism about value defended in this and the preceding chapters.

2. Nietzsche on Perspectivism, Knowledge, and Affects

Perspectivism is discussed in detail in only two passages in the works Nietzsche chose to publish: Section 354 of *The Gay Science* (GS 354) and the Third Treatise, Section 12 of *On the Genealogy of Morality* (GM III:12). The term itself, *Perspektivismus*, is used only in GS 354 (where it is equated with "phenomenalism"[3]). GM III:12 uses several

[2] Remember that Nietzsche was trained as a classical philologist (what we would now call a classicist), and was almost entirely self-taught in philosophy, starting in the late 1860s. Scholarship has shown that he was heavily dependent on secondary sources for his understanding of the history of philosophy, but he did read many primary texts on his own. Moreover, secondary literature at that time tended to quote extensively from the primary sources.

[3] I asked an excellent PhD student here at the University of Chicago, Joshua Fox, to look into the question of why Nietzsche would have equated perspectivism and "phenomenalism." His research was sufficiently illuminating, that I want to quote a good bit of it here:

> The term "Phänomenalismus" appears ten times in Nietzsche's writing—once in *Gay Science* 354, once in *Anti-Christ* 20, and eight times in unpublished *Nachlass* material. All uses are from the period between 1885 and 1888. In the *Anti-Christ* passage, Nietzsche describes Buddhism as having a phenomenalist epistemology, citing its focus on suffering instead of sin as an example. In *Nachlass* fragment 9[126] from the fall, 1887 journals, Nietzsche lists phenomenalism—alongside Schopenhauer—under the heading "epistemic pessimism." *Nachlass* fragment 2[184] from the fall, 1885—fall, 1886 period presents phenomenalism as making the following pronouncement: "Der Phänomenalismus: wir wissen nichts von einem 'Ding an sich.'" In all other cases, the term phenomenalism appears in arguments for the unreliability of so-called "facts of consciousness"—it is because phenomenalism operates even in the case of self-observation that we cannot trust conscious representations of our own mental states.
>
> These uses of the term phenomenalism are consistent with its typical philosophical use in the latter half of the nineteenth century. The term was applied to any view which limited human understanding to a world of appearances (i.e. a world which was in some sense a

cognate terms—*Perspektiven* (perspectives), *perspektivisches Sehen* (perspective seeing), *perspektivisches "Erkennen"* (perspective "knowing")—but never *Perspektivismus*. GS 354 was part of the Fifth Book added to the second edition of *The Gay Science* some five years after the first four "books" appeared (1881); in other words, the Fifth Book was written around the same time as GM III:12 (1886). One might hope an interpretation of perspectivism could show how these two passages fit together.

Briefly—and simply by way of introduction—GS 354 claims that our conscious "knowledge" of the world is influenced by evolutionary pressures: what we take ourselves to know is only that which serves the needs of the species, as it were. Such knowledge is relative to perspective, but this is the *human perspective*, one we cannot escape in virtue of being human. I will call this *Global Humeanism*, since it supposes, with Hume, that the non-rational dispositions towards forming certain kinds of beliefs are so widely shared (due to evolutionary pressures on Nietzsche's view—not Hume's, obviously) that they are *typical of being human* and thus give rise to a common body of beliefs about the world that are socially useful, even if false (or unwarranted).[4] By contrast, GM III:12 advances a superficially different claim, namely, that all knowledge is dependent (in some sense to be specified) on affects. GM III:12 advances this thesis, in particular, against the possibility Schopenhauer held out of affect-free knowledge: for Nietzsche, all knowledge—even of space, time, and causality—is dependent on the affects. This will form the crux of the continuity between the passages, as I will argue below. In the end, I will argue, GM III:12 calls our attention to the role affects play only in what comes to our cognitive attention, not in constituting what really exists.

product of human subjectivity)—for the phenomenalist, in other words, human knowledge was necessarily knowledge of a phenomenal world. A wide variety of different views were taken to be phenomenalist in this sense. It was sometimes equated with idealism [citations omitted]—views like Berkley's which equated reality and appearance were identified as phenomenalist. However, the term was also applied to views like those of Kant and Schopenhauer which limited human knowledge to the realm of appearance, but still drew a distinction between appearance and reality, asserting the existence of an unknowable reality (a thing in itself) behind the apparent world...

Nietzsche would have already been familiar with the term from earlier readings. Thus, Brobjer notes that Nietzsche likely read Hans Vaihinger's *Hartman, Dühring und Lange: Zur Geschichte der deutschen Philosophie* in 1876 (Brobjer 2008: 156), which made use of the term in connection with a discussion of the difference between Hartmann and Dühring's views - Dühring's assertion of "die absolute Realität der Aussenwelt" is contrasted with the "absoluten Phänomenalismus" of Hartmann (Vaihinger 1876:43). Likewise, Nietzsche read Friedrich Ueberweg's *Grundriss der Geschichte der Philosophie* in 1867–1868 (Brobjer 2008: 67), which made wide use of the term—notably equating it with idealism on multiple occasions in discussion of Berkley, while also using it to describe Kant's view that we can only understand the world as filtered through subjective organizing principles that may or may not actually apply to its reality...

[4] "Global Humeanism" is a kind of "species relativism" that was common in Germany in the late nineteenth century, one often associated with forms of psychologism according to which putative laws of logic are really just facts about the psychology of our species; one sees resonance of those ideas in Nietzsche too, though his view about the status of logic is not obviously consistent throughout his writings (sometimes he writes as if logic really is a priori, and not simply because evolution selected for such inferences in creatures like us). See generally Kusch (1995).

2.1 Gay Science 354

GS 354 begins with a puzzle: why should thinking, feeling, willing, and remembering be conscious, since each could transpire without being conscious, without "seeing itself in a mirror" (as Nietzsche puts it)?[5] The answer Nietzsche proffers is that these mental states become conscious because of the need to communicate with others: "consciousness is . . . a net of communication between human beings; it is only as such that it had to develop." Here Nietzsche echoes Herder's view that conscious thinking is articulated in language (as Nietzsche puts it: "the development of language and the development of consciousness . . . go hand in hand"), but (this is Nietzsche, not necessarily Herder) language develops only as "required by social or herd utility," which consists in communicating what is common in experience (not what is distinctively individual). Nietzsche equates this with "perspectivism": "all becoming conscious [i.e., becoming *aware of*] involves a great and thorough corruption, falsification, reduction to superficialities," i.e., the superficialities conducive to socially useful communication (superficial precisely because they pick out only what is common to different experiences and thus useful for social coordination: cf. BGE 268 for a similar argument). In context, it seems clear Nietzsche does not mean this point to apply to brute perceptual consciousness (e.g., experiencing redness or sweetness), but rather to the linguistically articulable awareness of our own mental life, or the mental lives of others, as well as observable features of the world we inhabit.[6] His conclusion: "We simply lack any organ for knowledge, for 'truth': we 'know' (or believe or imagine) just as much as may be *useful* in the interests of the human herd, the species . . . ."

There are two key ideas at the conclusion of GS 354. First, unlike some recent Anglophone philosophers (e.g., Street 2006: 130–1), Nietzsche recognizes that evolutionary forces affecting human cognition do not necessarily prefer true to false belief—even in the case of ordinary knowledge about the empirical world (cf. Stich 1978: 55–60, for an earlier, and more plausible Anglophone assessment: natural selection favors false positives or false negatives over accuracy in perceptual reports whenever the former confer reproductive advantage). This point will be especially true with regard to claims about our mental lives, since these are only useful for social coordination to the extent that they identify *common* features, not individual or idiosyncratic ones: what my pain upon being bitten by the snake is *really* like is irrelevant compared to the fact that *you want to avoid it!*, which is what others in my community need to "know." Nietzsche's claim is that our conscious knowledge is subject to evolutionary pressures which are only accidentally truth-tracking but are essentially reproductive-fitness-tracking: thus we lack a capacity for knowledge (without quote marks), having only an ability to "know" what is useful for the "herd" (since Nietzsche takes the average type of person to be the upshot of natural selection). Call this aspect of Nietzsche's view in GS 354

[5] I return in detail in Chapter 5 to Nietzsche's understanding of consciousness.

[6] Cf. Riccardi (2015: 225), which offers an illuminating discussion of why Nietzsche takes introspection to be an inadequate way to acquire self-knowledge, partly in the context of GS 354.

Skeptical Darwinism. As he puts it elsewhere, errors that "proved to be useful and helped preserve the species" persisted, since "those who hit upon or inherited these had better luck in their struggle for themselves and their progeny" (GS 110). Examples of such (alleged) errors include "that there are enduring things; that there are equal things; that there are things, substances, bodies; that a thing is what it appears to be; that our will is free; that what is good for me is also good in itself" (GS 110).[7] From a certain kind of radically naturalistic view, common in the nineteenth century and familiar to Nietzsche, most of these claims were, indeed, false or unwarranted. (Of course, one kind of NeoKantian view arrives at the same conclusion, but for a different set of [transcendental idealist] reasons.)

Second, Nietzsche is a *Global Humean*: he assumes that these evolutionary pressures operate to produce massive convergence on certain so-called "errors," the ones essential to human coping with the world and with our fellow humans.[8] This was a common view in the late nineteenth century, travelling under the label "species relativism," and eventually sparking the anti-naturalist (anti-psychologistic) reaction that gave birth to both the phenomenological and analytic traditions, in, respectively, Husserl and Frege (cf. Kusch 1995). Thus, in the preface of *Beyond Good and* Evil, Nietzsche calls "perspective" "the basic condition of all life."[9] In the final book of *The Gay Science*, added in 1886, he goes further, noting that whether all existence is perspectival "cannot be decided even by the most industrious and scrupulously conscientious analysis and self-examination of the intellect; for in the course of this analysis the human intellect cannot avoid seeing itself in its own perspectives, and *only* in these. We cannot look around our own corner" (GS 374). In consequence, "we cannot reject the possibility that [the world] *may include infinite interpretations*" but that is neither here nor there for essentially the pragmatic reasons articulated in the famous *Twilight* passage on how the "true" world (i.e., Kant's noumenal realm) finally became recognized as a "fable": since such a world is "unattainable" it is also "unknown" so "[c]onsequently not consoling, redeeming, obligating," in other words useless (TI IV). Thus, any interpretations that are unavailable to us are practically irrelevant.

There is an obvious loose resonance here with the twentieth-century idea of "Neurath's boat," popularized in the Anglophone literature by Quine: we can only ask and answer questions about what there is and what we know from within some existing interpretation of the world, which means there is no neutral standpoint from which we can rule out radically different interpretations let alone adjudicate among them. There may be radically different interpretations, of course, but that can hardly matter for those of us who cannot possibly occupy the perspective from which they arise. And what perspectives we can, in fact, occupy is determined by the

[7] Cf. GS 112: "We operate only with things that do not exist: lines, planes, bodies, atoms, divisible time spans, divisible spaces."

[8] Nietzsche plainly thinks some of these errors are dispensable, e.g., about the good and about free will.

[9] *[D]as Perspektivische, die Grundbedingung alles Lebens*. The contrast is made with Plato, who spoke *vom reinen Geiste and vom Guten an sich* (of pure spirit and the good in itself).

evolutionary limits set on cognition. In sum, Nietzsche's Global Humeanism, with its Skeptical Darwinian component, must set the baseline against which all our other epistemic pursuits proceed. (I am here so far only describing Nietzsche's view, neither endorsing nor rejecting it. I shall have more to say about the merits, below.)

2.2 On the Genealogy of Morality III:12

GM III:12 appears, initially, to be a different passage about perspectivism, but it is important to recall its context within the argument of the Third Treatise of the *Genealogy*. The main topic of the Third Treatise is *why* ascetic ideals—ideals of self-denial ["chastity, poverty, humility"], ideals that "deny life"—have been so appealing to human beings, figuring, as they do, in all the world's major religions. Against those who think this asceticism is a mere legacy of religious superstition, now abolished by a scientific age, Nietzsche claims—in what is intended as a dramatic surprise of the essay—that *even* science, with its faith in the absolute value of truth, also embodies the ascetic ideal (cf. GS 344 for a similar claim, also from Book V; and see Leiter 2015a: 213 ff. for detailed discussion: Nietzsche's idea, in brief, is that error is a necessary condition of life, thus an obsessive overvaluation of truth would be a threat to life itself).

Well before Nietzsche defends that latter hypothesis in the Third Treatise (in GM III:23), however, he also claims that Kant's transcendental idealism expresses the ascetic ideal, because of its doctrine that "*there is* a realm of truth and being, but reason is firmly *excluded* from it!" (GM III:12). Kant's doctrine is ascetic, on this account, *not* because it overvalues truth, but because it denies that we have any access to the real or objective truth about the world as it is in-itself: this is supposedly ascetic because it treats as mere appearance the only living world there is (the "phenomenal" world in Kant's terms). So whatever Nietzsche's perspectivism amounts to, it cannot mean that "the world" is cognitively off-limits, lest it fall prey to the asceticism of Kant's view. This latter point is crucial to any reading of GM III:12.

Nietzsche's discussion of perspectives (GM III:12) is then introduced as an alternative, non-Kantian, and non-ascetic way of thinking about "objectivity," one in which objective knowledge is *not* a matter of knowledge of a noumenal world.[10] Nietzsche writes:

> To see differently in this way for once, the *will* to see things differently, is no small discipline and preparation of the intellect for its coming "objectivity"— understood not as "contemplation without interest" (which is, as such, a non-concept and an absurdity), but as *having in our power* our "pros" and "cons": so as to be able to engage and disengage them so that we can use the *difference* in perspectives and affective interpretations for knowledge. From now on, my philosophical colleagues, let us be more wary of the dangerous old conceptual fairy-tale which has set

[10] To be clear, Kant himself did not think that objectivity demanded knowledge of the noumenal world—for Kant, the objectivity of our knowledge *of the phenomenal world* was secured by the fact that the human mind necessarily imposed structures on phenomenal experience. But Nietzsche is following the post-Kantian skeptics who thought that the real upshot of transcendental idealism is that we are forever blocked from actual objective knowledge.

up a "pure, will-less, painless, timeless, subject of knowledge" [quoting Schopenhauer]... —here we are asked to think of an eye which cannot be thought at all, an eye turned in no direction at all, an eye where the active and interpretive powers are to be suppressed, absent, but through which seeing still becomes a seeing-something, so it is an absurdity and non-concept of the eye that is demanded. There is *only* a perspective seeing, *only* a perspective "knowing"; the *more* affects we allow to speak about a thing, the *more* eyes, various eyes, we are able to use for the same thing, the more complete will be our "concept" of the thing, our "objectivity." But to eliminate the will completely and turn off all the affects without exception, assuming we could: well? Would that not mean to *castrate* the intellect?

The first thing to notice is that this passage claims *only* that *knowing* is perspectival, not that truth is. That leaves open the possibility that there is a non-perspectival truth about the world, though the pragmatic dismissal of the noumenal world from *Twilight* mentioned earlier would explain why Nietzsche thinks such a truth would be irrelevant *if it transcended all possible* perspectives creatures like us (our species) could adopt. But Nietzsche's point in GM III:12, I suggest, is far more banal and entirely consistent with his dismissal of the "noumenal world" as a symptom of asceticism: namely, that the world is sufficiently complex that the parts we attend to for purposes of acquiring knowledge are determined by our affects or interests, thus the more of them that are brought to bear the more we would know about the world (the more truths about the world we will know). That certainly fits with the visual analogy that Nietzsche offers: if I view an object from many different angles and perspectives, I will, indeed, acquire more first-hand visual knowledge of it. (The visual analogy would also imply that some perspectives do not give us knowledge [a point I emphasized in Leiter 1994], but Nietzsche does not say that explicitly—indeed, all he says explicitly is that the more perspectives that are deployed, the greater our "objectivity" [Nietzsche's quotes].) I think this banal point is, in fact, central to Nietzsche's meaning: the world is overflowing with possible cognitive targets, and our affects (or interests) determine which ones we pick up upon on any given occasion. Let us call this Nietzsche's "Busy World Hypothesis": there is so much we *could* know, that what we do end up cognizing depends on our affects and interests. The Busy World Hypothesis will both help us understand why Thucydides is Nietzsche's paradigm of a perspectival knower, as it were, and how GM III:12 is, in fact, continuous with GS 354. I return to both points shortly, but first let us press further on the analogy that is central to GM III:12.

Knowing is like seeing, according to Nietzsche, in that knowing, like seeing, is *dependent* (in some sense to be specified) on a perspective (an *interest* or *affect*). Christopher Janaway has argued that affects are "constitutively necessary conditions of the knower's knowing anything at all" (Janaway 2007: 212), but this talk of dependence (or "constitutively necessary conditions") is ambiguous between two possibilities, which are apparent in the case of visual perspectives. I cannot have direct knowledge (by "acquaintance," as it were) of what the bottom of the table looks like unless I lie on the floor and look up at it: my perspective "constitutes" what I know in the sense that

I could not be acquainted with how the bottom of the table appears except by occupying the relevant perspective.[11] Call this a case of *epistemic constitution*:[12] the perspective makes a particular bit of cognition of an objective feature of the world possible.

But there is a stronger constitutive sense of a visual perspective, in which it is not simply the necessary causal precondition of "knowledge" (or awareness of [acquaintance with] some aspect of the world), but in which the object of purported knowledge depends *for its existence* on the perspective from which it is seen. The oasis in the distance that appears to the man lost in the desert and dying of thirst is constitutively dependent on the perceiver in this second, "metaphysical" sense: only for that perceiver, under those circumstances and in those conditions, does the object (the oasis) appear (it is a mirage, after all). When perspectives *metaphysically constitute* an object, there is, in reality, no such object, and so any "knowledge" of it is illusory. Values are, for Nietzsche, metaphysically constituted in this way, since Nietzsche is an anti-realist, someone who denies that there are any mind-independent facts about value as I argued in Chapters 1 and 2. In other words, values are like the hallucinated "oasis" in a crucial respect: their existence is relative to the person, or the type of person, who perceives them. There may be an objective (psychological) fact that events have particular value for particular persons (just as there is an objective psychological fact that a man dying of thirst in the desert perceives an oasis in the distance), but there is no objective or observer-independent fact about the *real* value of events.

Of course, if *no values* are mind-independent, then that must be true of *epistemic values* as well: judgments about what is warranted or justified to believe must also be mind-dependent. I see no reason to think Nietzsche would deny that: indeed, it is the whole point of his Global Humeanism that "creatures like us" have a tendency to deem justified certain kinds of claims about the world, even if they are not from a species-independent point of view.[13] And Global Humeanism, recall, is one of the upshots of GS:354, with herd-reproducing forces explaining the epistemic values and the resulting beliefs that triumph. But since we cannot do without most of these epistemic values—since we cannot occupy any other perspective—they form the baseline for all our epistemic pursuits. This fits with a point that Janaway has correctly emphasized, namely, that GM III:12 is clearly referring to Schopenhauer. In particular, while Schopenhauer agreed with Kant that the knowing subject imposes upon experience various forms and categories like space, time, and causality, Schopenhauer, unlike Kant, deemed even these to be products of the human "will," that is, of "human needs, interests, and affects" (Janaway 2007: 193). That view is suggestive, obviously, of the

[11] We can ignore "knowing" what the bottom of the table looks like based on testimony or other inferential sources of knowledge—Nietzsche makes clear with the reference to the eye in GM III:12 that perceptual knowledge is the relevant analogy.

[12] I follow Janaway in using the language of "constituting," but what is really at issue is the "causal precondition" of knowing something.

[13] Is there such a point of view? Nietzsche is not always clear about this.

doctrine I have been calling Global Humeanism, the one we find in GS 354 as well. As Janaway goes on to note,

> Schopenhauer polarizes will and intellect, and likes to tell us that while the brain is the focus of the intellect, the genitals are the focus of the will. Hence when Nietzsche speaks of "castrating the intellect" [in GM III:12] he makes a direct assault on Schopenhauer's aspiration towards a will-free operation of the intellect: we must accept the intellect as essentially will-driven...
>
> (Janaway 2007: 200)

In other words, when GM III:12 rejects the possibility of Schopenhauer's "pure, will-less, painless, timeless, subject of knowledge" he is affirming that even the Schopenhauerian intellect is "essentially will-driven" (i.e., affect-driven): there is *contra* Schopenhauer, never any "contemplation without interest." Thus Nietzsche leaves us with the view that the only knowing possible for us—including that involved in the Kantian intuitions of space and time and the categories of the understanding—is causally dependent on human interests and affects.

And now the continuity between GS 354 and GM III:12 should be clear: both passages presuppose the Busy World Hypothesis, and thus that what we believe "depends" (in the epistemic or causal sense) on affects—both our belief in the familiar Kantian phenomena (e.g., space, time, causality), but also our beliefs more generally. Both GS 354 and GM III:12 involve a kind of naturalized Kantianism, or what I have been calling Global Humeanism (or what was, at the time, denominated species relativism): whereas Kant treats the uniformity of human judgment on these matters as transcendental conditions on the possibility of knowledge, Nietzsche treats them as simply consequences of our cognitive propensities as shaped by evolutionary forces. But GM III:12 also calls attention to the role affects play in what we take ourselves to know beyond the Kantian case, i.e., the cases where we can turn on, and turn off, as it were, *certain* affects in the course of inquiry. In other words, Nietzsche has a two-level view: Global Humeanism (or naturalized Kantianism) means that at bottom what we know and believe is *relative to creatures like us* (that is species relativism, proper), but against that species-specific baseline, there are many things we can know in the species-relative sense depending on how we deploy our affects in the Busy World.

2.3 *Janaway on perspectivism*

Christopher Janaway proposes that GM III:12 is not "a generalization about all knowing"—as the Global Humeanism of *The Gay Science* passage appears to be—but applies only to cases like "knowledge about the various phenomena of morality" (2007: 209), the obvious subject of the *Genealogy*. Of course, when Nietzsche repudiates the possibility of "contemplation without interest" he is also repudiating a possibility related to purported aesthetic knowledge or appreciation (Kant's central case), suggesting that the target is broader than just morality and encompasses other claims about value. Yet there is nothing in GM III:12 itself that circumscribes its claim about cognition to evaluative phenomena—and, as I will argue below, Nietzsche's paradigmatic knower, Thucydides, illuminates primarily psychological phenomena, not ethical or aesthetic ones. And if affects are non-cognitive, and they even play a role in, e.g., knowledge about causation, then it is hard to see why GM III:12's claims should be circumscribed in the way Janaway proposes.[14]

Janaway argues that affects are "constitutively necessary conditions of the knower's knowing anything at all" because "even if scientific investigation has to be construed as a form of knowledge purged of all affects" it could still be that "knowing something *only* scientifically gives us a poorer understanding of it than knowing it through a variety of psychological, imaginative, rhetorical means—affect-arousing means—in addition to those of science" (Janaway 2007: 212). Janaway's idea seems to be that we cannot really understand the psychological truths about morality (e.g., that it arises from *ressentiment* or, that it manifests internalized cruelty) that Nietzsche's genealogy reveals unless we are affectively engaged by them. That is hardly obvious, for reasons I will return to in a moment. But I also want to take issue with Janaway's contrast between *Wissenschaft* and Nietzsche's own method. Any method that reliably produces knowledge of what is true is a *Wissenschaft*, and Janaway and I both agree that Nietzsche takes his method in the *Genealogy* to deliver such knowledge. The relevant contrast is not with "science" per se, but with science as practiced by "scholars."

Recall that Nietzsche concedes in *Beyond Good and Evil* (BGE 6) that *Gelehrten* (scholars), those who are really scientific (*eigentlich wissenschaftlichen*) men may have an actual "knowledge drive" (*Erkenntnisstrieb*), such that one can wind them up like a clock and they get to work acquiring knowledge: "it is almost a matter of total indifference... whether the 'promising' young worker turns himself into a good philologist or an expert on mushrooms [*Pilzekenner*] or a chemist." This is because, according to Nietzsche, the scholar's real affective attachments lie elsewhere: "in his family, or in making money, or in politics." As Janaway puts it: Nietzsche "regards it as possible, in exceptional cases, to pursue knowledge in disconnection from the sum of one's affects and drives, but this type of 'little clockwork mechanism' cannot be the basis of a general theory of knowing, nor an accurate guide to the nature of knowing subjects" (2007: 216). The "clockwork" case is not, however, exceptional; universities suggest it is the norm, as I am sure Nietzsche would agree.[15] But the key point is that Nietzsche thinks there is genuine *wissenschaftlich* activity aiming at knowledge which affects do *not* even epistemically constitute—except in the explanatorily otiose sense that they reflect an *Erkenntnisstrieb*—though affects do influence it indirectly and non-constitutively,

[14] The contemporaneous species relativism in German philosophy included no such restriction to the moral domain.

[15] Nietzsche observes that "scholars, insofar as they belong to the spiritual middle class, can never catch sight of the really great problems and question marks; their courage and their eyes simply do not reach that far—and above all, their needs which led them to become scholars in the first place, their inmost assumptions and desires that things might be such and such, their fears and hopes all come to rest and are satisfied too soon" (GS 373). The passage goes on to attack, as examples, Spencer's attempt to reconcile egoism and altruism, as well as reductionist materialist views, which cannot give an account of what it is really like to hear music.

insofar as the *Erkenntnisstrieb* operates in service of "family, or in making money, or in politics." The affective arousal required for knowledge of morality is still part of a *Wissenschaft*, just one fundamentally different from that of scholars, at least on Janaway's account, which I will now dispute.

According to Janaway's ambitious hypothesis, affective arousal illuminates aspects of the object (i.e., morality) that a merely "scientific" understanding misses. More precisely, on Janaway's reading, we really do *not know* what morality is like unless our affects of disgust, contempt, and anger are aroused by Nietzsche's genealogy of our morality. But why should that be true? In what sense do we not "know what morality is" absent such arousal? This is the central issue for Janaway's attempt to circumscribe perspectivism, to keep it away from knowledge claims generally. I will argue this attempt fails.

Perhaps an analogy with the Freudian hypothesis about transference and its role in therapy might help. On Freud's view, the psychoanalyst can tell the patient that he has an unconscious wish to kill his father, and even adduce all the relevant evidence from the patient's behaviors, relationships, dreams, jokes, slips of the tongue and so on that supports that hypothesis. And yet, on the Freudian view, the patient does not *really* know he harbors such an unconscious wish until he transfers the unconscious murderous rage at his father on to the analyst, until he consciously experiences the wish *transferred* upon the analyst. We might say that, absent transference, the patient only acquires what Bertrand Russell used to call "knowledge by description" or "propositional knowledge," rather than "knowledge by acquaintance."[16]

I propose a slight modification of the Russellian categories to capture what is at stake here. Let us say that an agent has propositional knowledge when he believes that X and has good reasons for affirming such a belief. Let us say that an agent undergoes *belief fixation* (as I called it in Chapter 3) when he has propositional knowledge of X and is motivated to act on his belief. When an agent has undergone *belief fixation* the agent is "acquainted" with the relevant facts. Not everyone who affirms the proposition X has undergone belief fixation: the hallmark of belief fixation is that the agent who affirms X is motivated to act upon his belief X. The key to Freudian transference is belief fixation. This is what is at issue in the therapeutic context: it is not enough for the patient to believe (propositionally) that he has a particular unconscious wish; he must believe it in such a way that he is then *motivated* to act, for example, to reject the actual wish, accede to it, take steps to repress it, etc.

Might this framing of the issues help Janaway's case for limiting GM III:12 just to knowledge of morality? Janaway's claim is that when Nietzsche arouses the readers' affects towards morality they come to know something different, namely, something about morality's origins, motivations, and real nature, things they would not have otherwise known. But all the Freudian analogy shows is that agents would not have acquired fixated beliefs in the absence of affective arousal, not that they would not be able to

[16] I am grateful to Ken Gemes for suggesting the Russellian terminology in this context.

understand (know propositionally) Nietzsche's hypotheses about the psychological origins of morality. Many readers, after all, are convinced by Nietzsche that the slaves feel *ressentiment* towards the masters based on the evidence in GM I, and conclude that the slaves are quite right to feel that way, and celebrate their victory. It seems like one can have propositional knowledge of the claims Nietzsche is making in his *Genealogy* without sharing in Nietzsche's contempt for slave morality or his desire to throw off its shackles.

I have argued for many years (e.g., Leiter 2002) that Nietzsche's primary aim is to transform the false consciousness of some of his readers—nascent higher human beings—about the dominant morality: he wants them to see that what passes for morality is actually *bad for them*, and thus inspire them to throw off its shackles. Nietzsche, we might say, aims at producing knowledge about morality that *motivates* action, and the only kind of knowing that does that is propositional knowledge (or acquaintance) accompanied by an affect (or, as a Humean might say, by a desire): that is, Nietzsche aims to produce belief fixation, at least among select readers. Mere "scholars" in Nietzsche's sense do not aim for belief fixation: what they know is a matter of practical indifference.

Unfortunately for Janaway, these considerations do not help his reading, since belief fixation does not seem to be what GM III:12 is about. Recall the crucial recommendation of the passage, namely, "*having in our power* our 'pros' and 'cons'... so as to be able to engage and disengage them so that we can use the *difference* in perspectives and affective interpretations for knowledge." GM III:12 recommends an approach that contributes to knowledge (no quote marks this time), not to motivation or action. And on this reading, there are facts about morality's origins and motivations that transcend particular perspectives, but which an aggregation of affective perspectives will illuminate. On this way of thinking about the perspective metaphor, there is a way things are independent of any particular perspective (albeit what that fact is will be constrained by Global Humeanism), and if we maximize our epistemic angles on the moral phenomena, we will increase our "objectivity." (Nietzsche puts "objectivity" in quotes in GM III:12 precisely because he is denying, as Janaway has plausibly argued, the Schopenhauerian view that cognition is epistemically independent of the will or affect.[17]) Nietzsche's admiration of Thucydides is, I believe, the key to understanding what he is after, since Thucydides, as Nietzsche understands him, is the paradigm

[17] On the *epistemic constitution* account, knowers are knowing more about the actual object, whose existence and character does not depend on the perspectives from which it is known. To be sure, the epistemic constitution view differs importantly from Kant's, in the sense that it does not treat the object-in-itself as cognitively unavailable. Yet from GS 354 and GS 374, we know that Nietzsche thinks that we can never get beyond the human perspective—"we cannot look around our own corner" (GS 374)—and thus "we cannot reject the possibility that [the world] *may include infinite interpretations*" but from perspectives ("corners") we can never occupy (GS 374). The upshot of Global Humeanism and Skeptical Darwinism is that there may be a world beyond our ken, but a world like that is of no practical relevance to human beings. That is consistent with the idea that GM III:12 involves only epistemic constitution: after all, we have already granted that Global Humeanism forms the backdrop for all knowing, including that which is the subject of GM III:12.

of knowing that GM III:12 describes. We shall see that the kind of psychological knowledge Thucydides provides depends on affects in a far weaker sense than that of producing belief fixation, and much closer to what the Busy World Hypothesis should lead us to expect.

2.4 Perspectivism in Thucydides

Nietzsche praised Thucydides, his primary representative of Sophistic culture, for exemplifying the "*culture of the most impartial* [or "unprejudiced" (*unbefangensten*)] *knowledge of the world*" one "which deserves to be baptized with the name of its teachers, the Sophists" (D 168). Nietzsche's admiration of Thucydides in these respects is consistent with his own perspectivism in both *The Gay Science* and the *Genealogy* senses. The "knowledge of the world" Thucydides' *History* conveys is obviously *not* knowledge of the physical or biological world, but rather a special kind of psychological knowledge, namely, *about human beings and their motivations*: he illuminates what they *value*, what events *mean* to them, and thus why they act as they do. Thucydides is "impartial" in that he is willing to accurately describe their motivations and values, even when they are offensive to conventional moral sensibilities, or even to Thucydides' own judgment of the merits. Thucydides can do this precisely because he can "engage and disengage" his own "pros and cons"—his own sympathies and antipathies—in order to enhance knowledge of why the actors in the Peloponnesian War did what they did. Unlike Plato, as Nietzsche notes, Thucydides "does not revile or belittle those he does not like..." (D 169).[18] He portrays them as they are.

Thucydides' standard device in the *History* is to put into the mouths of his speakers their *real* intentions and concerns, even if they would be shocking or offensive to observers. The classic example is the famed speech that, in Thucydides' fictional recounting, the Athenians deliver to the vanquished Melians:

> For our part, we will not make a long speech no one would believe, full of fine moral arguments—that our empire is justified because we defeated the Persians, or that we are coming against you for an injustice you have done to us....Instead, let's work out what we can do on the basis of what both sides truly accept: we both know that decisions about justice are made in human discussions only when both sides are under equal compulsion [i.e., only among equals does right prevail over might]; but when one side is stronger, it gets as much as it can, and the weak must accept that...
>
> Nature always compels gods (we believe) and men (we are certain) to rule over anyone they can control. We did not make this law, and we were not the first to follow it; but we will take it as we found it and leave it to posterity forever, because we know that you would do the same if you had our power, and so would anyone else. (Thucydides: V.89, V.105)

Nietzsche's own commentary on this particular dialogue highlights what he admires about Thucydides' rendering of the event:

[18] Ironically, but not surprisingly, Nietzsche was sometimes closer to Plato than Thucydides on this score!

Do you suppose perchance that these little Greek free cities, which from rage and envy would have liked to devour each other, were guided by philanthropic and righteous principles? Does one reproach Thucydides for the words he puts into the mouths of the Athenian ambassadors when they negotiated with the Melians on the question of destruction or submission?

Only complete Tartuffes [i.e. Socrates and Plato] could possibly have talked of virtue in the midst of this terrible tension—or men living apart, hermits, refugees, and emigrants from reality-people who negated in order to be able to live themselves—

The Sophists were Greeks: when Socrates and Plato took up the cause of virtue and justice, they were *Jews* [i.e. promulgators of Judeo-Christian, or slave, morality] or I know not what—Grote's tactics in defense of the Sophists are false: he wants to raise them to the rank of men of honor and ensigns of morality—but it was precisely their honor not to indulge in any swindle with big words and virtues—. (WP 429)

Socrates and Plato are not impartial: they let their moral indignation color their perception of what was going on around them; Thucydides, although he surely disapproves of the unbridled lust for glory and power that leads Athens to ruin (which is the story his *History* tells), nonetheless resists moralized denunciations in favor of exposing the actual motivations that drive the Athenians. The Athenians, after all, did not speak to the Melians as Thucydides portrays them, just as the victors in every war rarely speak so directly to the vanquished. All talk the language of "justice" and "fairness" and "philanthropic and righteous principles," but what Nietzsche admires about Thucydides is that he puts into the mouths of his Athenians victors *their actual beliefs and motivations*—hence Thucydides' "impartiality." In psychological reality, self-interest and lust for power drive everyone in this dialogue: the Melians think there is a question of justice at stake, since "justice" is the only card they have to play having been defeated; the Athenians may talk the talk of justice too, but in reality they think exactly as Thucydides portrays them, given their superior military position. Thucydides honors the perspectivism dictum (of GM III:12) of "allow[ing]...more eyes" to speak about the event in order to increase " 'objectivity' " precisely by recording the way in which the same event appears differently to the differing types whose perspectives he records. Are the Athenians really behaving unjustly towards the Melians? Are the Melians really demanding genuine justice from the Athenians? The answer to both questions is presumably negative for Nietzsche, given his anti-realism about value. The singular talent of Thucydides is his ability to represent how the meaning of what is transpiring *really* seems to each of the opposed parties.

A different passage, later in the Third Treatise of the *Genealogy*, helps illuminate the kind of perspectivism Thucydides exemplifies. GM III:24 says that "doing violence, pressing into orderly form, abridging, omitting, padding, fabricating, falsifying... belong[] to the *essence* of all interpreting" (GM III:24). Superficial readers sometimes infer from passages like this—with its reference to "all interpreting"—that Nietzsche is committed to a radical subjective relativism about all claims to "knowledge," yet the context of this remark is of decisive importance in understanding perspectivism, since the passage only purports to describe what "interpreters" actually do. But to whom then is Nietzsche referring?

Recall that the "ascetic priest" was said by Nietzsche in GM III to have interpreted "a piece of animal psychology" (GM III:20), namely, the internalization of cruelty which first gave rise to bad conscience, the latter being a fact about human psychology. The "priestly reinterpretation of the animal's 'bad conscience' (cruelty turned backwards)" turned it into guilt and the feeling of "sin," the "most dangerous doom-laden feat of religious interpretation" in history (GM III:20). The reinterpretation of the psychological fact—internalized cruelty—tells the agent what that fact means, namely, that the agent is a sinner and should feel guilty. Yet self-cruelty admits, obviously enough, of many other interpretations as to its meaning. *This case is clearly the paradigm case of "doing violence...fabricating, falsifying" that Nietzsche has in mind.* It is the ascetic priest who, in this instance, is engaged in fabricating, falsifying, and so on; the facts about "animal psychology" are what they are independent of the ascetic priest's imposition of meaning.

The *meaning* of the internalization of cruelty on Nietzsche's account is determined from one affective perspective or another; in itself, the psychological phenomenon has no meaning. It is *not true*, after all, that humans are sinners, and we know Nietzsche does not think it is true:[19] what is true is that *human beings suffer,* that *they have internalized their cruel instincts*, and that "*meaningless suffering is unbearable*" (GM III: 28), i.e., it leads to suicidal nihilism. The latter are claims in descriptive (if speculative) psychology/anthropology; it is only from particular perspectives (e.g., the ascetic priest's) that these psychological facts are assigned *meaning* or *value*. The way this operates in the case of the ascetic ideal is, of course, the central concern of the Third Treatise of GM, and only by understanding the ways in which it operates can we contribute, as GM III:12 has it, to knowledge about how human beings behave and why they take ascetic moralities seriously, the central topic of GM III. Nietzsche here proceeds as Thucydides does: he describes how things seem from a particular evaluative perspective that he does not share, though unlike Thucydides, Nietzsche's polemical hostility to the perspective in question is rather more obvious.

In the Third Treatise, Nietzsche goes on to remark that the "ascetic priest has ruined the health of the soul wherever he has come to power" (GM III:22), though as the first line of the next section makes clear, it is a matter of ruining "health and taste" [*Gesundheit* und...*Geschmack*] ["health," of course, is a term of endorsement for Nietzsche, meaning one has a certain kind of "taste"]. Thus, Nietzsche presents his own polemic against *The New Testament* as compared to the *Old* as involving him "stand[ing] alone in my taste regarding this most esteemed, most overestimated scriptural work (the taste of two millennia is *against* me)," yet adds that, notwithstanding, "I have the courage of my bad taste" (GM III:22). In other words, his claims about the

[19] As Nietzsche puts it: " 'sinfulness' in humans is not a factual state but rather only the interpretation of a factual state, namely of a physiological disgruntlement—the latter seen from a moral-religious perspective that is no longer binding on us" (GM III:16).

meaning of the *Old* as against the *New Testament* reflect Nietzsche's *type* (with its admittedly "bad" taste) against the ascetic's *type*. *Different types have different tastes*, and as Zarathustra says, "all of life is a dispute about tastes" (Z II: 13).

But if all life is a dispute about tastes, and understandings of internalized cruelty vary by the type of person who experiences it, then someone, from the outside, trying to understand these phenomena will need to be able to represent all these different affective perspectives in order to understand what is really going on. And this will require the inquirer to suspend his own opinions about the differing metaphysically constitutive perspectives on questions of meaning, given that those opinions will have been aroused in the first place by the perspectives he finds appealing. That ability to have "*in our power* our 'pros' and 'cons' " so as to be able to engage and disengage them so that we can use the *difference* in perspectives and affective interpretations for knowledge is the ability in which both Thucydides and (sometimes) Nietzsche excelled; as a result, they increased our knowledge of the phenomena they analyzed: in the Busy World of human affairs, they were able to suspend their own unfavorable judgments long enough to notice the competing affective perspectives brought to bear.

3. Defending Nietzsche's Naturalism about Value

Nietzsche's perspectivism, based on the actual texts, should be rather banal in the post-Quinean world. All expressions of knowledge may depend on "will" or "affect," but evolutionary pressures select in favor of some of these affects, such that most "creatures like us" converge on many epistemic values, albeit not all. Yet beyond that baseline, the Busy World Hypothesis reminds us that which particular objects of cognition command our attention will be influenced by our other affects and interests, and that this epistemic constitution plays an important role in what we know about the world. Such conclusions are familiar from philosophy of the last century, a point we return to below.

Of course, Nietzsche's own philosophical context is defined by NeoKantianism and species relativism—hence the particular expressed form of what I have been calling his Global Humeanism and Skeptical Darwinism. Even though we post-Quinean readers are less disposed to call beliefs "errors" just because their warrant derives from dispositions subject to evolutionary forces and less likely to think species-relative forms of justification are not really cases of knowledge when they are relative to the human species, we do share with Nietzsche the crucial claim that the sciences sort the wheat from the chaff when it comes to the "real" and the "knowable" (with or without the quote marks). It is that naturalism which drives all Nietzsche's views in moral psychology, as we have seen already and will see in the chapters to follow. Is naturalistic anti-realism about value, including epistemic value, of the Nietzschean kind, defensible?

Let us begin by stating clearly the special problem for naturalists like Nietzsche about value and normativity, including epistemic value and normativity. The explanatory modalities of the empirical sciences do not make any reference to deontic or normative properties related to *reasons*, as distinct from nomic or descriptive ones. Naturalistic explanations operate in the idiom of *causes*, not *norms*, and casual mention of norms in such explanations are always shorthand for causal explanations that are norm-free: e.g., "Oedipus gouged out his eyes when he discovered the wrongful things he had done," is really shorthand for, "Oedipus gouged out his eyes when he *came to believe* he had married his mother and killed his father, because he *felt* these actions were shameful." An adequate naturalistic explanation does not depend on it being a fact (or true) that it was wrongful to murder one's father and marry one's mother; it does not depend on it being a fact (or true) that one has a reason not to murder one's father or marry one's mother (see Leiter 2001; cf. Chapters 1 and 3). An adequate naturalistic explanation depends only on facts about the psychological states in which Oedipus found himself and the facts about human behavior in the world; it might also depend on psycho-social or anthropological facts about the belief and attitudes of others in the relevant community in which Oedipus lived. But what it does not depend on is that it is *shameful*, independent of how Oedipus or his compatriots feel, to marry your mother and kill your father, or that it is wrongful, independent of how Oedipus and others feel, to marry your mother and kill your father. For the naturalist, including Nietzsche, what we call normativity is simply an artifact of the psychological properties of certain biological organisms, i.e., what they *feel* or *believe* or *desire* (or are *disposed to feel, believe, or desire*).

Even putting issues of semantics to one side (as I have argued we must do in Chapter 1), there remains an interlocking set of metaphysical, epistemological, and, for want of a better word, practical or first-personal worries about value and normativity for naturalists of the Nietzschean stripe. We may summarize them as follows. First, naturalism is self-refuting, since the naturalistic outlook itself presupposes *epistemic* norms whose status is not naturalistically vindicated. Second, naturalism imposes domain-specific standards on domains of thought where they do not belong. Third, naturalism fails to do justice to the real, practical nature of normativity from the first-person point of view of deciding what one ought to do: it can explain what we *call* normativity, but it cannot explain *real* normativity.[20] I shall take these up in turn.

3.1 Naturalism is self-refuting

The naturalist supposes that we should treat the methods and thus the results of the empirical sciences as arbiters of what is true and what we should treat as "knowable."[21] But why do so unless those methods and results are themselves *normatively sound*, that is, justified by epistemically relevant considerations? Yet we may then ask: are those "epistemically relevant considerations" themselves to be interpreted as results of the

[20] I take it that "real normativity" means standards of what one ought to do or believe that are not dependent for their binding force on the attitudes, feelings, or beliefs of persons.

[21] This could be species-relative "knowledge" of course.

empirical sciences? Clearly not, on pain of circularity, but even apart from worries about circularity, it is not at all clear that these norms constitute scientific results as opposed to being presuppositions of scientific method. So that means the naturalist commends epistemic norms that are, themselves, not vindicated naturalistically: hence self-refutation.

This objection would be correct if the defense of naturalism were that epistemic norms favored it. *But this is not and can not be the defense of naturalism.* Quine, the leading Anglophone naturalist, was not ideally clear on this issue, sometimes being rather glib about the circularity problem, but I take it the right response to the worry is apparent in the famous closing observations in his "Two Dogmas of Empiricism":

> As an empiricist I continue to think of the conceptual scheme of science as a tool, ultimately, for predicting future experience in the light of past experience. Physical objects are conceptually imported into the situation as convenient intermediaries—not by definition in terms of experience, but simply as irreducible posits comparable, epistemologically, to the gods of Homer. Let me interject that for my part I do, qua lay physicist, believe in physical objects and not in Homer's gods; and I consider it a scientific error to believe otherwise. But in point of epistemological footing the physical objects and the gods differ only in degree and not in kind. Both sorts of entities enter our conception only as cultural posits. The myth of physical objects is epistemologically superior to most in that it has proved more efficacious than other myths as a device for working a manageable structure into the flux of experience. (1951: 41)

The interest in predicting the future course of experience[22] is, it would seem, a widely shared interest, one that facilitates crossing the street, cooking a meal, indeed, living a life. On this kind of view, we should be naturalists because *naturalism works*, not because it is "true" or "justified" in some sense either independent of or dependent upon naturalistic criteria. "Naturalism works" may sound like a slogan, but it is a slogan with real significance. Consider: thanks to the true beliefs of aerospace engineers (and, behind them, physicists and chemists), the plane that brought me to a lecture in London *actually brought me here*, that is, several tons of metal tubing and associated electronics rose tens of thousands of feet into the sky, with me strapped inside, and moved faster than any natural thing can on the ground, and deposited me in the place I was aiming to go—and not in the middle of the ocean or the middle of a desert—and did this without incinerating, mutilating, or otherwise killing me. Imagine telling a Homeric era farmer that, "In the future, farmers like you will be able to travel through the clouds in special tubes to faraway places you have heard of in stories, and do that in the time it takes you to ride a horse to the neighboring village." To be sure, the ontology of Homeric gods licenses telling stories about such magic, but the ontology of aerospace engineers allows the farmers and the professors to actually experience it. That airplanes work is not an epistemic warrant, but that airplanes work gives us the pragmatic explanation why creatures like us are disposed to treat the epistemology that underlies aerospace engineering as the benchmark of the true and the knowable. The

[22] I here mean the future course of actual events in the world, not "experience" in the phenomenalist's sense.

reasons for being a naturalist in the first place are not question-begging epistemic reasons; they are pragmatic ones, that almost everyone—including the anti-naturalists—actually accept in practice.[23] Naturalism thus makes its claim on us in virtue of its resonance with our attitudes, our practical interests in coping with the future course of our experience in the world.[24]

Notice that the locution "reasons for being a naturalist" really means "what explains why creatures like us are affectively disposed to take naturalistic epistemic criteria seriously." Someone could "reasonably" reject these reasons; but "reasonably" is, itself, a pro-attitude term of endorsement, meaning only that someone could feel indifferent to epistemic norms that, when applied, produce certain outcomes—outcomes like planes taking off and landing where they are supposed to. That epistemology bottoms out in practical interests should hardly be a surprising conclusion for a naturalist. Let us recall two important lessons from naturalistically-minded twentieth-century philosophy. First, from the famous Duhem-Quine thesis (Duhem 1914; Quine 1975, 1990) about the under-determination of scientific theories by evidence, we know that there are not even any scientific hypotheses that are epistemically obligatory, in the sense of required by logic and evidence.[25] This is because any recalcitrant evidence elicited in a test of a hypothesis is compatible with the hypothesis as long as we are willing to give up the background assumptions (i.e., the auxiliary hypotheses) such a test requires. In choosing among competing hypotheses and background assumptions, we must always fall back on evaluative considerations that "nature" does not adjudicate among, considerations such as theoretical simplicity, methodological conservatism, and consilience (cf. Quine and Ullian 1978).[26] Second, unless there were a plausible *substantive* conception of rationality (there does not appear to be one, alas), then rationality, including any internalist norm of epistemic warrant, is itself instrumental, imposing

[23] Other kinds of apparent self-refutation objections have appeared in the literature: Kim (1988), for example, argues that the notion of "belief" itself is normative, in the sense that a Quinean naturalized psychology of belief-formation must help itself to normative views to individuate those mental states that arise in response to sensory input as instances of "belief." More recently, Wedgwood (2007) has argued that the "intentional" is an inherently normative notion, so to the extent naturalists help themselves to intentional explanations (as all the great naturalists from Hume to Nietzsche do) they necessarily presuppose normative standards for individuating intentions. But the naturalist can help himself to any normative concepts that do useful naturalistic work in, e.g., individuating explanatorily important mental states.

[24] That naturalism "works" in the sense described in the text might seem like too lax a criterion. Why not think, for example, fictionalist naturalism—act as if we believe, rather than actually believe, whatever best explains our experience—would be just as good as actual naturalism? The only colorable answer is that it would not be: maintaining a make-believe posture is much harder than believing, which is why make-believe occupies so little of our lives. Skepticism about "naturalism works" usually trades, I suspect, on understating how well a naturalistic view really works in both ordinary and theoretical life.

[25] I acknowledge that the inveterate dogmatic realist may think this is merely an *epistemic* point, not a metaphysical one: there could still be *real epistemic values*; after all, we just do not know what they are or how to apply them. That is a logically possible position, but I am with Quine in thinking that if the *actual successful sciences* do not disclose such epistemic values, then it is dubious that reality demands any particular set of them.

[26] Scientific theories are none the worse for the naturalist in depending on logic, evidence and non-epistemic evaluative considerations: if the resulting theories work well for creatures like us, what more is there to expect?

normative constraints only on the means chosen to realize our ends, whatever they may happen to be. Thus, even norms for belief are hostage to ultimate ends, and so particular beliefs are unwarranted (that is, irrational) only relative to the believer's ends, a point Peter Railton pressed twenty years ago against those who thought there was a firm fact/value distinction (see Railton 1986a). That conclusion would also hardly be surprising to a naturalist like Nietzsche, who clearly appreciated (as we have seen repeatedly) the extent to which theoretical questions were driven by practical ends and interests.

Naturalism is, then, not self-refuting, since what commends naturalistic norms is not their warrant but their resonance with our practical interests and attitudes. This is quite consistent, unsurprisingly, with the Global Humeanism we have attributed to Nietzsche all along.

3.2 Naturalism imposes domain-specific standards where they do not belong

Someone who acknowledged the resonance of naturalistic epistemic norms with our practical attitudes might nonetheless object that such norms, while great for air travel and crossing the street, do not really help when it comes to coping with the prospect of death and suffering, or figuring out how to treat their neighbors. Why think naturalistic norms for belief should dominate the epistemic field, especially since, as we have just conceded, naturalism is not epistemically or, more broadly, rationally obligatory? Why think it should govern our talk and thought about norms outside the domain of phenomena for which we seek causal explanations? Maybe naturalistic norms "work" in certain domains, and that's enough; but why treat them as binding in other domains? That is the objection I wish to consider now.

The late Ronald Dworkin posed an extreme version of this challenge in 1996, but since then it has been taken up by his friends, including Thomas Nagel (1997), Derek Parfit (2011b), and T.M. Scanlon (2014).[27] The core thought that animates the anti-naturalists is this: even if causal or explanatory power is the criterion of the real and the knowable in the domain of the natural sciences, there is no reason to treat it as the arbiter of the real and the knowable in other domains of thought and inquiry. Call this view *Domain Separatism*. Domain Separatists hold that metaphysical and epistemological criteria vary with the subject-matter of cognitive domains and that it is an error to impose naturalistic criteria appropriate, for example, in empirical scientific inquiries, on to other domains. Domain Separatists thus endorse a version of the doctrine of "separate but equal": separate metaphysical and epistemic criteria for each domain, but all the domains are equal in terms of cognitive status, that is, stating truths and generating knowledge.

[27] The sociology of philosophy (especially contemporary philosophy), including its networks of friends, plays a much larger role in what views are taken seriously than the discipline's hyper-rational self-image would suggest. Nietzsche was acutely aware of this; cf. Leiter (2018).

The crucial question, obviously enough, is how we demarcate domains as the Domain Separatist would have us do? Dworkin says that while causal explanatory power "does seem appropriate to beliefs about the physical world" (1996: 119), it makes no sense for moral beliefs "[s]ince morality and the other evaluative domains make no causal claims" (1996: 120). But that is plainly false as we saw in Chapter 1: the moral explanations literature from the 1980s onwards—recall Brink, Railton, Cohen, Sturgeon, and others—is replete with examples of the role of causal claims in ordinary normative discourse (e.g., "Of course he betrayed them, he's an evil person"). It is perfectly reasonable then, even on the terms established by normative discourse itself, to inquire whether these explanations are *good* ones, let alone *best* explanations for the phenomena in question (see Chapter 1 and Leiter 2001 for a negative answer to this question).

Scanlon's recent view is more nuanced than Dworkin's (see especially Scanlon 2014: 21–2). Scanlon allows that there are "mixed" normative claims, ones that involve or presuppose claims about natural facts (and presumably could involve or presuppose causal claims in particular). But at the same time he affirms the core of Domain Separatism, namely, that it "makes most sense" he says to "not privilege science" but instead to endorse a view that,

> takes as basic a range of domains, including mathematics, science, and moral and practical reasoning. It holds that statements within all of these domains are capable of truth and falsity, and that the truth values of statements about one domain, insofar as they do not conflict with statements of some other domain, are properly settled by the standards of the domain that they are about. (2014: 19)

I note in passing that Scanlon gives no real argument for demarcating domains other than saying he thinks it "makes most sense"[28] to think of things his way. This betrays, I think, a deep peculiarity of much philosophy, including most Anglophone philosophy of the past half-century, namely, that it treats subjective reports of what "makes most sense" as data points with epistemic weight, as opposed to psycho-social artifacts that admit of explanation. But I will bracket that skeptical doubt here, even though a thorough-going naturalist should not: the psychology and sociology of inquirers, especially in a field as devoid of clear cognitive standards as philosophy, is an apt topic for systematic empirical investigation.

But back to Scanlon's version of Domain Separatism. Prior to saying it "makes most sense" to demarcate domains, Scanlon does note one consideration that might favor Domain Separatism, namely, the difficulties naturalists like Quine have in accounting for certain abstract mathematical truths, ones that do not seem indispensable for our best scientific theories. The latter kinds of abstract mathematical truths are worrisome for precisely the reason that Domain Separatists like Dworkin and Scanlon hope to invoke against the naturalist in the moral or practical case: namely, that it seems there

[28] Later, Scanlon says the idea of "domains" is just "common sense" (2014: 23), but that common sense embraces falsehoods is, from my philosophical standpoint, neither probative nor surprising.

are *clear* truths in this domain, which we should be loath to give up. If the Quinean (or Nietzschean) naturalist cannot capture all the abstract truths of mathematics with his causal/explanatory criterion for the real and the knowable, then so much the worse for the Quinean, so the Domain Separatist suggests.

That intuition is *prima facie* plausible in the mathematical case, but precisely for the reasons it is dubious in the moral case, a point that requires emphasis. Remember: the fact that there is massive cross-cultural and cross-temporal convergence on mathematical truths among inquirers, a kind of convergence that seems hard to explain away sociologically or psychologically, is precisely what makes it tempting to reject any metaphysical or epistemological criteria that made the convergence inexplicable on epistemic grounds, that is, as manifesting sensitivity to the mathematical truths in question. (In fact, convergence, like divergence, demands an explanation, and truth is not the only candidate even in cases of convergence, but we may bracket that here.) Importantly, nothing comparable is true in the moral case (recall the arguments in Chapter 1): we do not even have the requisite convergence in moral opinions that might create a defeasible presumption in favor of truth. The most striking fact about philosophical inquirers in the moral domain is that they agree about almost nothing, not about the priority of the right versus the good, or about the criterion of right action, or the criterion of goodness, or about whether the right and the good are even the fundamental ethical categories. Massive failure of convergence in the ethical domain ought to worry the moral realist.[29] Scanlon is certainly sensitive to this concern and so appeals to such purportedly uncontroversial truths about practical reason like, "The fact that a person's child has died is a reason for that person to feel sad" (2014: 2), which is, unfortunately for Scanlon, almost precisely the thesis that the Stoics quite intelligibly denied.[30] We should allow, however, that there might well be some odd practical claims that strike most creatures like us (i.e., members of our species) as correct—e.g., don't torture babies for fun—but such irrelevant outliers do not come close to the enormous cross-cultural convergence in the mathematical case.

So how, then, do we ultimately demarcate domains on Scanlon's view? Scanlon makes a variety of comments regarding how to think of "domains"—for example, that a domain should be "understood in terms of concepts that it deals with, such as number, set, physical object, reason, or morally right action" (2014: 19)—and he even purports to allow that "there can be meaningful 'external' questions about the adequacy of reasoning in a domain" (2014: 21). In the end, though, Scanlon echoes Dworkin in his own discussion of Gilbert Harman's "best explanation" argument for moral antirealism (Harman 1977). Harman, recall, argued that since the best explanation of why we might judge it wrongful for a bunch of young hoodlums to douse a cat with lighter fluid and set it aflame need make no reference to it actually being wrong to do so, only

[29] It worries Parfit, of course, in *On What Matters,* and he tries to argue that, in fact, all major theories converge. For some doubts, see Blackburn (2011) and Sandis (2011).

[30] Cicero, *Tusculan Disputations.* Book 3 ch. XIV. (Thanks to Martha Nussbaum for this reference.)

to facts about our psychology and our socialization, that we, therefore, have no reason to think it is *really* or *objectively* wrongful. Against Harman's view, Scanlon writes:

> [T]here is no reason to accept Harman's [best explanation] requirement as he formulated it—as a perfectly general requirement applying to all domains—since they do not all aim at the same kinds of understanding (e.g., at the best causal explanations of the world that impinges on our sensory surfaces). (2014: 27)

We may grant that moral talk and "understanding," assuming there is such a thing, does not aim primarily at causal explanation, even if, as we remarked earlier, moral talk sometimes helps itself to causal explanations—but Scanlon is more cautious than Dworkin, since he does not deny *outright* the relevance of causal explanation to moral thought, only that moral thought has other primary aims. But does it follow from this concession that there really is, as Scanlon claims, *no reason* to accept causal explanatory power as a marker of the real and the knowable even in the moral domain? That strong claim seems to overstate the case. Causal explanatory power has exercised pressure on attempts to make sense of the world precisely because, since the scientific revolution, our understanding of the world was purged of supernatural causes, such as gods and ghosts, because such entities have no causal explanatory power. We appear to know and understand more, as a result of this epistemically motivated cleansing. Why not say, then, that *all* domains that aim at *understanding* have a reason to take seriously the most successful markers of actual understanding we have? Indeed, the history of human inquiry since the scientific revolution is the history of purportedly domain-specific reasoning being subjected to scrutiny from scientific domains whose concepts and ontologies seemed to warrant more epistemic credence. Perhaps there is only *one* domain, the domain of human attempts to make sense of the world in all its baroque complexities, and to do so in terms that warrant some degree of epistemic confidence?

We may put the challenge to the Domain Separatist more precisely. Domain Separatists maintain that metaphysical and epistemological criteria vary with the subject-matter of purportedly "cognitive" domains and that it is an error to impose naturalistic criteria, appropriate, for example, in natural scientific inquiries, on to other domains. But in what domain do we locate the Domain Separatist thesis itself? What domain determines that a particular domain is, in fact, "cognitive"? By what domain's criteria is it supposed to be an error to ask whether practical reasoning satisfies naturalistic criteria? I suppose it will be tempting to say at this point that these claims are located in the domain of philosophy, that it falls to something called "philosophical reasoning" to adjudicate overreaching by one domain against another. But naturalists deny that there is something called "philosophical reasoning" that stands apart from the kinds of reasoning that work in the various natural and human sciences, so that response either begs the question against the naturalist *or* amounts to an admission that there is a meta-domain of reasoning, something the naturalist accepts, and which is precisely what the naturalist relies on in adjudicating the metaphysical and epistemological *bona fides* of all other domains. Either way, it seems, the Domain Separatist loses.

Or does she? Even if the Domain Separatist eschews the question-begging response of invoking the non-naturalist philosophical domain as the one that adjudicates the boundaries between domains, she can still ask the naturalist: why think the meta-domain of reasoning about which domains are cognitive should be governed by naturalistic standards of reasoning? That question is especially pressing because naturalistic standards of reasoning are, as I have already conceded, not rationally obligatory, but commended, instead, by our practical attitudes and interests.

Here I think there is no better answer to the Domain Separatist than the fact that the deliverances of naturalistic norms generally work well for creatures like us. No one finds it surprising, after all, that if we relax naturalistic constraints, we will get a promiscuous ontology, replete with moral facts, spirit facts, gustatory facts, aesthetic facts, theological facts, and so on. Someone might, of course, prefer more moral, spiritual, and gustatory facts, and the like, in their ontology, but that is not, by itself, an argument against naturalism, unless one thinks the epistemic norms that license belief in such facts answer to equally or more important practical attitudes of creatures like us. The naturalist, to be sure, noting the extent to which *all of us* are invested in naturalistic norms because they work so well in coping with the future course of experience, might then point out the pressures created by consistency (another preference of our species)—though that, too, is an epistemic attitude that is also not epistemically obligatory. And consistency in application of epistemic norms across domains might well yield in the face of the practical need for certain kinds of facts, such as facts about reasons. This brings us to what, I take it, has to be the real objection to the naturalist about normativity: namely, that he has not explained real normativity—that is, the bindingness of standards independent of our attitudes—and that explaining the real normativity of reasons is indispensable for creatures like us when we are trying to figure out what to do (or believe).[31]

3.3 The naturalist has not explained "real" normativity

Perhaps the naturalist can explain our normative talk and judgments in terms of certain psychological states of inclination and aversion, and complicated variations on those, but that does not explain *normativity*, since it does not explain why it is actually wrong to do X or why there is an overriding reason to do Y. Explaining the existence of normative talk in terms of normative attitudes is not the same as explaining normativity, and the former is all my naturalist has offered.

On this issue, I want to begin by noting my agreement with the anti-naturalists and my disagreement with certain kinds of contemporary Humean naturalists. For many contemporary Humean naturalists think they can give a naturalistic account of "real" normativity in terms of psychological states like desire and thus deflect the anti-naturalist's worry about the status of real normativity. But here I think an arch

[31] Thanks to Claire Kirwin for forcing me to think about this issue, though she will not agree with my response.

anti-naturalist like Scanlon gets it exactly right: there is, he says, an "evident lack of intrinsic normative significance of facts about desires" (2014: 6): the significance of desire is, as Scanlon says, merely causal. Here is how Scanlon puts it at greater length:

> The question [for the Humean]...would be whether identifying facts about reason with non-normative facts would explain reasons or eliminate their normativity. The "action guiding" force of reasons, on such a theory, would seem to be purely causal and explanatory. If the fact that one has a strong reason not to do *a* (and no countervailing reason to do *a*) is just a natural fact about what will satisfy one's desires, then this fact might explain one's failure to do *a*. But it does not explain why believing that one has such a reason (believing that this natural fact obtains) can make it irrational for one to do *a*. (2014: 6)

The problem is that the claim that it is "irrational for one to do *a*" means, for the naturalist, nothing more than some people or even all people might *feel* that you should not do *a*. The failed NeoHumean response to the problem of normativity underlines what it means to *really* be a naturalist about normativity. Of course, the NeoHumean naturalist has not explained *real* normativity, as Scanlon complains, because real normativity does not exist: *that is the entire upshot of the naturalist view*. There are no *reasons* whose existence and character is independent of human attitudes; there are only human attitudes which lead us to "talk the talk" of reasons, to feel that we should act one way rather than another. And if *real* normativity does not exist, if only *feelings* of inclination and aversion, compulsion and avoidance, actually exist, then that means that all purportedly normative disputes bottom out not in reasons but in the clash of will or affect. That is why, as A.J. Ayer correctly observed some eighty years ago, "when we come to deal with pure questions of value, as distinct from questions of fact...we finally resort to mere abuse" (1936: 147). Rhetorically, abuse has many uses, but its predominant role in moral discourse, including among philosophers,[32] should be a red flag that we are far removed from the fabled "space of reasons" in this arena.

Now what about the person deciding what she ought to do? If the naturalist is right, how does it help her? The answer has to be that it does not. The naturalist about

[32] Anscombe, an apologist for Catholic dogma, is notorious in this regard. See her two-sentence paper in *Analysis*: "The nerve of Mr. Bennett's argument is that if A results from your not doing B, then A results from whatever you do instead of B. While there may be much to be said for this view, still it does not seem right on the face of it." (Anscombe 1966) Anscombe does not always treat her interlocutors as generously as she does Bennett: "But if someone really thinks, *in advance*, that it is open to question whether such an action as procuring the judicial execution of the innocent should be quite excluded from consideration—I do not want to argue with him; he shows a corrupt mind." (Anscombe 1958: 17). Among consequentialists too, rhetorical abuse sometimes presents itself as an offer for self-approbation. Consider Smart: "Or would you, as a humane and sympathetic person, give a preference to the second universe? I myself cannot help feeling a preference for the second universe. But if someone feels the other way I do not know how to argue with him." (1973: 28) Consider also Wolf's use of "scare-adjectives" (remarked upon by Sommers 2007: 327): "A world in which human relationships are restricted to those that can be formed and supported in the absence of the reactive attitudes is a world of human isolation so cold and dreary that any but the most cynical must shudder at the idea of it." (Wolf 1981: 391) Della Rocca's epigraph to "The Taming of Philosophy," is here apt: "Don't mistake the fact that you don't like my view for an argument against it"(Della Rocca 2013: 178).

normativity gives us a third-person account of what normativity is, namely, certain kinds of psychological states that grip certain kinds of biological organisms, and move them to action or inaction. From the standpoint of the person thinking about what she ought to do, all this is irrelevant: she operates in the domain of illusion Nietzsche so well appreciated. She will act on the feelings of inclination and aversion she has, subject to the constraints they impose upon her beliefs about what is the case, though she will not understand herself to be doing so. In thinking about whether she should act upon any particular inclination or aversion, she will be causally influenced by her other inclinations and aversions, including the inclinations and aversions common in her community, though she will not, again, think of them under that description. So-called practical deliberation from the first-person standpoint—to the extent it even matters causally (see Chapter 5)—is shot through with illusion and falsehood, a plausible assessment from both a Nietzschean and empirical psychological point of view.

Those who think practical philosophy is a cognitive subject—as opposed to what it actually is, namely, a kind of armchair sociology of the moral etiquette of bourgeois philosophy professors—typically object to the naturalist at this point by noting that an agent faces comparable questions of *theoretical normativity*, questions about what she ought to believe.[33] Here I obviously differ—as this whole Chapter has made clear—from twentieth-century naturalists and moral skeptics like Ayer and Stevenson, who ignored this problem, and agree with naturalists and moral skeptics like Nietzsche, who did not: I think the issue is the same. Even in the theoretical domain, there is no real normativity, that is, no norms of belief or epistemic value the agent *must* adhere to, as I argued earlier. If epistemology proper, the systematic account of what one "ought" to believe (even in the species-relative sense of epistemic ought), gives the appearance of a more robust discipline it is only because its primary data points—namely, the claims of the successful empirical sciences—are clearer and more widely accepted, precisely because of their resonance with our practical interests. But that also means that epistemology proper is also a kind of armchair sociology, though one that can be discharged more responsibly from the armchair since its data points—the epistemic norms manifest in the practices of the successful sciences—are ones that can be studied in illuminating ways by reading books and journals.

For Nietzsche's kind of naturalist, there is no metaphysical difference *in kind* between moral and epistemic values—both are artifacts of attitudes common among

[33] See, for example, Korsgaard's (2012) *3AM* interview: "there is no more reason to doubt that reason plays a role in guiding human actions than there is to doubt that reason plays a role in forming human beliefs. In fact there is less, since people believe much crazier things than they do. And all of [Rosenberg, Pat Churchland, and Leiter] are dedicated to the project of working out what we have good reason to believe. If they came to the conclusion that reason doesn't play much of a role in forming most people's beliefs most of the time, they wouldn't give up that project themselves. They are interested in the kinds of questions that arise when we are trying to use reason to figure out what to believe. As a moral philosopher, I'm interested in questions that arise when we are trying to use reason to figure out what to do." But naturalists about epistemology realize that epistemic normativity is a descriptive enterprise, not a normative one: the question is not what we have good reason to believe, the question is what epistemic norms are operative in successful sciences.

creatures like us—but that latter point is still compatible with a radical difference in *degree* between them. For the Global Humean, recall, creatures like us generally converge in our epistemic attitudes because the norms those attitudes endorse do so well at meeting widely shared human needs and interests, such as predicting the future course of experience, as I argued earlier. Consider epistemic norms like the following: treat normal perceptual experience as *prima facie* veridical, honor logical inferences, and employ the inductive method in empirical inquiry. These epistemic norms do, indeed, seem to facilitate successful navigation of the world and prediction of the future course of experience. Something like this, I suspect (or hope), was Hume's own view, though unlike Hume, the other great modern naturalist Nietzsche does not think natural dispositions converge as well in the ethical case. That would explain why the great insight Nietzsche attributes to the Sophists concerns "the multiplicity (the geographical relativity) of the moral value judgments [*Moralischen Werthurtheile*]" (WP: 428), not *all* value judgments, in other words, but the distinctively moral ones (cf. Chapter 1). The key difference in the case of theoretical normativity is that creatures like us share enough attitudes and interests to allow meaningful debates about warrant and justification. Global Humeanism in the domain of theoretical norms gives the appearance of "real" normativity; if the same were true in the practical domain, we would not get *real normativity* there, just Global Humeanism about the practical. But, *contra* Humean optimism, that is not what we find.

If we have no *real* reason to believe the same or act the same, and thus we may not believe the same or act the same, given that our underlying psychological states (our attitudes) vary, what follows? What follows is basically what Ayer and Stevenson correctly diagnosed not quite a century ago: where people share attitudes, reasoning about what one ought to do and what one ought to believe is possible; where people do not share attitudes, reasoning is not possible and only force prevails in a dispute, whether that is the rhetorical force of producing a change in attitudes by whatever means are effective or the physical or lawful force of suppressing contrary attitudes.[34] An agent deciding what to do or what to believe is in the grips of particular normative attitudes, some practical and some theoretical, and has no reason to discount them since after all *they are her attitudes*—although, as Nietzsche noticed, she might discount them if she were in the grips of a non-naturalistic view of what had to be true of her attitudes for them to move her, that is, if she thought they had to be something more than *her attitudes*. But that I like Japanese food better than Thai food is a fact about my gustatory attitudes, yet it seems none the worse for that: why wouldn't I eat Japanese food if *that's my gustatory attitude*? My moral and epistemic attitudes are more ambitious in their scope—for example, they are not indifferent to *your* attitudes on similar questions—but they are not, on the naturalistic view, different from the gustatory attitudes in their metaphysical or epistemological status. We can easily imagine

[34] If philosophers were more attuned to reality, they would investigate the differing kinds of *force* operative in human affairs.

a world—since such worlds have existed—in which perceptual evidence is not treated as even defeasibly veridical, in which the so-called "scientific method" is dismissed, and in which the dominant epistemic values are what the holy book says or what the holy leader declares. Worlds governed by such epistemic norms tend to have features we modern, post-Enlightenment folk find unpleasant, but that is, itself, another attitudinal response. If enough of our fellows share our attitudes, then darkness recedes, and Enlightenment triumphs. But those are facts about people's attitudes, as influenced by their pleasures and pains, their inclinations and aversions, their loves and hatreds, and not about real normativity. For naturalists, there is no real normativity, but normative judgment, and its role in the lives of creatures like us, is easy enough to explain, even if the explanation bottoms out in a kind of brute power. In this respect, Nietzsche really is the "philosopher of power," though far more sensitive to its various manifestations than his typically vulgar acolytes.

PART II

Freedom, Agency, and the Will

5

Nietzsche's Theory of Agency

The Will and Freedom of the Will

1. Introduction: Free Will, Moral Responsibility, Determinism

By the "will," philosophers typically mean whatever the source of, or capacity for, action is supposed to be in a person: this could be the person's desires, intentions, their values, their reasons for acting, or the "self" in some other sense.[1] The will, so understood, is *free* if either:

(1) the future is open, i.e., it is possible for the agent to act otherwise than s/he does (call this "Alternate Possibilities" freedom of the will—or, for short, AP free will); or
(2) the agent has the right kind of control over his/her actions, such that the agent (or the agent's will) counts as the real "source" of the actions (call this the "Control" sense of free will).[2]

In the contemporary philosophical literature, a classic and influential Control account is due to Harry Frankfurt according to which the will is free if one acts on the (first-order) desire that one desires to be effective in action; addicts, on this account, are not acting freely because they experience their addiction as a compulsion that they would prefer not to act upon, but cannot resist doing so (Frankfurt 1971).[3] In the modern tradition, to be morally responsible (i.e., to be the proper target of moral praise or blame for one's actions[4]) the actions must result from a free will, which has always meant a will that could have willed otherwise (something Frankfurt denies is

[1] Nietzsche, who denies the causality of the will, as we will see, does not deny the causal efficacy of something like desires or the "self" understood Nietzsche's way: his dispute is with the attempt to identify any of these candidates for the "will" with a *free* will.

[2] I shall follow the lead of two leading contemporary authors who, noting that some are skeptical about the idea of a "will," note that they "will write in terms of free action and of acting freely when discussing free will" (McKenna and Pereboom 2016: 9–10, 11).

[3] Frankfurt argues, through some rather fanciful and arguably question-begging thought experiments, that "alternate possibilities" are not needed for free will or moral responsibility. Nietzsche, like the Christian tradition, assumes that free will requires AP, as I discuss below in the text.

[4] One can think of *moral* praise and blame as involving the idea that the person *deserves* the praise or blame, and that certain moral emotions are warranted: e.g., guilt in the case of blame.

necessary).[5] This modern tradition traces back to the Stoics (who introduced the idea of a will that "assents" to particular actions) and early Christianity, in particular. Alexander of Aphrodisias in the Second Century A.D. was the first to explicitly hold that *freedom to do otherwise* is a condition for voluntary action and therefore responsibility: he is the first explicit theorist of AP free will (Frede 2011: 100, 177). It will turn out that there is an aspect of Nietzsche's own views that has a superficial resonance with Control views, a topic to which I return in Chapter 6.

The general threat to freedom of the will is supposed to come from *determinism*. Robert Kane's gloss on this broad family of views (2005: 5–6) is particularly useful for our purposes:

> Doctrines of determinism have taken many historical forms. People have wondered at different times whether their choices and actions might be determined by fate or by God, by laws of physics or laws of logic, by heredity and environment, by unconscious motives or psychological or social conditioning, and so on. But there is a core idea running through all historical doctrines of determinism that reveals why they are a threat to free will—whether the doctrines be fatalistic, theological, logical, physical, psychological, or social. According to this core idea:
>
> An event (such as a choice or action) is *determined* when there are conditions obtaining earlier (such as the decrees of fate or the foreordaining acts of God or antecedent causes plus laws of nature) whose occurrence is a sufficient condition for the occurrence of the event. In other words, it *must* be the case that, *if* these earlier determining conditions obtain, then the determined event will occur.

To be sure, in modernity, God is dead and classical physical determinism is often claimed to be false due to quantum physics (though it remains unclear how that would help free will). But even without *classical* (i.e., *nomological*) *determinism* (given any state of the world at time T, the laws of nature will determine the next state of the world at T+1), free will can still be threatened—in either the AP or Control Senses of free will—if what we do is causally determined by the environment, by our physiology, by our unconscious psyche, or some combination of these forces. Nietzsche's kind of "determinism" is certainly neither the nomological nor theological kind, but it is one that appeals centrally to the role that physiology and unconscious drives play in determining action (this will be Nietzsche's "fatalism," to which we return below).

Incompatibilists, as the term is used in the philosophical literature, deny that free will and moral responsibility are compatible with the causal determination of the will in any form. Nietzsche is, I will argue, a kind of incompatibilist, but not the kind common

[5] In an influential article, at least in Anglophone philosophy, Gary Watson (1996) proposed a distinction between "accountability" responsibility and "attributability" responsibility. The former designates the conventional issues in the literature on free will and moral responsibility, namely, whether the agent is morally responsible and thus praiseworthy or blameworthy for his acts. The latter, by contrast, speaks only to whether an action is attributable to a person (to the person's "real self"), in a way that a reflex or a compulsion or an action that results from addiction is not. Calling an attributable action a case of "responsibility" seems to me more misleading than illuminating, and throughout I will assume that the primary issue for Nietzsche and the bulk of the Western tradition is what Watson calls accountability. I return in Chapter 6 to Watson's distinction.

in the Christian (i.e., anti-naturalist) traditions of philosophy, i.e., so-called "libertarian" incompatibilists who accept the incompatibility of freedom, moral responsibility, and causal determinism but believe that the will can sometimes stand outside the deterministic causal order and thus be free and morally responsible (Kant is the most infamous case, with which Nietzsche was familiar). Nietzsche is what we now call a "Hard Incompatibilist" (or "Hard Determinist"), someone who accepts the truth of determinism (albeit in a particular Nietzschean form), accepts that freedom and causal determination of the will are incompatible, and who concludes, accordingly, that no one has free will or is morally responsible.[6]

By contrast, so-called "Compatibilists" believe the causal determination of action is compatible with free will and moral responsibility. The crucial claim for many Compatibilists is that actions must be causally determined *in the right kind of way* (I will refer to these views as "Causal Compatibilism"); for another group of Compatibilists (probably the majority in the recent Anglophone literature[7]), as long as agents are "responsive" to relevant reasons for acting, they can be morally responsible (hereafter "Reasons-Responsive Compatibilism"). I hope to show that Nietzsche is a Hard Incompatibilist who also has arguments against Compatibilism in both forms as well. But let us begin with what Nietzsche actually says on the subject of free will and moral responsibility.

2. What Nietzsche Says about Free Will and Moral Responsibility

It behooves us to start with some texts, since (as we will see in Chapter 6), moralizing readers of Nietzsche often want to present him as still committed to freedom of the will in some sense sufficient for responsibility. All scholars concede that the early *Human, All too Human* (1878) reflects a Hard Incompatibilist position, since Nietzsche was here in the grips of Schopenhauer's Kantian view about the status of free will in the phenomenal world, i.e., the world as it appears to us, governed, as it is, by causal laws. As Nietzsche says in this early work, "No one is responsible [*verantwortlich*] for his deeds, no one for his nature; to judge is to be unjust" (HAH 39; cf. HAH 106). But we

[6] In recent Anglophone literature, Derk Pereboom (2001) and Galen Strawson (1994) have defended this view, the latter with explicit reference to Nietzsche, though they defend it on very different grounds. Spinoza is the most important historical antecedent for Nietzsche, and we will discuss Nietzsche's views in relation to Spinoza's in Chapter 6. Strictly speaking, Hard Incompatibilists also hold that free will and moral responsibility are incompatible with causal *indeterminism*; I suspect Nietzsche would agree, though the texts underdetermine that point.

[7] Versions of something like this view are defended by, *inter alia*, Susan Wolf, Dana Nelkin, John Martin Fischer, Mark Ravizza, Michael McKenna and others. From a Nietzschean point of view, this literature seems like a rearguard action to salvage moral responsibility in the face of the failures of both Humean (including Frankfurt-style) Compatibilism and libertarian Incompatibilism. The main data point in its favor—namely, that it allows us to salvage "ordinary" practices of moral praise and blame—is irrelevant for Nietzsche, who accords no special priority to existing practices, which are the targets of his critiques. I shall have more to say about this strand of recent Anglophone Compatibilism later in the chapter.

can put HAH to one side[8] since evidence of Nietzsche's skepticism about freedom and responsibility remains plentiful in his mature corpus of the 1880s, long after he has broken free of Schopenhauer and NeoKantianism. Thus, at the start of the decade, in *Daybreak*, he writes:

> Do I have to add that the wise Oedipus was right that we really are not responsible for our dreams—but just as little for our waking life, and that the doctrine of freedom of will has human pride and feeling of power for its father and mother? (D 128)

This is a typical Nietzschean strategy: to explain belief in freedom of the will by the ulterior motivations we have for accepting it rather than by its real existence, since in reality, we are as little responsible for what we do in real life as for what we do in our dreams. It is hard to imagine a more bracing denial of freedom and responsibility. The same themes are sounded in one of his very last works, *The Antichrist*:

> Formerly man was given a "free will" as his dowry from a higher order: today we have taken his will away altogether, in the sense that we no longer admit the will as a faculty. The old word "will" now serves only to denote a resultant, a kind of individual reaction, which follows necessarily upon a number of partly contradictory, partly harmonious stimuli: the will no longer "acts" [*wirkt*] or "moves" [*bewegt*]. (A 14)

Denial of the causality of "the will" (more precisely, what we *experience* as willing) is central to Nietzsche's skepticism about free will (a point to which we return below) and also explains why he frequently denies "unfree will" as well: what we experience as "will" does not, in fact, cause our actions, so the causal determination or freedom of *this* will is irrelevant. In *Daybreak* (124), he writes:

> We laugh at him who steps out of his room at the moment when the sun steps out of its room, and then says: "*I will* that the sun shall rise"; and at him who cannot stop a wheel, and says: "*I will* that it shall roll"; and at him who is thrown down in wrestling, and says: "here I lie, but *I will* lie here!" But, all laughter aside, are we ourselves ever acting any differently whenever we employ the expression "*I will*"?

If the faculty of the will "no longer 'acts' or 'moves'" (A 14)—if it is no longer causal—then there remains no conceptual space for the Causal Compatibilist idea that the right kind of causal determination of the will is compatible with responsibility for our actions, since the will is epiphenomenal. If, as Zarathustra puts it, "thought is one thing, the deed is another, and the image of the deed still another: the wheel of causality does not roll between them" (Z I, "On the Pale Criminal")—a pithy statement of the point of the D 124 passage—then there is no room for moral responsibility: I may well identify with my "thoughts" or my will, but if they do not *cause* my actions, how could I possibly be responsible for them? (This is Nietzsche's crucial argument against Causal Compatibilism, to which we return later.)

[8] Though do see HAH 39 for a statement of skepticism about free will and responsibility that is echoed in later work.

In the central discussion of free will and responsibility in the *Genealogy*, Nietzsche writes:

> For just as common people separate the lightning from its flash and take the latter to be a *deed*, something performed by a subject called lightening, so popular morality also separates strength from the expressions of strength as if there were an indifferent substratum behind the strong person which had the *freedom* to manifest strength or not. But there is no such substratum... [T]he suppressed, hiddenly glowing affects of revenge and hate exploit this belief [in the subject] and basically even uphold no other belief more ardently than this one, that *the strong are free* to be weak, and the birds of prey are free to be lambs:—they thereby gain for themselves the right to hold the bird of prey *accountable* [*zurechnen*]... [The weak] *need* the belief in a neutral "subject" with free choice, out of an instinct of self-preservation, self-affirmation, in which every lie is sanctified. (GM I:13)

The "will" that was denied as a faculty in the other passages is now here dubbed a "substratum" that stands behind the act and chooses to perform it, or not. But there is no such faculty, "will," or substratum, choosing to manifest strength or weakness; there just is the *doing*, no doer who bears the responsibility for it. The discussion of "The Four Great Errors" in *The Twilight of the Idols* is to the same effect. As Nietzsche writes in conclusion there:

> Today we no longer have any pity for the concept of "free will": we know only too well what it really is—the foulest of all theologians' artifices, aimed at making mankind "responsible" in their sense... [T]he doctrine of the will has been invented essentially for the purpose of punishment, that is, because one wanted to impute guilt. (TI VI:7)

Once again, Nietzsche's denial that the will (or, more precisely, what we experience as the will) is a causal faculty—the central argument of this chapter of *Twilight*, as I discuss below—is juxtaposed with a psychological explanation for why people would nonetheless be motivated to believe in freedom and responsibility. Once we abandon this "error of free will" we should, in turn, abandon the concepts picking out the reactive attitudes whose intelligibility depends on it, concepts like "guilt." Zarathustra well describes the required revision to our thinking about freedom and responsibility that results: " 'Enemy' you shall say, but not 'villain'; 'sick' you shall say, but not 'scoundrel'; 'fool' you shall say, but not 'sinner' " (Z I: "On the Pale Criminal"). The abandoned concepts—that of villain, scoundrel, and sinner—are all ones that require freedom and responsibility that would license blame, while the substitute concepts (enemy, sick, and fool) merely describe a person's condition or character, without supposing anything about the agent's responsibility for being in that condition or having that character.

Any account of Nietzsche's theory of agency must show how it is consistent with these pervasive themes in the Nietzschean corpus. Nietzsche, I will argue, endorses a Hard Incompatibilist position because he is a "fatalist" (in a sense to be explained) and fatalism is incompatible with AP Free Will (in either compatibilist or incompatibilist forms) and, indeed, given Nietzsche's reasons for it, also with other existing

Compatibilist views of free will. I begin by laying out Nietzsche's fatalism; subsequent sections will turn to his reasons for being a fatalist, including the misleading phenomenology of willing, the epiphenomenalism of conscious mental states, our inability to introspectively identify the motives on which we act, and Nietzsche's hypothesis about the real genesis of action.

3. Fatalism

In earlier work (Leiter 1998, 2002), I have defended the view that Nietzsche believes that the possible trajectories of each individual's life are fixed in advance in virtue of an individual's nature, that is, the physiological and psychological facts that make the person who he is. (In Chapter 7, I will offer evidence that Nietzsche is right.) It is striking that Nietzsche endorses fatalism in this sense from the beginning of his philosophical career until the very end. In 1878, for example, he praises Schopenhauer for his "insight into the strict necessity of human actions" adding that we confront "a brazen wall of fate [*des Fatums*]: we *are* in prison, we can only *dream* ourselves free, not make ourselves free" (HAH II:33). As noted earlier, Nietzsche rejects the nomic determinism about the phenomenal world that undergirds Schopenhauer's view and Nietzsche's own view in HAH. Yet in his next work, *Daybreak*, he still suggests that what looks like purposive and intentional action is nothing more than the *necessary*[9] course of events playing itself out:

> [P]erhaps there exists neither will nor purposes, and we have only imagined them. Those iron hands of necessity which shake the dice-box of chance play their game for an infinite length of time; so that there *have* to be throws which exactly resemble purposiveness and rationality of every degree. *Perhaps* our acts of will and our purposes are nothing but just such throws—and we are only too limited and too vain to comprehend our extreme limitedness: which consists in the fact that we ourselves shake the dice-box with iron hands, that we ourselves in our most intentional actions do no more than play the game of necessity. (D 130)

Anticipating the later themes of *Ecce Homo* (to which I return, below), Nietzsche writes in *The Gay Science*: "*What does your conscience say*? —'You shall become the person you are'" (GS 270). A few years later, in *Beyond Good and Evil*, Nietzsche observes that:

> [A]t the bottom of us, really "deep down," there is, of course, something unteachable, some granite of spiritual *fatum*, of predetermined [*vorherbestimmer*] decision and answer to predetermined selected questions. Whenever a cardinal problem is at stake, there speaks an unchangeable [*unwandelbares*] "this is I." (BGE 231)

In his last productive year, Nietzsche writes that, "The single human being is a piece of *fatum* from the front and from the rear, one law more, one necessity more for all that is yet to come and to be" (TI VI:6). In *Nachlass* notes from the same year, he claims that "the voluntary is absolutely lacking... everything has been directed along certain lines

[9] This is presumably a kind of token-necessity, though whether there can be such necessities without laws of nature is not an issue Nietzsche appears to have thought about.

from the beginning" (WP 458) and that, not surprisingly, "one will become only that which one is (in spite of all: that means education, instruction, milieu, chance, and accident)" (WP 334). His famous doctrine of "amor fati"—"that one wants nothing to be different, not forward, not backward, not in all eternity" (EH II:10)—takes on a new significance against the background of his fatalism: since nothing *could*, after all, have been different, the affirmative attitude towards life which Nietzsche famously commends would require, then, that we accept things the way they are.

The most striking evidence of Nietzsche's fatalism comes from how he tells the story of his own life in *Ecce Homo*. The subtitle of the work, recall, is "How One Becomes What One Is" (*Wie man wird, was man ist*): it is a story of how one's life unfolds in a way determined by one's nature.[10] Nietzsche's highly stylized "autobiography" is, in fact, organized around two ironies. Autobiographies are standardly extended exercises in self-congratulation, but whereas the typical autobiography pursues this end while trying not to be obvious about it, Nietzsche simply declares plainly the point of the project, that is, to show, as his chapter headings put it, "Why I Am So Wise" (EH I), "Why I Am So Clever" (EH II), and so on. This is autobiography as *unabashed* self-congratulation.

These megalomaniac chapter headings have led some readers to think that the book is a work of incipient madness, but I find that implausible in light of the actual answer Nietzsche proffers for the title questions. For though Nietzsche, indeed, thinks himself

[10] Some interpreters try to resist the fatalistic implications. For example, Richard Rorty, commenting on the subtitle, writes as follows:

> In the sense Nietzsche gave to the phrase, "who one actually is" does not mean "who one actually was all the time" but "whom one turned oneself into in the course of creating the taste by which one ended up judging oneself." The term "ended up" is, however, misleading. It suggests a predestined resting place. (1989: 99)

Rorty does not, in fact, try to ground this interpretive claim in a reading of *Ecce Homo* (he cites only Alexander Nehamas as authority, to whom I return, below). Yet the misunderstanding of Nietzsche's point is hinted at by Rorty's mistranslation: one becomes "*what*" [*was*] one is, according to Nietzsche, not "who" [*wer*] one is. Speaking of "what" rather than "who" fits with the naturalistic objectification of the person that one would expect from a philosopher who views persons as having many immutable, determining characteristics, such that one may ask of a human being, as one may ask of a tree, "*What* is it made of essentially?"

Nehamas's own reading of the EH subtitle is defended on different, but equally problematic, grounds. For example, commenting on the famous section "On the Despisers of the Body" (Z I:4), Nehamas claims that those who despise the body do so because of "the belief that they have a stable self" (1985: 251 n. 6). But Zarathustra nowhere in the passage disputes the existence of a stable self; to the contrary, he equates the real self with the body, and describes how this body determines what we do even as we imagine otherwise. "Your self [the body]," says Zarathustra, "laughs at your ego and at its bold leaps. 'What are these great leaps and flights of thought to me' it says to itself. 'A detour to my end. I am the leading strings of the ego and the prompter of its concepts.'"

Nehamas also argues that the idea of an underlying, essential self is incompatible with Nietzsche's "general denial of the idea of a reality that underlies appearance" (1985: 173). Yet *this* denial is for Nietzsche a denial of the *metaphysical* distinction between the "merely" apparent, sensible realm and a supra-sensible, unknowable reality (as drawn, e.g., by Kant; cf. TI: IV); it could hardly involve a denial of the difference between superficial states (like consciousness) and the underlying, causally efficacious states (which are, in principle, knowable), like the unconscious drives or the body. For this latter distinction is plainly central to Nietzsche: for example, when he calls consciousness "surface and skin—which, like every skin, betrays something but *conceals* even more" (BGE 33) (cf. EH II: 9: "consciousness *is* a surface").

wise, clever, and the author of good books, there is nothing, in fact, self-congratulatory about his answer to the questions *why* he is so wise, so clever, and the rest. This is because the argument of *Ecce Homo* reflects Nietzsche's fatalism: his being so "wise," so "clever" was simply a lucky stroke of nature, not something that can be credited to him *qua* free agent.

Indeed, the book begins on precisely that note: "The good fortune of my existence," says Nietzsche in the first line, "lies in its fatality [*Verhängniss*]" (EH I:1). As a result, the answer to the apparently self-congratulatory "why" questions is roughly this: "It was a lucky fact of nature that I, Nietzsche, was a healthy organism, that is, the type of creature that instinctively does the right things to facilitate its flourishing."[11] "I have always *instinctively* chosen the *right* means against wretched states" (EH I:2; first emphasis added), declares Nietzsche. As the argument of *Ecce Homo* makes explicit, this means choosing (instinctively or necessarily) the right nutrition, the right climate, the right forms of recreation, "everything that deserves to be taken seriously in life" (EH IV:8).[12] Nietzsche wrote such wise and clever books for the same reason the tomato plant grows tomatoes: because it could not have done otherwise. There is no self-congratulation involved in simply reporting what had to be, and Nietzsche evinces none. To the contrary, as he remarks in the quotation with which the book opens: "How could I fail to be grateful [dankbar] to my whole life?" This very way of putting the question, however, suggests a sharp divide between the "life"—which runs its necessary course—and the conscious "self" which views the life as though a spectator upon it.

Fatalistic themes pervade *Ecce Homo*. Explaining why he returned to Rome while writing *Zarathustra*, Nietzsche comments that "some fatality was at work" (EH III: Z-4). He declares that "*amor fati*" is the mark of "greatness": that one does not merely "bear what is necessary . . . but *love*[s] it" (EH II:10). Later he remarks (not surprisingly) that "*amor fati* is my inmost nature" (EH III: CW-4). The depth of Nietzsche's fatalism regarding his own life becomes most apparent in a long passage from the second chapter of *Ecce Homo*. Nietzsche is here discussing his development as a philosopher, after noting that, "To become what one is, one must not have the faintest notion *what* one is" (EH II:9). He continues:

> Meanwhile the organizing "idea" that is destined to rule [*die zur Herrschaft berufne*] keeps growing deep down—it begins to command; slowly it leads us *back* from side roads and wrong roads; it prepares *single* qualities and fitnesses that will one day prove to be indispensable as means toward a whole—one by one, it trains all *subservient* capacities before giving any hint of the dominant task, "goal," "aim," or "meaning."

[11] Cf. EH I:2: "I took myself in hand, I made myself healthy again: the condition for this—every physiologist would admit that—is *that one be healthy at bottom*."

[12] Cf. EH II:10: "these small things—nutrition, place, climate, recreation, the whole casuistry of selfishness—are inconceivably more important than everything one has taken to be important so far."

> Considered in this way, my life is simply wonderful. For the task of a *revaluation of all values* more capacities may have been needed than have ever dwelt together in a single individual—above all, even contrary capacities that had to be kept from disturbing, destroying one another... [Their] *higher protection* manifested itself to such a high degree that I never even suspected what was growing in me [*was in mir wächst*]—and one day all my capacities, suddenly ripe [*reif*], *leaped forth* [*hervorsprangen*] in their ultimate perfection. (EH II:9)

Here Nietzsche looks back at his own life almost as a third-person observer, astonished and pleasantly surprised to see how it all turned out so well. It would be as if an apple tree, unaware of its true nature, never "suspect[ing] what was growing" in it, were suddenly to discover one day its fruit "suddenly ripe" and "leap[ing] forth."[13] We now have the answer to the book's subtitle "how one becomes what one is?" The answer: by making no special effort *consciously directed toward that end*, because one becomes what one is *necessarily*.

Nietzschean fatalism is unusual in the history of fatalistic ideas in philosophy, but we can now state its contours more precisely (I largely follow, with some modifications, the account in Leiter 2002: 81–7). According to Nietzsche the fatalist, a person's life proceeds along a fixed trajectory, fixed by "natural" facts about that person ("type-facts" in the sense introduced earlier [Introduction, Section 1]). Nietzsche the fatalist views a person like a plant: just as, say, the essential natural facts about a tomato plant determine its development (e.g., that it will grow tomatoes and not, say, corn), so too the essential natural facts about a person determine its development as well. Of course, the precise development of a tomato plant—whether it "flourishes" or wilts—is affected (causally) by a host of other factors that do not constitute the "essence" of the plant: for example, the soil in which it is planted, the amount of water and sunshine it receives, and the like. So the natural facts about the tomato plant *circumscribe* the possible trajectories, though they themselves do not uniquely determine which of these is realized. Nietzsche holds the same view about persons: natural facts about a person circumscribe what that person becomes, though within the limits set by the natural facts, the precise details of what a person becomes depend (causally) upon other factors. More formally, then, we can say that according to Nietzschean Fatalism:

> Natural facts about a person are *causally primary* in fixing the trajectory of that person's life.
> Natural facts, in turn, are "causally primary" with respect to some effect (i.e., some life trajectory) insofar as:
> (1) they are always necessary for that effect; though
> (2) they may not be sufficient for it.

[13] Cf. Schopenhauer's observation in *On the Freedom of the Will* that trying to use "talk and moralizing" to "reform" a man's "character... is exactly like the attempt... by means of careful cultivation to make an oak produce apricots" (1985: 54).

So, for example, natural facts (e.g., about metabolism, genetic inheritance, body type, and strength) are causally primary with respect to being a professional basketball player, in the sense that (1) to become a professional basketball player it is always *necessary* to have the right natural characteristics (height being only the most obvious), though (2) these natural characteristics are typically not sufficient to guarantee that one becomes a professional basketball player (e.g., not all tall, physically fit people become professional basketball players).[14] Nietzschean Fatalism is compatible, then, with the idea that factors other than natural facts about the person may still play a causal role in the trajectory of a person's life—within the limits circumscribed, of course, by the natural facts. For Nietzsche's fatalism to have any bite, of course, it must turn out that the natural facts significantly circumscribe the possible trajectories. I shall assume, with Nietzsche, that they do so, in this sense: the fundamental facts about one's *character and personality* are fixed by natural facts ("type-facts"), and thus

[14] Ken Gemes and Christopher Janaway object to this account as follows:

> The gloss [Leiter] gives on natural facts being causally primary with respect to some effect is that such facts are necessary but possibly not sufficient for the relevant effect. But this is an extraordinarily weak gloss; our having heads is a necessary but not sufficient condition for our becoming philosophers, but we would not want to say that our having heads is causally primary with respect to our becoming philosophers. And, while Leiter puts "essential" in scare quotes, one worries that in as much as essential properties are typically taken to be unchangeable this saddles Nietzsche with a view that weights the causal role of nature rather heavily over that of nurture. (2005: 733)

I have in this book and earlier work repeatedly documented the many places where Nietzsche embraces the idea of an "unchangeable" or "essential nature," but the more important point here is that an M-Naturalist, whether Nietzsche or Hume, *ought* to emphasize the causal role of nature over that of nurture, precisely in order to—as Barry Stroud puts it in describing Hume's view—"explain[] various and complicated... happenings in terms of relatively few extremely general, perhaps universal, principles" (Stroud 1977: 3). This is why Hume seeks "a completely general theory of human nature," since one of the features that marks it as aspiring to the scientific is precisely its *generality*, namely, its attempt to transcend real and vivid cultural particulars to see what all these disparate cultural artifacts have in common, namely, their genesis from tendencies rooted in the nature of the human.

The other part of Gemes and Janaway's critique—concerning the "weakness" of the necessary, but not sufficient, characterization of what it is for an explanans to be "causally primary"—simply exploits a familiar problem about empiricist analyses of causation, from Hume to Mackie: namely, that they flounder on the problem of picking out the regular "correlations" that count for purposes of causation or, in the case of Mackie, in specifying the conditions that are merely non-causal "background" conditions when we pick out the INUS cause of an event (where the INUS cause is "an insufficient but necessary part of an unnecessary but sufficient condition" for the event happening). Having a head does not cause anyone to be a philosopher (even if it is a necessary condition), but having the genetic make-up of a tomato is surely a key part of the best causal explanation of why a particular seed grows into a tomato plant. It would be astonishing—or simply gross anachronism—to think Nietzsche has a good explanation of how we mark this difference, especially when so many philosophers who have thought systematically about the problem do not. But that does not change the fact that ordinary and scientific practice recognizes the distinction. Indeed, Nietzsche gives every sign of being a sensible M-Naturalist on this score, and not a disreputable metaphysician, when he describes "science" as simply "the healthy concepts of cause and effect" (A 49). Let science and the application of scientific methods decide what is a cause and what is not; we may then help ourselves to whatever kinds of causes work. We may, at least, be confident that no interesting theory will develop around an explanation of philosophers in terms of their having heads, while *every* sensible scientific explanation of plants growing tomatoes will appeal to the genetic make-up of tomato plant seeds. If Nietzsche is right (an issue to which we return especially in Chapter 7), then the same will be true about the correct naturalistic account of moral beliefs and attitudes.

how one responds to differing circumstances and environments is also causally determined by these natural type-facts. But the actual circumstances in which a person finds himself are plainly not fixed in advance by the natural facts about a person. In this sense, Nietzschean Fatalism differs from the sort of fatalistic doctrine associated with Calvinism, in which all the details of one's life are determined in advance.

Let us call "Classical Determinism" the view that for any event *p* at a time *t*, *p* is necessary given the totality of facts prior to *t*, together with the actual laws of nature. "Classical Fatalism," by contrast, is the view that whatever happens had to happen, but not in virtue of the truth of Classical Determinism.[15] Classical Fatalism involves the notion of some sort of non-deterministic, perhaps even non-causal *necessity*. Finally, we will call "Causal Essentialism" the doctrine that for any individual substance (e.g., a person or some other living organism) that substance has some "essential" properties that are causally primary with respect to the future history of that substance, i.e., they non-trivially determine the space of possible trajectories for that substance.[16] Notice that Causal Essentialism entails neither Classical Determinism nor Fatalism. Unlike Determinism, Causal Essentialism is compatible with there being no laws of nature (which seems to be Nietzsche's view). Unlike Fatalism, Essentialism does not entail that any particular outcome to a person's life is *necessary* (since Causal Essentialism only *circumscribes* trajectories, but does not necessitate any particular one).

Nietzsche's Fatalism involves *only* Causal Essentialism. Nietzsche is neither a Classical Determinist nor a Classical Fatalist. That is, he holds only that there are essential natural facts about persons that significantly circumscribe the range of life trajectories that person can realize and that, as a result, make one's life "fated," not in the classical sense, but in the sense that what we become is far more constrained, in advance, than we had ever realized. And Causal Essentialism is clearly sufficient for supporting the generic worry about determinism with which we began: it necessitates, together with other facts beyond the agent's control, the agent's actions, thus rendering impossible both AP free will and (for reasons to be set out in detail, below) Control free will.

4. The Phenomenology of Willing

Recall Section 124 of *Daybreak*, where Nietzsche sets the primary issues that shall occupy us here in trying to understand his theory of the will. Nietzsche writes:

> We laugh at him who steps out of his room at the moment when the sun steps out of its room, and then says: "*I will* that the sun shall rise"; and at him who cannot stop a wheel, and

[15] Strictly speaking, Classical Determinism would not entail Classical Fatalism, since the outcomes necessitated under Classical Determinism are *contingent* on the past and on the laws of nature. (I am grateful to Rob Koons for help in thinking through these distinctions.)

[16] I view talk of "essences," as I take it Nietzsche does too, *sans* metaphysical baggage. Nietzsche can agree with Quine that "relative to a particular inquiry, some predicates may play a more basic role than others, or may apply more fixedly; and these may be treated as essential" (Quine 1981: 120–1). Cf. Nietzsche's reference to "the weakness of the weak" as "their *essence* [*Wesen*]...their sole, ineluctable, irremovable reality" (GM I:13).

says: "*I will* that it shall roll"; and at him who is thrown down in wrestling, and says: "here I lie, but *I will* lie here!" But, all laughter aside, are we ourselves ever acting any differently whenever we employ the expression "*I will*"?

I take it to be uncontroversial that this last question is rhetorical, and that the intended answer to this question is: "no, it is no different at all" (as the voluminous textual evidence reviewed earlier in this chapter would suggest). What we need to understand here is why Nietzsche thinks that when we act and say "I will," it is no different, and no less ridiculous, than when he "who steps out of his room at the moment when the sun steps out of its room... says '*I will* that the sun shall rise.' "[17]

If it is really true that this analogy holds, then it follows that the experience of willing which precedes an action does not track an actual causal relationship: the experience of willing is epiphenomenal with respect to the action. As Nietzsche notes in *The Gay Science*, "the feeling of *will* suffices for" a person "to assume cause and effect" (GS 127), but it will be the burden of Nietzsche's argument to show that this assumption is mistaken. Thus, an adequate account of Nietzsche's theory of the will and action will require us to get clear about three claims: first, the phenomenology of "willing" an action, the experience we have which leads us (causally) to conceive of ourselves as exercising our will (to say "I will"); second, Nietzsche's arguments that the experiences picked out by the phenomenology are not causally connected to the resulting action; and third, Nietzsche's account of the actual causal genesis of action. On the latter score, we shall turn to some recent work in empirical psychology that, in fact, supports precisely Nietzsche's skepticism that our "feeling" of will is a reliable guide to the causation of action.

Nietzsche recognizes that we often *feel* as if we are exercising free will, but he is unusual among philosophers in scrutinizing that experience, breaking it into its component parts. The resulting account is admittedly a *revisionary* one—it is not ultimately designed to *vindicate* the epistemic reliability of the feelings involved—but it is, Nietzsche claims, the correct account of those feelings. The key discussion comes in Section 19 of *Beyond Good and Evil*, whose account of the phenomenology of willing bears quoting at length:

[I]n every act of willing there is, to begin with, a plurality of feelings [*Gefühlen*], namely: the feeling of the state *away from which*, the feeling of the state *towards which*, and the feeling of this "away from" and "towards" themselves. But this is accompanied by a feeling of the muscles that comes into play through a sort of habit as soon as we "will," even without our putting "arms and legs" into motion. Just as feeling—and indeed many feelings—must be recognized as ingredients of the will, thought must be as well. In every act of will there is a commandeering thought,—and we really should not believe this thought can be divorced from the "willing," as if some will would then be left over! Third, the will is not just a complex of feeling and thinking; rather it is fundamentally an *affect* [*ein Affekt*]; and specifically the affect of the command. What

[17] Nietzsche himself makes the point clear just a few sections later in the same work, noting "that we really are not responsible for our dreams—but just as little for our waking life" (D 128).

is called "freedom of the will" is essentially the affect of superiority with respect to something that must obey: "I am free, 'it' must obey'—this consciousness lies in every will. . . . A person who *wills*—, commands something inside himself that obeys, or that he believes to obey."[18]

Let us use an example to flesh out Nietzsche's account. Sitting at the computer, I wonder whether I should go downstairs to see what the children are doing. I "decide" to do so, and so begin to rise from my chair. I *feel* as if I have willed the movement: I feel the *moving away* from the desk and computer, the *moving towards* the door, and I *feel* the physical, or muscular, movement as well. Let us call all this complex of feelings, for ease of reference, "the bodily feelings."

These bodily feelings are not, however, sufficient for the experience of will: they are merely *qualitative*, merely the "raw" feeling of "away," "towards," of muscles contracting, limbs moving. We still need the "commandeering thought"—that's Nietzsche's label, which I will use in what follows—namely, the thought, "I will get up from the desk and go downstairs" or some suitable surrogate. But the bodily feelings and the commandeering thought are still not enough, according to Nietzsche, for the experience of willing. This is perhaps Nietzsche's key claim. For the experience of willing is, according to Nietzsche, essentially the *meta-feeling*—the "affect" Nietzsche calls it—of commanding. "Affect" is not being used here in its Freudian sense of psychic energy or "charge," but as something closer to feeling once more. By the "affect of the command," Nietzsche means the *feeling* that the *thought* (i.e., the propositional content, such as "I will get up from the desk and go downstairs"[19]) brings about these other bodily feelings, i.e., of "away from," "towards," of, in a word, movement; and that this commanding is *who I am*. By *identifying* with the commandeering thought—by taking that to be "who I am"—we *feel* superior, we experience this affect of superiority. So we have the experience of willing when the person identifies himself with a certain propositional content (the commandeering thought "I will get up from the desk and go downstairs") that one takes to be commanding the bodily feelings, i.e., the feeling that attach to the "towards," "away from" and the muscular sensations; and this identification produces the meta-feeling of superiority which is the feeling of willing. In short, one experiences willing when one *feels* as if the bodily qualia are obeying the thought, and that the commanding thought is who one is.

As Nietzsche recognizes, there is something paradoxical here, since, as he observes in the same section of *Beyond Good and Evil*:

[W]e are, under the circumstances, both the one who commands *and* the one who obeys, and as the obedient one we are familiar with the feelings of compulsion, force, pressure, resistance,

[18] Clark and Dudrick (2012: 180 n. 2) object that the latter half of "*ich bin frei, 'er' muss gehorchen*" should be translated as "he must obey," not "it must obey" (they believe this possible difference in translation supports an alternative reading of the passage—I return in notes, below, to their interpretation). But "he must obey" makes no sense with reference to the "something that must obey." That something is obviously *the body* (*der Leib*), the muscles, arms, and legs Nietzsche has just been discussing: and since *der Leib* is a masculine noun, "er" makes perfect sense in German, but not when translated literally as "he" in English.

[19] It might be more apt to put the propositional content in the imperative form, so that it does not sound merely like a prediction!

and motion that generally start right after the act of willing. On the other hand, however, we are in the habit of ignoring and deceiving ourselves about this duality by mean of the synthetic concept of the "I." (BGE 19)

In other words, talk of "I"—as in "*I* will go downstairs"—obscures an elemental fact: it's my body that is "obeying" my will, so "I" am also one who obeys, as well as one who commands. Of course, we don't experience it, or think of it, that way: we identify the "I" with the feeling of *commanding*, not the feeling of obeying. Thus, our experience of the "I," our identification of it with the commandeering thought, itself requires an explanation: *why* do we not identify ourselves with the *commanded* feelings and movements, why do we, instead, identify ourselves with the superiority of the *commandeering thought*?

Here is what Nietzsche offers by way of explanation in the same passage:

[T]he one who wills believes with a reasonable degree of certainty that will and action are somehow one; he attributes the success, the performance of the willing to the will itself, and consequently enjoys an increase in the feeling of power that accompanies all success. "Freedom of the will"—that is the word for the multi-faceted state of pleasure of one who commands and, at the same time, identifies himself with the accomplished act of willing.[20]

We identify, then, with the *feelings of command* rather than those of obedience because identifying with the former increases pleasure (it is pleasant to feel the body "obeying" and thus pleasant to feel as if we are exercising free will)—so the explanation might seem straightforwardly hedonistic. But this would be too quick, since the real explanation, as often happens in Nietzsche, is cast in terms of feelings of power, which, *in turn*, produce pleasurable sensations. We need not resolve the issue here of the primacy of the desire for pleasure or desire for power as the fundamental explanatory mechanism;[21] for the phenomenology all that matters is that it be true that there *is* a feeling of pleasure attendant upon the sensation of willing, *even if* that feeling derives from a feeling of power.

So now we have Nietzsche's account of the *phenomenology* of willing from *Beyond Good and Evil* (and I should add that there is no more systematic account in the corpus that conflicts with it): we *feel* as though we are exercising free will when we *identify* with the "commandeering thought" which we feel is superior to, and being obeyed by, the myriad qualitative experiences involved in movement, that is, the bodily feelings; and we so identify because of the feelings of pleasure and power that arise from the "affect of superiority" that flows from that identification.

[20] What then of *unsuccessful* actions, which presumably one can also experience as being freely willed, although not "accomplished"? Suppose, for example, I decide to get up from the computer to see what the children are doing, but fail to do so (perhaps one of my kids has glued me to the chair!). Although the action is unsuccessful, all the requisite components for the experience of free will are present (e.g., I can feel the requisite bodily movements, even if they are not brought to completion).

[21] In *The Gay Science*, Nietzsche offers the apparently stronger claim on behalf of hedonism that for all willing "a representation of pleasure and displeasure is needed" (GS 127). Unfortunately, there is no elaboration of the thought, and so it is not clear that the *representation* might not itself be prompted by an experience of *power*: in any case, nothing in the discussion there rules it out.

5. What We Experience as Willing is not Causally Efficacious

The crucial idea in Nietzsche's theory of the will is that the phenomenology of willing, no matter how vivid, does *not* in fact mirror or reflect or—as I shall say in what follows—*track* an actual causal relationship. That is, the feeling of superiority that attaches to the "commandeering thought" with which we identify is not, in fact, identical with anything that actually stands in a causal relationship with the resultant action. Recall that Nietzsche writes in the long section from *Beyond Good and Evil* that we have been scrutinizing:

> the one who wills [i.e., who has the experience of willing] believes, in good conscience, that willing *suffices* for action. Since it is almost always the case that there is will only where the effect of command, and therefore obedience, and therefore action, may be *expected*, the *appearance* translates into the feeling, as if there were a *necessity of effect*. In short, the one who wills believes with a reasonable degree of certainty that will and action are somehow one; he attributes the success, the performance of the willing to the will itself, and consequently enjoys an increase in the feeling of power that accompanies all success... (BGE 19)

To put it in quasi-Humean terms, Nietzsche claims that because the complex of bodily feelings, commandeering thought, and meta-feeling are fairly constantly conjoined with succeeding bodily actions, we naturally infer (since it increases "the feeling of power") that the will has caused the subsequent actions. How, then, has the phenomenology misled us, according to Nietzsche?

Remember that the experience of will for Nietzsche has three components: the bodily feelings; the commandeering thought; and the meta-feeling of superiority, i.e., the feeling that the thought commands everything else. It is the meta-feeling (perhaps the pleasure attendant upon the meta-feeling) in turn that leads us to identify with the thought, rather than with the parts of our body that are commanded.

In debunking the phenomenology as a reliable guide to causation, Nietzsche's target is the *commandeering thought*, rather than the bodily feelings or the meta-feeling. And his argument is brilliantly simple. He starts from another bit of phenomenology, namely that, "a thought comes when 'it' wants, and not when 'I' want" (BGE 17). Nietzsche's target in this *particular* passage is the famous Cartesian doctrine, "I think, therefore I am." But, Nietzsche points out, from the fact that there is thinking, it does not follow that *I*, i.e., some subject or agent, is doing the thinking, and so it does not follow that I exist. As Nietzsche puts it:

> It is...a *falsification* of the facts to say that the subject "I" is the condition of the predicate "think." It thinks: but to say the "it" is just the famous old "I"—well that is just an assumption or opinion, to put it mildly, and by no means an "immediate certainty." In fact, there is already too much packed into the "it thinks": even the "it" contains an *interpretation* of the process, and does not belong to the process itself. (BGE 17)

Even if the explicit target in this particular passage is the Cartesian "I," the surrounding context makes clear the real target, namely, the will. The preceding section of *Beyond*

Good and Evil, for example, treats the "I think" and the "I will" as both being common, but mistaken, examples of "immediate certainties;"[22] while the following section returns explicitly to an attack on "free will," only to be followed by the long passage, Section 19 of *Beyond Good and Evil*, on which we have been focusing.

Now what does Nietzsche's phenomenological claim here mean? What does it mean to say a thought comes when "it" wants, not when "I" want? Because we are talking about thoughts that "come," I take it Nietzsche must mean thoughts that come to consciousness. And his point is that our "thoughts" appear in consciousness, without our having willed them: "*ein Gedanke kommt, wenn 'er' will, und nicht wenn 'ich' will.*" We need to be careful here since, after all, Nietzsche is engaged in an attack on the existence of will, so he can't believe that there is any sense in which I could genuinely will a thought into existence. But he can't, of course, presuppose that conclusion here without begging the question. Rather, we must take the talk of willing here to refer to the *experience of willing*, which Nietzsche, as we have seen all along, concedes is real enough.

So Nietzsche's phenomenological point then comes to this: a "thought" that appears in consciousness is *not* preceded by the *phenomenology of willing* that Nietzsche has described, that is, there is no "commandeering thought" preceding the conscious thought to which the meta-feeling (the affect of superiority) attaches. (Even if there were such a commandeering thought in some instance, this would just create a regress, since not every commandeering thought will be preceded by the experience of willing.) Since we do not *experience* our thoughts as willed the way we experience some actions as willed, it follows that no thought comes when "I will it" because the experience to which the "I will" attaches is absent.

Notice the clever structure of this argument, which is entirely *internal* to the perspective of the agent who takes himself to possess a will. For what Nietzsche does is point out that the criterion of willing that agents themselves treat as reliable guides to a causal relationship—namely, the phenomenology already described—is, in fact, completely absent in the case of thoughts (or, at least, in the case of the thought that starts an inferential chain of thinking which involves the experience of willing). As an introspective matter, it seems Nietzsche is plainly correct about this point, that is, most thoughts arrive in consciousness, unbidden, as it were, by any exercise of will. But if we do not experience our thoughts as willed, then it follows that the actions that follow upon our experience of willing (which includes those thoughts) are not caused in a way sufficient to underwrite ascriptions of moral responsibility.[23]

Nietzsche's conclusion—that our experience of willing does not, in fact, make us morally responsible for our actions—requires two premises. The first premise is this: the decisive component of the experience of will—namely, the commandeering

[22] Schopenhauer affirms the latter, Descartes the former.

[23] There is independent empirical evidence that the thoughts we are aware of are caused by non-conscious forces of which we are wholly unaware: for a useful, recent overview, see Oakley and Halligan (2017).

thought—is, itself, causally determined, at some point, by something other than the will, since thoughts that come into consciousness are causally determined by something other than the will.[24] (What the "something else" is we shall return to.) The second premise is Incompatibilism.[25] Since we have shown that the "commandeering thought" that is part of the experience of will is not *causa sui*, it follows that the will it helps constitute is not *causa sui*, and thus any actions following upon that experience of willing could not support ascriptions of moral responsibility.

[24] I am going to speak of "caused" and "causally determined" interchangeably, without meaning to prejudge issues about probabilistic causation—issues that, in any case, were unknown to Nietzsche.

[25] Owen and Ridley object (2003: 73–4) that the rest of the passage (BGE 21) undermines the point noted in the text. They write: "it must be a mistake to attribute to Nietzsche...the view that the will is 'unfree' in the sense of being causally determined, since he explicitly rejects that position" (73). But in what sense precisely does Nietzsche "reject" that claim?

One possibility is that Nietzsche, in BGE 21, is still in the grips of the NeoKantian view (via Friedrich Lange) that "cause and effect" are merely features of the phenomenal world, not of "things in themselves." If Nietzsche abandons, as even Owen and Ridley do not dispute (2003: 74), this NeoKantian view, then Nietzsche's argument against being *causa sui* is unaffected: if nothing in the "phenomenal" world can be self-caused, and the modifier "phenomenal" is doing no work, then it follows that nothing can be "self-caused" *simpliciter*. Owen and Ridley seem to acknowledge this point, but then add another objection (2003: 74):

> [Even granting Nietzsche's rejection of "Lange's Neo-Kantian skepticism concerning the reality of causation], if the argument against the *causa sui* as a piece of "superlative metaphysical nonsense" still holds once the Neo-Kantian view has been abandoned, then so too does the argument against classical determinism. That Nietzsche later came to accept the reality of causation, in other words, has no effect on the logical point that we draw from the passage, namely, that the opposite of a piece of nonsense is itself a piece of nonsense.

But Nietzsche does not speak of "superlative metaphysical nonsense," he says rather that the idea of the *causa sui* reflects a "longing for 'freedom of the will' in the superlative metaphysical sense," that is, in contemporary terms, some kind of libertarian free will. Even allowing that Nietzsche deems the idea of the *causa sui* nonsensical—he does say it "is the best self-contradiction that has even been conceived" even though he does not call it "superlative metaphysical nonsense" (a quote Owen and Ridley simply invent)—it does not follow, logically or otherwise, that an opposed doctrine is also nonsensical, unless that opposed doctrine shares the premise that renders the first self-contradictory. But what makes the idea of the *causa sui* incredible is the idea that one can "pull[] yourself by the hair from the swamp of nothingness up into existence" (BGE 21), and *that* is precisely the idea that is repudiated by the view that the will is causally determined. Nietzsche's purported argument against this latter doctrine depends entirely on the NeoKantian skepticism about causation that even Owen and Ridley concede he later abandons. This, in turn, explains precisely why there was no point in quoting that portion of the passage: the argument against the "unfreedom of the will" is a bad argument, depending on a NeoKantian doctrine Nietzsche himself came to repudiate. By contrast, the argument against the *causa sui* is sound in its own right, independent of the NeoKantian skepticism, and an argument consistent with other claims Nietzsche makes in this and subsequent works.

Clark and Dudrick (2012: 94–7) offer a different reading of Nietzsche's point about causation in BGE 21, one compatible with my point about Incompatibilism. They suggest that by the "in itself" Nietzsche means not the Kantian noumenal realm but "the natural or empirical world, the world as it appears from the viewpoint of the natural sciences," a usage Kant himself sometimes employs (Clark and Dudrick 2012: 95). With regard to this world, Nietzsche is, as Clark and Dudrick persuasively argue, a Humean about causation: "we find in the world itself...only regular patterns of succession, constant conjunction of similar events" (2012: 95). The "reification" of cause and effect to which he objects, then, is the failure to recognize the role of the mind in projecting *necessity* on to these constant conjunctions: "Nietzsche's objection is not to making causal claims or to taking such claims to be true, but only to interpreting causal claims in a way that involves 'reification' or projective mislocation" (2012: 96).

Now it must be conceded that the phenomenology of willing argument, as I have reconstructed it, simply takes for granted the truth of Incompatibilism. Why Nietzsche takes this view for granted is not hard to see: it is deeply embedded in Western moral and religious thought, tracing back to Alexander of Aphrodisias in the Second Century A.D. as we noted at the start of the chapter. As Galen Strawson has noted, the Incompatibilist idea of responsibility "has for a long time been central to the Western religious, moral and cultural traditions" (Strawson 1994: 8). Of course, if the *causa sui* were really a "self-contradiction" (BGE 21), as Nietzsche puts it, then the phenomenology of thoughts argument would be superfluous (cf. Clark and Dudrick 2012: 184 n. 3): *nothing* could be *causa sui* if it were a logical or conceptual impossibility. But this is rhetorical excess on Nietzsche's part, since it is quite clear we can conceive of something *causa sui*, namely, God. (The *causa sui* may be a physical impossibility *in this world*, but it is not a conceptual or logical impossibility, despite Nietzsche's rhetorical overreach.) Indeed, in BGE 21, Nietzsche goes on to state what is at issue in wanting to be *causa sui* quite clearly: it is "the longing to bear the entire and ultimate responsibility for your actions yourself and to relieve God, world, ancestors, chance and society of the burden," but in fact we do not bear such "entire and ultimate responsibility" of the kind that libertarian incompatibilists have long thought necessary for freedom of the will, for we are plainly not responsible for the thoughts that immediately precede our actions.

Does this argument—the "argument from the phenomenology of thoughts" (as I shall call it), i.e., the argument that they come when they want, not when I want—leave compatibilist conceptions of free will untouched? For the argument from the phenomenology of thoughts does not rule out the possibility that our experience of willing misleads us as to our *real will*, and that this *real will* does, in fact, stand in the appropriate causal relationship with actions. Of course, this "real will," if it exists, had better be one that the agent can claim as his own if we are to then saddle the agent with responsibility for the actions it produces. We turn to these issue in Section 7, below.

6. Confusing Cause and Effect

To see what the other argument for the epiphenomenality of the will might be, we need to remember Nietzsche's commitment to the Doctrine of Types that we first mentioned in the Introduction.[26] Recall that Nietzsche thinks that human beings are marked by type-facts—physiological facts and facts about their unconscious drives—that largely explain their values and behavior. We can see Nietzsche's Doctrine of Types clearly at work in his theory of the will when we move from *Daybreak* and *Beyond Good and Evil* to another significant discussion of the will in the late Nietzschean corpus: "The Four Great Errors" section of *Twilight of the Idols*.

[26] See Introduction, Section 1.

Three of the errors Nietzsche discusses here pertain to causation: he calls them "the error of confusing cause and effect" (1–2), "the error of false causality" (3), and "the error of imaginary causes" (4–6). The fourth "great" error, by contrast, is "the error of free will" (7–8), though there is, in fact, no argument given in these concluding sections of the chapter for why free will is an error (instead Nietzsche offers one debunking explanation of why people might be motivated to believe in free will apart from its reality). The inference the reader is plainly supposed to draw is that the "error of free will" follows from the errors about causation discussed in the preceding sections. If we can reconstruct the argument that emerges from those sections, then, we shall have identified Nietzsche's other main reason for viewing the will as epiphenomenal and thus for rejecting free will.

The first error, that "of confusing cause and effect," can be summarized as follows: given two regularly correlated effects E1 and E2 and their mutual "deep cause," we confuse cause and effect when we construe E1 as the cause of E2, missing altogether the existence of the deep cause. Let us call this error "Cornarism" after the example Nietzsche uses:

> Everybody knows the book of the famous Cornaro in which he recommends his slender diet as a recipe for a long and happy life... I do not doubt that scarcely any book (except the Bible, as is meet) has done as much harm... The reason: the mistaking of the effect for the cause. The worthy Italian thought his diet was the *cause* of his long life, whereas the precondition for a long life, the extraordinary slowness of his metabolism, the consumption of so little, was the cause of his slender diet. He was not free to eat little *or* much; his frugality was not a matter of "free will": he became sick when he ate more. (TI VI:1)

In other words, what explains Cornaro's slender diet *and* his long life is the same underlying fact about his metabolism. Cornaro's mistake was to prescribe his diet for all without regard for how individuals differed metabolically, metabolism being the relevant type-fact in this context.[27]

Even if we grant Nietzsche all the facts as he presents them, this would not yet help show that there is no free will, unless the error involved in Cornarism extended beyond

[27] There is an important ambiguity introduced by the Cornaro example in what Nietzsche means by claiming that the experience of willing does not track a causal relationship. On one reading—call this *the Will as Secondary Cause*—slow metabolism (the relevant type-fact about Cornaro) would explain why Cornaro ate a slender diet, and the fact that he ate a slender diet explains his longevity. If we take this version as an analogue of willing, then the will is, indeed, causal, but it is not the *ultimate* cause of an action: something *causes* the experience of willing and then the will causes the action. On a more ambitious reading—*the Will as Epiphenomenal*—the slow metabolism explains *both* the slender diet and the longevity, but there is no causal link between the latter two. The Cornaro example itself most plausibly suggests the Will as Secondary Cause (surely the slender diet makes a *causal* contribution to the long life), yet the passage with which we began, from *Daybreak*, suggests the Will as Epiphenomenal instead: if the "I will" is really analogous to the person "who steps out of his room at the moment when the sun steps out of its room, and then says: '*I will* that the sun shall rise'" (D 124), then there is no causal link between the experience of willing and the resulting action, just as there is no causal link between the person who wills the sun to rise and the rising of the sun. I will argue, below, that the stronger claim about the epiphenomenal status of conscious willing is the primary claim Nietzsche defends.

cases such as diet and longevity. But that is exactly Nietzsche's contention, since in the very next section he saddles morality and religion quite generally with Cornarism. According to Nietzsche, the basic "formula on which every religion and morality is founded is: "Do this and that, refrain from that and that—then you will be happy! Otherwise..." Cornaro recommended a slender diet for a long life; morality and religion prescribe and proscribe certain conduct for a happy life. But, says Nietzsche,

> [A] well-turned out human being... *must* perform certain actions and shrinks instinctively from other actions; he carries the order, which he represents physiologically, into his relations with other human beings and things.

So morality and religion are examples of Cornarism: the conduct they prescribe and proscribe in order to *cause* a "happy life" are, in fact, *effects* of something else, namely the physiological order represented by a particular agent, one who (as Nietzsche says) "*must* perform certain actions," just as Cornaro *must* eat a slender diet (he is "not free to eat little *or* much"). That one performs certain actions *and* that one has a happy life are themselves both effects of the physiological order. If we grant Nietzsche the Doctrine of Types, then there is indeed reason to think that Cornarism is a feature of morality too, since morality fails to recognize the crucial role of type-facts in determining one's actions, even the moral values one accepts.

That brings us to the next "error," that of "false causality," the mistake of thinking we know what causation is because of our introspective confidence in what we take to be the causal powers of our own mental life. Nietzsche explains:

> We believed ourselves to be causal in the act of willing: we thought that here at least we caught causality in the act. Nor did one doubt that all the antecedents of an act, its causes, were to be sought in consciousness and would be found there once sought—as "motives": else one would not have been free and responsible for it. Finally, who would have denied that a thought is caused? That the "I" causes the thought? (TI VI:3)

We already know, of course, from the phenomenology of thought argument who it is that denies that thoughts are caused by the "ego," by some internal agency, such that one would be "free and responsible" for them. And Nietzsche soon makes clear in this section of *Twilight of the Idols* that his view remains unchanged:

> The "inner world" is full of phantoms...: the will is one of them. The will no longer moves anything, hence does not explain anything either—it merely accompanies events; it can also be absent. The so-called *motive*: another error. Merely a surface phenomenon of consciousness—something alongside the deed that is more likely to cover up the antecedents of the deeds than to represent them...
>
> What follows from this? There are no mental [*geistigen*] causes at all. (TI VI:3)

In the last line, Nietzsche must mean only that there are no *conscious* mental causes, since it is obvious that psychological causes are central to Nietzsche's diagnostic and explanatory practices. Indeed, in other passages, he is explicit that the target of this critique is the picture of conscious motives as adequate to account for action. As he writes in *Daybreak*, "we are accustomed to exclude all [the] unconscious [*unbewusst*] processes from the accounting and to reflect on the preparation for an act only to the extent that it is conscious" (D 129), a view which Nietzsche plainly regards as mistaken, both here and in the passage quoted above. The theme of the "ridiculous overestimation and misunderstanding of consciousness" (GS 11) is a recurring one in Nietzsche. "[B]y far the greatest part of our spirit's activity," says Nietzsche, "remains unconscious and unfelt" (GS 333; cf. GS 354). But what does this skepticism about conscious mental causes really amount to?

6.1 *Skepticism about the causal efficacy of consciousness*

We cannot understand Nietzsche's doubts about the causal efficacy of conscious mental states unless we first understand how he proposes to demarcate the conscious/unconscious distinction, since Nietzsche, like Freud after him, utilizes extensively causal explanation of behavior in terms of unconscious mental states. One instructive reading of Nietzsche on this score is due to Katsafanas (2016); seeing why this interpretation fails will be useful in arriving at a more satisfactory account of Nietzsche's view.

Katsafanas distinguishes between three ways of thinking about the unconscious, all of which share the idea that what is unconscious is "not introspectively accessible" (2016: 21). The question is what explains the obstacle to introspection. On what we may call the "Leibniz view" (this is my label, like all those below, not Katsafanas'), the unconscious states are too weak or fine-grained "to be introspectively sensed" (Katsafanas 2016: 21) (think of hearing the "crash" of a wave on the beach) (cf. Riccardi 2017 for more on this sense of the unconscious). On what we can call the "Herder view," unconscious thoughts are inaccessible because not linguistically articulated (2016: 20–1). Finally, on Freud's view, unconscious mental states are inaccessible because repressed (2016: 21). The Leibniz, Herder, and Freud views all seem to play a role in different passages in Nietzsche, though it is something like the Herder view that is crucial, a point I return to, below.

On Katsafanas' interpretation, however, Nietzsche holds none of these three views. Rather, according to Katsafanas, Nietzsche believes that "conscious mental states are those with conceptual content, whereas unconscious mental states are those with nonconceptual content" (2016: 46). Distinguishing the conscious and unconscious in terms of *conceptual* content would certainly provide a clean demarcation, but it is not Nietzsche's view. To try to show that for Nietzsche all and only conscious mental states are necessarily *conceptually articulated*, Katsafanas relies on two passages: GS 354 which explicitly endorses the Herder view (e.g., Nietzsche writes that "the development of language and the development of consciousness . . . go hand in hand") and BGE 268 for the proposition that "[w]ords are acoustical signs for concepts." Katsafanas needs the latter because nothing in GS 354 claims that consciousness is conceptual (let alone *uniquely* conceptual), only that "conscious thinking [unlike the unconscious version] *takes the form of words, which is to say signs of communication*" (GS 354). Only if one supposed that conceptual content had to be linguistically articulated would one get

Katsafanas' desired conclusion, but GS 354 pointedly does not say that. The fragment of the BGE passage might help[28] *except* that it goes on to say, beyond what Katsafanas quotes,[29] that "concepts... are more or less definite image signs [*Bildzeichen*] for often recurring and associated sensations, for groups of sensations" (BGE 268). That makes clear that concepts, on Nietzsche's view, do not depend on words, words being merely "acoustical" ways of representing concepts, while "image signs" actually *are* concepts. This suggests rather strongly that Nietzsche is working with a familiar notion of concepts as "mental representations," a bit like "ideas" in the manner of Hume.

That Nietzsche distinguishes between linguistic and conceptual articulation is rather important, since the alternative view that treats conceptual articulation as necessarily linguistic would generate a host of problems for Nietzsche's entire corpus. Let me just mention the most obvious one here in the text:[30] much explanation in terms of the unconscious—as Nietzsche's moral psychology makes clear—depends on the unconscious states having conceptual content, which is fine if conscious states only require linguistic articulation, but a problem on Katsafanas' view. Katsafanas' response to this kind of (natural) concern is unsatisfactory. Katsafanas admits that Freud's explanations of behavior in terms of unconscious mental states often turn on those states being conceptually articulated, but Katsafanas retorts that many Freudian explanations are "highly contentious" (2016: 70). That is true but irrelevant since Nietzsche's own explanations are also often contentious while at the same depending on conceptually articulated content: for example, and most famously, the kind of "sour grapes" mechanisms at work in the slave revolt in morality. Katsafanas responds, further, that if Freud-style explanations depend on mental states with conceptual content, then "Nietzsche will label these states *conscious*" (2016: 70). But the latter claim has no basis in Nietzsche's texts; it is simply a dogmatic reaffirmation of Katsafanas' assertion that conscious mental states have conceptual content, but nonconscious ones do not.

[28] Of course, that Xs are Ys does not show that Ys are necessarily Xs! Katsafanas can cite only a *Nachlass* passage making the stronger claim.

[29] Katsafanas returns to more of the passage at (2016: 37), but for a different purpose.

[30] There are other problems. On the Leibniz view of the unconscious, for example, perceptions can have determinate but non-articulable content, which, for Katsafanas, must be nonconceptual content. He introduces some suggestive textual evidence from Schopenhauer and Nietzsche that "unconscious" perceptions "involve a mere discriminatory ability" while "conscious ones... involve a classifying awareness that presents the perceived object as a token of some type" (2016: 34). But the unconscious perception must have a *determinate* non-conceptual content. Katsafanas usefully discusses contemporary views about nonconceptual content (though without noting that none of them think nonconceptual content is unconscious), but then, surprisingly, suggests that the account of nonconceptual content for "perceptual states" can be extended "to other kinds of mental states as well" (2016: 37), such as "believing" and "calculating" (2016: 38). Katsafanas is thinking of accounts of subpersonal information-processing based on a causal theory of information, but even putting aside the interpretive question about whether this could be Nietzsche's view, it is still inadequate to account for the kind of rich forms of unconscious explanation that both Nietzsche and Freud deploy, as I discuss in the text. Ultimately, it is mysterious how such an account of human thinking and reasoning could work. Katsafanas appeals to what Schopenhauer calls "intuitive knowledge," which is really just a kind of know-how (the billiard player knows how to make his shot without knowing the "science of mechanics" as Schopenhauer puts it). Katsafanas claims this "displays a form of thinking and believing," but it is not plausible that Nietzsche's explanations of behavior in terms of unconscious motives can all be assimilated to "know-how" (even assuming that know-how actually involves unconscious beliefs).

Since there is no evidence that the conscious/unconscious distinction is marked by conceptual articulation, *contra* Katsafanas, how might it be marked? GS 354 already gives us the answer, though Katsafanas's confusion of conceptual with linguistic articulation obscured its real point: for it is linguistic articulation that is really crucial to how Nietzsche understands consciousness (that is, Nietzsche follows Herder on this point). I will here follow the powerful philosophical and exegetical account developed by Riccardi (2015, 2017).[31]

In GS 354, Nietzsche argues that "the development of language and the development of consciousness... go hand in hand," though as Riccardi points out (2015 : 225) that is hardly plausible with respect to, say, phenomenal consciousness: one can experience color or pain without any linguistic capacity; and surely non-human animals can have conscious perceptual experiences without having language (the dog sees the squirrel and chases it). The only kind of consciousness that plausibly requires linguistic articulation would be precisely the kind that Nietzsche focuses on in GS 354, namely, that which develops "only under the pressure of the need for communication," namely, that kind of consciousness necessary to coordinate our behavior with others. Here is what Nietzsche says:

Consciousness is really only a net of communication between human beings; it is only as such that it had to develop; a solitary human being who lived like a beast of prey would not have needed it. That our actions, thoughts, feelings, and movements enter our own consciousness—at least a part of them—that is the result of a "must" that for a terribly long time lorded it over man. As the most endangered animal, he *needed* help and protection, he needed his peers, he had to learn to express his distress and to make himself understood; and for all this he needed "consciousness" first of all, he needed to "know" himself what distressed him, he needed to "know" how he felt, he needed to "know" what he thought... [O]nly this conscious thinking *takes the form of words, which is to say signs of communication*, and this fact uncovers the origin of consciousness. (GS 354)

Riccardi suggests we view linguistic articulation as necessary for "self-consciousness," since that is the kind of consciousness that "requires the capacity to self-refer—a capacity we acquire by learning how to use the first-person pronoun" (2015: 225). Commenting on GS 354, Riccardi offers the following explication of Nietzsche's idea:

Suppose we were living in a primitive society, exposed to threats of all sorts and with utterly sparse resources and fragile skills to face them. The advantages, which in such a situation derive from one's belonging to a social group, are based on the capacity for mutual communication. In particular, this requires both that one be able to tell others what the content of one's mental states is and that others be able to understand what one is thereby saying. The first requirement can be met only if one is in a position, as Nietzsche has it, to "know" what distressed him, to "know" how he felt, to "know" what he thought, that is, if one has some kind of epistemic access to the content of one's mind. But this, Nietzsche argues, is precisely what it means to be conscious of them. (2015: 226)

[31] I believe most of what I want to argue, below, is compatible with the interesting account of "conscious" mental states as involving "inner speech" in Fowles (2019) as well.

Of course, this also requires us to "make use . . . of a shared set of mental terms," and that means, importantly, that "the access we have to ourselves is not *direct*, but rather *mediated* by whatever folk-psychological framework we learn from the surrounding environment" (2015: 226), which explains why Nietzsche thinks language falsifies our inner lives: this shared vocabulary "does not reflect the phenomenological richness and complexity of our inner life" since when the individual "conceptualizes her own states" she will necessarily "conform to the shared folk-psychological vocabulary" (2015: 233–4). After all, what my pain upon being bitten by the snake is *really* like is irrelevant compared to the fact that *you want to avoid bad sensations like this!*—which is all members of the community need to "know."

But the problem is even worse than that from the standpoint of the causal efficacy of what we consciously experience as willing, which brings us back to our central topic. As Riccardi puts it: "[G]iven that the conscious experience of our own willings is shaped by our linguistic practice, their real nature remains introspectively inaccessible. In other words, we simply fail to see that our willings are constituted by the complex and continuous interplay between" the unconscious parts of our psyche (or, in my terms, "type-facts") (Riccardi 2015: 238). Because self-conscious states, including those involved in the experience of willing, are linguistically articulated, and because the linguistic articulation of such states evolved under evolutionary pressure for social coordination, such conscious states do not represent the *actual causal genesis* of our actions.

There is an additional reason for thinking the kinds of self-conscious mental states that sometimes precede action are epiphenomenal, and this has to do with the fact that Nietzsche arguably holds something like a Higher-Order-Thought ("HOT") view of consciousness (Riccardi 2017 compiles the textual evidence in detail). On a HOT view, a target mental state is conscious insofar as another mental state (the higher-order-thought, as it were) has as its object the target state: as Nietzsche puts the idea, to "think, feel, will, and remember . . . would be possible without, as it were, seeing itself in a mirror," i.e., without being conscious (GS 354). We now have powerful evidence from research in the cognitive sciences (usefully reviewed, e.g., in Rosenthal [2008]) that the causal efficacy of a wide array of mental states does not depend on their being conscious (e.g., there is such a thing as unconscious mathematical calculation, among many other examples). Insofar as this includes the conscious mental states that precede action, we get a quite radical conclusion even when those states accurately represent the underlying motive for the action: that the state is conscious is not essential to its causal efficacy.

The significance of this for Nietzsche's skepticism about free will again becomes clear in Katsafanas' own reading of Nietzsche. For Katsafanas acknowledges that for Nietzsche our "motives" (e.g., our drives, affects) influence even what passes as reflection or deliberation about what to do (2016: 145–7). Yet Katsafanas, surprisingly, also claims that "conscious deliberation is causally efficacious" in what an agent does (2016: 147). His evidence, however, that conscious deliberation is causally efficacious

(2016: 150–4) consists of passages in which Nietzsche notes that the interpretation attached to a particular drive influences its manifestation (cf. the discussion of D 38 at 2016: 152). Yet Katsafanas himself also argues (correctly) that unconscious drives *interpret* (including interpreting *other drives* [cf. 2016: 148]), so that by itself cannot demonstrate the causal efficacy of conscious reflection or deliberation. The problem is that Katsafanas confuses the question "do interpretations we are conscious of causally affect our motives?" with the question "is our being conscious of the interpretation what makes it causally effective on our motives?" A positive answer to the first is compatible with a negative answer to the second. When Katsafanas turns to a version of the second question (as articulated by Riccardi [2017]), his attempt to defend an affirmative answer simply turns on his earlier, mistaken interpretation of Nietzsche's view of consciousness: Katsafanas thinks that the causal role of any "interpretation" must be conscious since interpretations have conceptual content and a "conscious state... is a conceptualized state" (2016: 155). But since the latter is neither Nietzsche's view, nor very plausible as a thesis in its own right, Katsafanas offers no reason to reject Riccardi's point that, following Rosenthal, a mental state's *being conscious* is irrelevant to its causal efficacy.

6.2 *The error of free will*

With this background, we may now return to the final error about cause and effect in *Twilight*, what Nietzsche calls the error of "imaginary causes" (TI VI:4). This error occurs when we invent, *post hoc*, causes to explain certain phenomena in our experience, phenomena that are, in reality, the cause of our invention. Nietzsche uses the striking example of dreams, though I'll modify the content of his example. Suppose while I am dreaming in the early morning hours, a police car, with siren wailing, passes by my window, but does not wake me. More often than not, into my dream will emerge a narrative which *explains* the sound: perhaps in my dream I suddenly find myself being pursued by police, in their cars, with *their* sirens wailing. As Nietzsche puts it: "The representations which were *produced* by a certain state have been misunderstood as its causes" (TI VI:4). That is, the dream police car, and the dream siren—themselves *actually* the product of the real, external sound of a siren—are now, in the dream, treated as the *causes* of that sound.

Once again, what is significant for Nietzsche is that, as he puts it, "*the whole realm of morality and religion belongs under this concept of imaginary causes*" (TI VI:6). Let us take just one of Nietzsche's examples. Christians, he says, might "explain" "agreeable general feelings" as being produced by "faith, charity, and hope... the Christian virtues" (TI VI:6). One feels well, at peace, content, because one practices these Christian virtues—or so the religious explanation goes. But, objects Nietzsche,

> [A]ll these supposed explanations are resultant states and, as it were, translations of pleasurable or unpleasurable feelings into a false dialect: one is in a state of hope *because* the basic physiological feeling is once again strong and rich... (TI VI:6)

So the Christian says, "That you have practiced the Christian virtues explains why you feel well and are at peace with yourself." In fact, says Nietzsche, there is a physiological explanation for why an agent who feels at peace with himself feels that way, and it is also an explanation for why he practices hope, faith, and charity. The structure of the criticism suggests, in fact, that the "error of imaginary causes" is just an instance of the first error, that "of confusing cause and effect," since, once again, one mistakes an "effect" (e.g., the feeling of hope) for the cause of something else (e.g., being at peace with oneself), when both are effects of an unrecognized "deep cause," i.e., "the basic physiological feeling" as Nietzsche has it in this example.[32] And as with the earlier error, this one seems to depend entirely on accepting Nietzsche's Doctrine of Types, his doctrine that the psycho-physical facts about a person explain their conscious experience and behavior.

How does it follow from the three errors about causation—really, *two* errors, since the last is just an instance of the first—that "free will" is also an error? The error of confusing cause and effect is a *general* error that afflicts morality because morality is based on a mistaken picture of agency: we think that certain moral prescriptions will bring about certain consequences for those who follow them, yet the ability and willingness to act on the prescriptions, and the enjoyment of the consequences are possible only for certain *types* of persons. An exercise of free will plays no role. Notice that this argument makes no claim about the phenomenology of willing.

The error of false causality is an error because we wrongly infer that we know what causation is from our *experience* of the will being causal; but the will is not, in fact, causal, which follows from the Doctrine of Types and the phenomenology of thoughts argument. But, on any account of free will and moral responsibility, the will must be causal (even if not *causa sui*), in order for agents to have free will and be morally responsible for their actions. Therefore, if the error of false causality is a genuine error, then it follows that there is no free will. Only this second error implicates the phenomenology of willing, since it claims that we are in error in thinking we know what causation is based on our *experience* of the will. And the argument says we are in error here because our experience of the will misleads us as to the causal powers of the will: "there are no mental causes at all" Nietzsche tells us.

In sum, Nietzsche offers two arguments for why the phenomenology of willing is not a reliable guide to the causation of action: the argument from the phenomenology of thoughts; and the argument from false causality, which depends on his Doctrine of Types, his related fatalism, and his skepticism about the causal efficacy of self-conscious mental states.

[32] So, too, in the case of dreams: one treats the dream police car as cause of the dream siren, when in fact both are caused by the *real* siren. What makes the case of "imaginary causes" a special instance of the error of confusing cause and effect is that in this case, E2 is itself a reflection of the deep cause. That difference, as far as I can see, does not matter for our purposes in the text.

7. The Real Genesis of Action

If the *experience* of willing does not, according to Nietzsche, illuminate how actions are brought about, what, then, *really* explains our actions? We have already pointed to the answer, since it was implicated at several points in the preceding. *Type-facts*—facts about the unconscious psychology and the physiology of agents—explain our actions. But rather than revisit the account Nietzsche offers, perhaps it may help to turn to some work in recent empirical psychology, much of which is powerfully synthesized by Daniel Wegner in his book *The Illusion of Conscious Will* (Wegner 2002), which sketches a picture of agency congenial to Nietzsche's view. Wegner, like Nietzsche, starts from the *experience* of willing, and, like Nietzsche, wants to undermine our confidence that the experience accurately tracks the causal reality. To do so, Wegner calls our attention to cases where the *phenomenology* and the *causation* admittedly come apart: one set of cases involve "illusions of control," that is, "instances in which people have the feeling they are doing something when they actually are not doing anything" (2002: 9) (think of a video game, in which you feel your manipulation of the joy stick explains the action on the screen, when in fact, the machine is just running a pre-set program). Another set of well-documented cases involve the "automatisms," that is cases where there is action but no "experience of will" (2002: 8–9) (examples would include ouija board manipulation and behaviors under hypnotism). Wegner remarks:

> [T]he automatisms and illusions of control...remind us that action and the feeling of doing are not locked together inevitably. They come apart often enough to make one wonder whether they may be produced by separate systems in the mind. The processes of mind that produce the experience of will may be quite distinct from the processes of mind that produce the action itself. (2002: 11)

If the cases in question do, indeed, show that the phenomenology of willing is not always an accurate guide to causation, they certainly do not show that this is *generally* true. But Wegner wants to establish Nietzsche's claim, namely, that the phenomenology of willing systematically misleads us as to the causation of our actions. And in the place of the "illusion of free will" as Wegner calls it, he proposes a different model according to which "both conscious willing and action are the effects of a common unconscious cause" (Holton 2004: 219), but the chain of causation does not run between the experience of willing and the action; rather, in Nietzschean terms, some type-fact about persons explains both the experience *and* the action (see the helpful diagram in Wegner and Wheatley 1999: 483; Wegner 2002: 68). As Wegner sums up his alternative picture of the causal genesis of action:

> [U]nconscious and inscrutable mechanisms create both conscious thought about action and the action, and also produce the sense of will we experience by perceiving the thought as cause of the action. So, while our thoughts may have deep, important, and unconscious causal connections to our actions, the experience of conscious will arises from a process that interprets these connections, not from the connections themselves. (Wegner 2002: 98)

Although Wegner's reasons for viewing the conscious experience of willing are not the same as Nietzsche's, Wegner adduces a variety of kinds of evidence that lends support to the view that conscious willing is epiphenomenal.

I want to concentrate on just one illustrative bit, already well known to students of the free will literature, but probably less familiar to those interested in Nietzsche. These are the studies by Benjamin Libet and colleagues (discussed in Wegner 2002: 50–5) examining the brain electrical activity (the "readiness potential" or "RP") that precedes an action (such as moving a finger) and the experience of willing. What the researchers found is that "the conscious willing of finger movement occurred at a significant interval *after* the onset of the RP (and also at a significant interval before the awareness of the movement)" (Wegner 2002: 53). According to Wegner, "These findings suggest that the brain starts doing something first... [t]hen the person becomes conscious of wanting to do the action" that the brain has already initiated (Wegner 2002: 53). Wegner (2002: 54) quotes Libet summing up the import of his findings as follows:

> [T]he initiation of the voluntary act appears to be an unconscious cerebral process. Clearly, free will or free choice of whether *to act now* could not be the initiating agent, contrary to one widely held view. This is of course also contrary to each individual's own introspective feeling that he/she consciously initiates such voluntary acts; this provides an important empirical example of the possibility that the subjective experience of a mental causality need not necessarily reflect the actual causative relationship between mental and brain events.

In other words, about a century after Nietzsche, empirical psychologists have adduced evidence supporting his theory that the phenomenology of willing misleads as to the actual causal genesis of action.

Of course, the correct interpretation of the Libet results is controversial.[33] But there are other places where empirical psychology has "caught up," as it were, with Nietzsche—or, more charitably, provided confirmation for Nietzsche's theory of the will (we will see more in Chapter 7). Wegner adduces support, for example, for what Nietzsche calls the "error of false causality" (Wegner 2002: 64 ff.), as well as the "error of confusing cause and effect" (Wegner 2002: 66 ff., 96 ff.). Automaticity phenomena generally in psychology vindicate Nietzsche's suspicions about the confusions concerning cause and effect in the psychological realm. As Oakley and Halligan (2017) sum it up:

> Over the past 30 years, there has been a slow but growing consensus among some students of the cognitive sciences that many of the contents of "consciousness," are formed backstage by fast,

[33] Alfred Mele (2006: 30–48) has mounted a sustained attack on Libet's interpretation of his results. Mele says that the onset of the conscious experience of willing after the RP "leaves it open that... rather than acquiring an intention or making a decision of which he is not conscious [at the time of the RP], the agent instead acquires an *urge* or *desire* of which he is not conscious," and which only becomes effective in virtue of the conscious intention (2006: 33). Although Mele's point gains some support from an interpretation of other experiments by Libet (discussed by Mele at 34–40), he establishes only that there is an *alternative* interpretation, not that his alternative is correct. But the resolution of the Libet–Mele dispute does not matter for Nietzsche's purposes, since Nietzsche is an incompatibilist, and the Libet results, even on Mele's rendering, show that *the causal trajectory* (whether that is an urge or an intention) leading to the action begins prior to the conscious intention to perform the action (whenever that occurs), and that is sufficient to defeat the *causa sui* conception of freedom of the will.

> efficient non-conscious systems. In our account, we take this argument to its logical conclusion and propose that "consciousness" although temporally congruent involves no executive, causal, or controlling relationship with any of the familiar psychological processes conventionally attributed to it... In other words, all psychological processing and psychological products are the products of fast efficient non-conscious systems. The misconception that has maintained the traditional conscious-executive account largely derives from the compelling, consistent temporal relationship between a psychological product, such as a thought, and conscious experience, resulting in the misattribution that the latter is causally responsible for the former.
> (Oakley and Halligan 2017: 1–2)

This, in a nutshell, is Nietzsche's picture of what is going on in action, though he arrived at it more than a century earlier.

As a final example, recall Nietzsche's own account of the genesis of action in the passage on "self-mastery" in *Daybreak* (D 109). Nietzsche begins this discussion by canvassing six different ways of "combating the vehemence of a drive [*eine Triebe*]." What follows is Nietzsche at his most psychologically astute, as he documents six different ways of mastering a powerful urge: for example, by avoiding opportunities for gratification of the drive, thus weakening it over time; or by learning to associate painful thoughts with the drive, so that its satisfaction no longer has a positive valence. One might think this is proto-cognitive-behavioral therapy of which Aaron Beck might approve! Notice, however, that in each case it involves treating oneself as an object for causal manipulation (which indeed is central to the picture underlying cognitive-behavioral therapy): since the drive will press for gratification in the presence of its object, avoid the object; since the drive seeks gratification and thus pleasure, associate unpleasant thoughts with the satisfaction to dampen the force of the drive.

Nietzsche is also concerned in this passage to answer the question as to the "ultimate motive" for "self-mastery," and it is this answer that takes him far from cognitive-behavioral therapy, but to the heart of his view of agency. Nietzsche explains the motive for self-mastery as follows:

> [*T*]*hat* one *wants* to combat the vehemence of a drive at all, however, does not stand within our own power; nor does the choice of any particular method; nor does the success or failure of this method. What is clearly the case is that in this entire procedure our intellect is only the blind instrument of *another drive*, which is a *rival* of the drive whose vehemence is tormenting us... While "we" believe we are complaining about the vehemence of a drive, at bottom it is one drive *which is complaining about the other*; that is to say: for us to become aware that we are suffering from the *vehemence* of a drive presupposes the existence of another equally vehement or even more vehement drive, and that a *struggle* is in prospect in which our intellect is going to have to take sides.

In the end, to be sure, the intellect "take sides" (*Partei nehmen*) but that is not the same as saying the intellect determines which side prevails: to the contrary, the intellect is a mere spectator upon the struggle. In short, the fact that one masters oneself is *not* a product of "free will," but rather an effect of the underlying type-facts characteristic of that person: namely, which of his various drives happens to be strongest. There is, as it were, no "self" in "self-mastery": that is, no conscious "self" who contributes anything to the process. "Self-mastery" is merely an effect of the interplay of certain unconscious drives, drives over which the conscious self exercises no control. A "person" is an arena in which the struggle of drives (type-facts) is played out; how they play out determines what he believes, what he values, what he becomes. But, *qua* conscious self or "agent," the person takes no active part in the process. As Nietzsche puts the same point, later, in *Beyond Good and Evil*: "The will to overcome an affect is, in the end, itself only the will of another, or several other, affects" (117; cf. also GM III:17). The will, in other words, or the experience of willing (in self-mastery), is itself the product of various unconscious drives or affects. Which is, in slightly different terms, exactly the theory of the will that some empirical psychologists have arrived at one hundred years after Nietzsche.

8. Against Compatibilism

If Nietzsche and the recent psychologists are correct, then the conscious mental states that precede our actions are themselves causally determined by non-conscious forces and are themselves causally inert with respect to the actions that follow. Even moralizing readers of Nietzsche will agree that these psychological facts would undermine free will and moral responsibility on an Incompatibilist view, but I want to conclude by emphasizing that they defeat Compatibilist accounts of the Control variety as well.

Causal Compatibilists starting with Hume share the thought that *the right kind* of causal determination of our actions is compatible with free will and moral responsibility. The *right kind of causal determination* is a kind that preserves the intuition at the core of Control accounts, i.e., that the agent controls or owns or identifies with the resulting action. Causal Compatibilist Control accounts (such as Hume's and Frankfurt's) confront a regress problem: identify a mental state preceding the action with which we "identify" (or from which we are not "alienated," per Watson), and one can reasonably ask *what makes it the case that the identifying mental state is ours*? After all, on Nietzsche's view, it would hardly be surprising if agents sometimes felt as if their first-order desires *belonged* to them, but what (causally) explains that *feeling of belonging*? How do I know that the *belonging desire* is one with which I identify (one that satisfies the Control account)?

Frankfurt offered an answer to the question of what is required for "identification" as follows:

> When a person identifies himself *decisively* with one of his first-order desires this commitment "resounds" through the potentially endless array of higher orders... The decisiveness of the commitment he has made means that he has decided that no further question about his second-order volition, at any higher order, remains to be asked. (Frankfurt 1971: 332, 333)

But having "no further question about his second-order volition" is just another psychological fact about the agent, one that might simply be a by-product of non-conscious forces over which the agent has no control and with which he cannot "identify" or "not identify" since he is wholly unaware of them.

Now Frankfurt is, happily, a Humean in his philosophical psychology: only desires are motivationally effective, and thus his attempted response to the "identification" problem is in terms of desires. But non-Humeans like Gary Watson find their point of entry to the dialectic at precisely this point. For Watson thinks that Frankfurt's hierarchy of desires leads to the regress problem just noted, so that what we need for a satisfactory account of Control over our actions is a *rational* judgment that particular actions have value. As Watson candidly puts it: "The doctrine I shall defend is Platonic in the sense that it involves a distinction between valuing and desiring which depends upon there being independent sources of motivation" (Watson 1975: 341). "Valuing" on this view involves "those principles and ends which [the agent]—in a cool and non-self-deceptive moment—articulates as definitive of the good, fulfilling, and defensible life" (1975: 346). Cogent objections have been raised to Watson's view (e.g., Velleman 1992: 472), but I do not want to get sidetracked into them, since Watson's kind of view is obviously a non-starter in a Nietzschean moral psychology: it has to introduce a source of motivation that is not fundamentally affective; and it requires the absence of moral conflicts and a kind of unity of virtue (lest one be alienated from the motives on which one acts). Crucially, while Watson acknowledges that "some desires, when they arise, may 'colour' or influence what appear to be the agent's evaluations," this can happen "only temporarily" (345), which is exactly what Nietzsche's moral psychology, including D 109, denies. So if a rationalist moral psychology is a non-starter for Nietzsche (as it is for all empirical moral psychology), then we are left with the regress problem familiar from Causal Compatibilist accounts.[34]

But what about Reasons-Responsive Compatibilism, the form that has arisen (at least in professional Anglophone philosophy) in the wake of the failure of Causal Compatibilism? If deliberation, or conscious reasoning about what one ought to do, is epiphenomenal (as Nietzsche argues), then it is hard to see how humans can be deemed "reasons responsive" such that they are morally praiseworthy and blameworthy for what they do: why should a non-causal correlation between certain antecedently consciously experienced reasons and a subsequent action ground moral responsibility? Barometers drop before storms, after all, but they do not cause them and are not blameworthy for them. If Nietzsche is right, the same type-facts that cause an experience of deliberation may also cause an action, but the "wheel of causality" does not roll between the deliberation and the doing.[35]

Nietzsche thinks that the *feeling* of free will is, at bottom, an epiphenomenon of a process in which conscious thoughts that are consistent with and temporally proximate to succeeding actions are misinterpreted as causal, when, in fact, both the

[34] While the later Watson (1996) casts the issue as one about "attributability" (see *supra* n. 5) the Nietzschean doubts about Watson's picture undermine even that possibility.

[35] Some Reasons-Responsive Compatibilists have gone so far as to suggest that one can be morally responsible as long as one's unconscious self is "responsive to reasons," but given that Nietzsche's conception of drives is that they are non-rational, it is hard to see how such a rearguard dialectical move will get off the ground.

thoughts and the actions themselves are causally determined by non-conscious, perhaps neurophysical aspects of the person. The upshot is that our actions are neither *causa sui, nor caused by any conscious state with which we might identify, nor are they reason-responsive*. To the extent, then, that Nietzsche continues to use the language of "freedom" and "free will"—and he does so in a variety of passages that we will consider in Chapter 6—he must use those concepts in revisionary senses unrecognizable to either of the two major traditions of thinking about free will in the modern era: on the one hand, the broadly Kantian identification of freedom with autonomous action, meaning action arising from rational self-legislation (or guidance), which grounds moral responsibility; and, on the other, the broadly Humean equation of freedom with acting on the basis of conscious desires or reasons. Neither traditional concept of freedom or free will is available to or embraced by Nietzsche the fatalist.

6

A Positive View of Freedom?

Many professional scholars—though fewer philosophically innocent readers—have resisted the idea that Nietzsche is a Hard Incompatibilist, denying freedom of the will in the senses associated with either the broadly Kantian or Humean traditions, as well as moral responsibility. I want to consider some of the objections of these scholars, though I will continue to maintain that Nietzsche denies that people ever act freely or are morally responsible for anything they do. I will also argue that Nietzsche engages in what Charles Stevenson (1938) would have called a "persuasive definition" of the language of "freedom" and "free will," radically revising the content of those concepts, but in a way that aims to capitalize on their positive emotive valence and authority for his readers.[1] I will concede at the end of this chapter, however, that there is a family resemblance between Nietzsche's idea of "freedom" and Spinoza's, though one that does not vindicate either the AP or Control senses of free will discussed in the prior chapter (though it has a superficial resonance with the latter).

I begin by examining in some detail the passages in Nietzsche that actually discuss freedom and free will and that are thought by some scholars to suggest he has a different view than the one I articulated and defended in Chapter 5. Scrutinizing the actual textual evidence will bring out the extent of Nietzsche's persuasive redefinition of the idea of freedom.

1. "The Sovereign Individual"

A favorite passage of moralizing readers of Nietzsche has become his discussion of the "sovereign individual" in the *Genealogy* and so it is with this lengthy, but complicated, passage that we should begin. Recall that the Second Essay of the *Genealogy* starts with a naturalistic question: how to "breed an animal" [*ein Thier heranzuzüchten*] which is able to make and honor a promise? The assumptions underlying this question are twofold. First, and most obviously, human beings are certain kinds of animals, trainable, like other animals, to be able to perform certain tasks. Second, as with other animals, one explains what they do (in this case, promise-making) not by appeal to their

[1] "A 'persuasive' definition is one which gives a new conceptual meaning to a familiar word without substantially changing its emotive meaning, and which is used with the conscious or unconscious purpose of changing, by this means, the direction of people's interests" (Stevenson 1938: 331).

exercise of some capacity for autonomous choice and decision, but in terms of the causal mechanisms (e.g., breeding) acting upon them which yield certain steady behavioral dispositions (in this case, again, being able to make and keep promises). Nietzsche then identifies two preconditions for promise-making: first, *regularity* of behavior and, second, reliable *memory*. Regularity is necessary because a promise-maker must be "answerable for his own *future*" (GM II:1), and one cannot be answerable for a future that is utterly unpredictable. Memory is essential for the obvious reason that only someone who can *remember* his promises can possibly honor them at a later date.

Two factors are singled out by Nietzsche as formative for the human animal in its development of regular behavior and a memory: the "morality of custom" and the role of pain in mnemonics. With "the help of the morality of custom and the social strait-jacket, man was *made* truly predictable [*berechenbar*, or calculable]" (GM II:2). Nietzsche here alludes to his own earlier discussion in *Daybreak* (cf. D 9), which, drawing on the etymological connection between *Sittlichkeit* (morality) and *Sitte* (custom), advanced "the plausible hypothesis that customs constituted the first morality, that traditional ways of acting played the same role during early human life that 'rarefied and lofty' moral codes, rules, and principles play today: that is, they provided criteria for moral right and wrong" (Clark and Leiter 1997: xxix–xxx). In this earlier discussion, Nietzsche's goal was a kind of naturalization of the (implausible) Kantian account of moral motivation as a matter of reverence for the moral law: Nietzsche proposes instead that it is "obedience to tradition" (and fear of the consequences of deviation from tradition) that really constitutes moral motivation, rather than some fictional "reverence" for a moral law (see Clark and Leiter 1997: xxx).

By the time he writes the *Genealogy*, Nietzsche is now more interested in the role of custom ("the social straitjacket") in making humans "truly predictable," i.e., regular in their behavior. This development eventually yields the individual with a conscience, whom Nietzsche refers to variously as a "sovereign" or "autonomous" individual (GM II:2). Here is the crucial passage:

> [W]ith the help of the morality of custom and the social straitjacket, man was *made* truly predictable. Let us place ourselves, on the other hand, at the end of this immense process where the tree actually bears fruit, where society and its morality of custom finally reveal what they were simply *the means to*: we then find the *sovereign individual* as the ripest fruit on its tree, like only to itself, having freed itself from the morality of custom, an autonomous super-ethical individual (because "autonomous" and "ethical" are mutually exclusive), in short, we find a man with his own, independent, durable will, who has *the right to make a promise*—and has a proud consciousness quivering in every muscle of *what* he has finally achieved and incorporated, an actual awareness of power and freedom, a feeling that man in general has reached completion. This man who is now free and who really does have the right to make a promise, this master of the *free* will, this sovereign—how could he remain ignorant of his superiority over everybody who does not have the right to make a promise or answer for himself, how much trust, fear and respect he arouses—he "*merits*" all three—and how could he, with his self-mastery, not realize

that he has necessarily been given mastery over circumstances, over nature and over all creatures with a less durable and reliable will? The "free" man, the possessor of a durable, unbreakable will, thus has his own *standard of value* in the possession of such a will: viewing others from his own standpoint, he respects or despises; and just as he will necessarily respect his peers, the strong and the reliable (those *with the right* to give their word),—that is everyone who makes promises like a sovereign, ponderously, seldom, slowly, and is sparing with his trust, who *confers an honour* when he places his trust, who gives his word as something which can be relied on, because he is strong enough to remain upright in the face of mishap or even "in the face of fate"—: so he will necessarily be ready to kick the febrile whippets who make a promise when they have no right to do so, and will save the rod for the liar who breaks his word in the very moment it passes his lips. The proud realization of the extraordinary privilege of *responsibility*; the awareness of this rare freedom and power over himself and his destiny, has penetrated him to the depths and become an instinct, his dominant instinct:—what will he call his dominant instinct, assuming that he needs a word for it? No doubt about the answer: this sovereign man calls it his *conscience*.

The "sovereign individual" is said to be the "fruit" [*Früchte*] of the long tradition of the morality of custom, but the tree bears this fruit at the point when the morality of custom is left behind: this individual is "autonomous" or "supra-ethical" (*übersittliche*) in the quite precise sense of being no longer bound by the morality of custom (*sitte*). He is the perfected animal, the one so perfected by the breeding of the morality of custom that he no longer needs the discipline of *sitte* to perform his "trick," as it were. And what exactly is the "trick" of this well-trained animal? Surely it bears emphasizing that he is described as having one and only one skill: he can make and keep a promise! And why can he do that? Because he can remember that he made it, and his behavior is sufficiently regular and predictable, that others will actually act based on his promises. This might explain why Nietzsche gives this self-important animal, the so-called sovereign individual, a suitably ridiculous and pompous name: he refers to him, in the original, as the "*souveraine* Individuum," a mix of French and (perhaps) Latin, meaning, literally, a sovereign atom—a phrase Nietzsche never uses again, anywhere, in the corpus.[2]

There is, however, more to GM II:2 than what I have emphasized so far, and this is brought out in the observation by Thomas Miles (2007) that "self-mastery" is central to the image of the sovereign individual, and that "[t]his self-mastery consists of a self-affirming conscience that guides the sovereign individual to take on great tasks and fulfill his commitments to them" (2007: 12).[3] As we have already noted, however, the

[2] Nietzsche never uses any possible cognate expressions anywhere in the corpus either—phrases like *souverän(e) Individuum* or *souveraine/souverän Mensch*. Nor does Nietzsche ever employ again in the corpus any of the distinctive phrases he uses to characterize or refer to this *souveraine Individuum*: e.g., *autonome übersittliche Individuum* or *Herr des freien Willens* or *Privilegium der Verantwortlichkeit* or *der Inhaber eines langen unzerberchlichen Willens*; these phrases appear only in GM II:2, and never again in the corpus. (I am indebted here to Nicholas Koziolek for research assistance.)

[3] Rutherford (2011: 525–9) also sees the "sovereign individual" passage as relevant to understanding "freedom" in Nietzsche's sense. We will return to his reading at the end of this chapter.

only "great [sic] task" concretely on offer by Nietzsche is that the sovereign individual can make a promise and keep it. This is not nothing, to be sure, but it seems *prima facie* hard to square with the overblown rhetoric of GM II:2, rhetoric to which Miles himself calls attention (2007: 13); for example:

> The proud realization of the extraordinary privilege of *responsibility*; the awareness of this rare freedom and power over himself and his fate [*Geschick*], has penetrated him to the depths and become an instinct, his dominant instinct:—what will he call his dominant instinct, assuming that he needs a word for it? No doubt about the answer: this sovereign man calls it his *conscience*. (GM II:2)

But Nietzsche, as we saw in detail in Chapter 5, denies—and not just once—that anyone has "freedom and power over himself and his fate" or that anyone has, as GM II:2 also claims, "mastery over circumstances [*Ümstande*]". The conclusion of "The Four Great Errors" from *Twilight of the Idols* is as clear as any passage in Nietzsche on the subject:

> [N]o one *gives* people their qualities, not God or society, parents or ancestors, not even *people themselves* (—this final bit of nonsense was circulated by Kant—and maybe even by Plato—under the rubric of "intelligible freedom"). *Nobody* is responsible for people existing in the first place, or for the state or circumstances or environment they are in. (TI VI:8)

That means, of course, that the sovereign individual, whose "privilege of *responsibility*" extends to "himself and his fate," indeed, to his "circumstances," is delusional, at least if he *really* believes any of this.

That conclusion is exactly what one should expect given Nietzsche's skepticism about free will that we encountered in Chapter 5. Recall, in particular, our discussion of the treatment of "self-mastery" of a troubling drive in D 109,[4] according to which "our intellect is only the blind instrument of *another drive*, which is a *rival* of the drive whose vehemence is tormenting us... [A]t bottom it is one drive *which is complaining about the other*" (D 109). The intellect, in short, is the "blind instrument" [*blinde Werkzeug*] of another drive, and thus the fact of self-mastery is just an effect of the underlying type-facts about that person, namely, which of his various drives happens to be strongest. Some "higher types" may, as we noted in Chapter 5, exemplify a unified hierarchy of drives that Nietzsche occasionally associates with the idea of "freedom" (an issue we return to, below), but we do not honor Nietzsche's admonition to read him free of moral prejudices if we then try to reconstruct this as a moral ideal (Kantian or Humean) of autonomy and responsibility.

In sum, we can agree with the emphasis of Miles on the "self-mastery" characteristic of the "sovereign individual," and still acknowledge that, given Nietzsche's conception of self-mastery, it is wholly compatible with his denial of free will and moral responsibility in so many other passages.[5]

[4] Chapter 5, Section 7.

[5] Miles also makes the good point (2007: 15) that the description of the "sovereign individual" in GM II:2 resembles the characteristics I argue Nietzsche associates with the higher type (Leiter 2002: 116–22).

2. Coherence and Freedom: A Consideration of Other Passages

Peter Poellner has offered another way of understanding Nietzsche's "positive" view of freedom as a kind of "substantive ideal" (2009: 152).[6] As Poellner describes it:

> [Freedom as a substantive ideal] is what seems to be at stake in many of those remarks where Nietzsche expresses admiration for people who, as he sees them, have succeeded in integrating an unusually great multiplicity of "drives" and evaluative commitments into a long-lasting, coherent whole. (2009: 152)

I think this is the best reading of what Ken Gemes in several papers has also argued (see especially Gemes 2009).[7] When Gemes speaks of Nietzsche as wanting to understand "genuine agency" (2009: 40) and wanting to change "his preferred readers from being mere conduit points of a vast array of conflicting inherited drives into genuinely unified beings" (2009: 45), I take him to understand Nietzsche as presenting us with an ideal of agency, one involving a kind of unity of the drives. Perhaps the "sovereign individual"

But there is no reason in Nietzsche to think being a "higher type" is anything other than a fortuitous natural fact—as Nietzsche took it to be in *his very own* case! (See Leiter 2002: 157–9). See the discussion, below, at the conclusion of this chapter about Spinoza and Nietzsche on freedom in connection with the reading by Rutherford (2011).

[6] Poellner also thinks there is an account of "freedom" in Nietzsche that is concerned with "a *transcendental* question: the constitutive conditions of full-fledged, autonomous rather than heteronomous, selfhood" (2009: 152). As Poellner explains it: "Nietzsche... seems to be interested, like Kant, not just in minimal agency, but in autonomous or free agency in a sense which it would be inappropriate to ascribe to a compulsive subject, or to an addict or acratic person—a slave of momentary affect and desire [GM II:3]—or to a very young child... What emerges from [GM II:2 on "the sovereign individual," and GS 335, 347] is that autonomy or freedom in the relevant sense is a matter of 'having a protracted will' and 'mastery over oneself' under the aegis of a 'conscience'" (GM II:2). This now makes the account sound like a "substantive ideal," the reading I focus on in the text, which I think is the best reading of Poellner's point, especially since I do not see any textual evidence that Nietzsche is even interested in the problem of akrasia.

[7] Gemes contrasts what he calls "deserts free will" with "agency free will." According to the latter, "the free will debate is intrinsically tied to the question of agency: what constitutes an action as opposed to a mere doing?" (2009: 33). To be sure, no one thinks that there can be free will or free agency if there is not a difference between *actions* and "mere doings," for example, mere bodily movements. Gemes goes on to say that "agency free will" is concerned with the question of "what makes for autonomy" (2009: 33), and then says later that "agency free will" is concerned with "the profounder question, 'What is it to act in the first place, what is it to be a self capable of acting?'" (2009: 39). Unfortunately, I do not see the textual evidence that these are Nietzsche's concerns. Gemes also says—without, once again, any evidence or citation—that those interested in "deserts free will" "tend to write as if we already have a notion of self and action more or less firmly in place and are only raising the question of whether such selves are ever to be held morally responsible for their actions" (2009: 39). It is true that writers on free will, both historically and at present, typically assume that they have a handle on the distinction between actions and "mere doings" (to use Gemes' terminology), but the "notion of self" is often precisely what is at issue for those Gemes would put in the "deserts free will" camp: is the self, for example, to be identified with our second-order desires, or is the self, or "will," merely an effect of other causes? Gemes appears to be after the distinction in Watson (1996) between the "attributability" of actions to an agent as opposed to holding the agent "accountable" (i.e., morally responsible) for those actions. As we argued in Chapter 5, Section 1, n. 5, it is not clear what any of this has to do with "responsibility" (Watson's concern), and we can add now that it is equally mysterious what this has to do with "freedom" (Gemes's concern). More strikingly, the Gemes/Poellner criterion for "free agency" is far more demanding than what either Frankfurt or Watson propose.

is meant to represent such an ideal as well, albeit opaquely. Yet the ideal itself does seem to be a recognizably Nietzschean one.

The question naturally arises, however, why this ideal should be associated with "freedom" or "free will": why not just say that Nietzsche's ideal agent has a certain pattern of coherent drives or dispositions (the pattern to be specified, of course) and leave it at that? "Freedom" is, after all, a promiscuous concept. In ordinary language, we say that someone just released from prison is a "free man," and we also say that someone who shuns conventional expectations—about careers or styles of dress or other social norms—is a "free spirit." But being unconstrained by physical limits (as in prison walls) or social conventions (as in expectations about career or appearance) does not raise philosophically interesting points about freedom of human agency, for Nietzsche or anyone else. We need much more evidence than an occasional use of the term "freedom" to conclude that Nietzsche has a philosophically important *positive* conception of freedom or free will.

Readers of Nietzsche know that he often employs familiar concepts in revisionary or highly deflationary senses: think of "soul," "power," and "willing." The same turns out to be the case, I believe, with Nietzsche's view of "freedom" and "free will." I agree with scholars like Gemes and Poellner that Nietzsche sometimes (though not very often) associates the language of "freedom" with certain kinds of persons—agents whose psychic economy has a certain kind of coherence—but in so doing he has engaged in what Charles Stevenson would have called a "persuasive definition" of "freedom": he wants to radically revise the content of "freedom" while exploiting the positive valence that the word has for his readers. This is because Nietzsche recognizes that to *really* transform the consciousness of his preferred readers he must reach them at a non-rational, even sub-conscious level, and one way to do so is to associate Nietzschean ideals with values in which his readers are already emotionally invested. And as Nietzsche notes in *The Gay Science*, values are "among the most powerful levers in the involved mechanisms of our actions" (GS 335). Thus by associating an ideal of the person with the evaluatively (i.e., emotionally) laden word "freedom," Nietzsche increases the likelihood that he can activate the causal levers of at least some readers that will lead them towards this new ideal. Yet from a purely descriptive point of view, he might just as well have called his new ideal agents "Causally Coherent," since his picture really has nothing to do with "freedom" at all: Nietzsche's ideal "unified" agent is just a kind of natural artifact, one whose drives interact constructively rather than destructively.[8] But with regard to his rhetorical aims, Nietzsche is shrewd to sometimes describe such natural artifacts as exemplars of "freedom."

Both Gemes and Poellner, like other writers in this genre, rely on a very small number of passages to support what they claim is Nietzsche's positive account of freedom. I want to examine these passages with some care—I have already dealt with GM II:2 in

[8] As we will see at the conclusion of the chapter, this may have something to do with Spinoza's idea of freedom, though his is one quite foreign to the rest of the modern tradition in philosophy.

this regard—since I think it will turn out that they do not generally support the readings Gemes, Poellner, and others want to give them. To be clear, I am not denying that Nietzsche highly values persons who, by natural fortuity, exhibit the kind of agency picked out, I take it, by Gemes' notion of "genuine agency" and Poellner's notion of "full personhood." But none of this has anything to do with "freedom" in the two most influential modern traditions of thought about freedom and responsibility, namely, the Humean and the Kantian (we return to the "Spinozistic" tradition, which may not be a tradition, below[9]).

What better place to start than with *Twilight of the Idols*, "Skirmishes of an Untimely Man," Section 38 which Nietzsche explicitly titles "My conception of freedom"? Here is how he introduces and explicates that concept:

> Liberal institutions cease to be liberal as soon as they are attained: later on, there are no worse and no more thorough injurers of freedom than liberal institutions. Their effects are known well enough: they undermine the will to power; they level mountain and valley, and call that morality; they make men small, cowardly, and hedonistic—every time it is the herd animal that triumphs with them: Liberalism: in other words, herd-animalization.

This introduction to "my conception of freedom" seems clear: one undermines *freedom* on Nietzsche's view by making "men small, cowardly, and hedonistic." Philosophical and religious traditions have had many views of freedom, to be sure, but I am not aware of any in which being big, brave, and indifferent to suffering loomed large, yet that appears to be precisely the concept of freedom Nietzsche invokes here. This passage continues:

> These same [liberal] institutions produce different effects while they are still being fought for; then they really promote freedom in a powerful way. On closer inspection, it is war that produces these effects, the war *for* liberal institutions . . . [W]ar educates for freedom. For what is freedom? That one has the will to assume responsibility for oneself [*den Willen zur Selbstverantwortlichkeit hat*]. That one maintains the distance which separates us. That one becomes more indifferent to difficulties, hardships, privation, even to life itself. That one is prepared to sacrifice human beings for one's cause, not excluding oneself. Freedom means that the manly instincts which delight in war and victory dominate over other instincts, for example, over those of "happiness." The human being who has *become free* [*der freigewordne Mensch*]—and much more the *spirit* who has become free—spits on the contemptible type of well-being dreamed of by shopkeepers, Christians, cows, females, Englishmen, and other democrats. The free man is a *warrior* [*Der freie Mensch ist Krieger*].

Assuming "responsibility" for oneself is, of course, not the same thing as actually being responsible for one's actions. The former is an attitude, a disposition, that of the warrior it turns out, since this attitude is equated by Nietzsche with, e.g., "indifference to difficulties, hardships, privation, even to life itself" and so on. There is no sense, ordinary

[9] There are echoes of it in Hegel (cf. Beiser 2005: 74 ff.), though it is unclear whether Nietzsche knew anything about those since the evidence suggests Nietzsche never read Hegel though he did read some of his own contemporaries "influenced" by Hegel (notably Hartmann).

or philosophical, in which "freedom" means pleasure in warfare—though warriors are, to be sure, usually thought to be big, brave, and indifferent to suffering! This is, quite clearly, "persuasive definition" in the sense Stevenson identified many decades ago.[10]

Of course, there are limits on "persuasive definitions" if they are still to persuade:[11] One could not persuasively define "dishwasher," for example, as "pleasure in warfare"! But "freedom," as we have already remarked, is a promiscuous concept, and Nietzsche exploits this fact in passages like the one from *Twilight* we are considering. In particular, he employs, to good effect here and elsewhere, the device of persuasively redefining a concept by first equating it with a common-sensically cognate concept (e.g., freedom and liberalism) but then arguing that the cognate phenomenon really involves something very different ("war"), until we end up with a radical revision of the original.

In Section 41 of the same chapter from *Twilight*, Nietzsche goes on to describe the "Freedom which I do *not* mean," namely,

> ...abandonment to one's instincts... [Today] the claim for independence, for free development, for *laisser aller* is pressed most hotly by the very people for whom no reins would be too strict... [T]hat is a symptom of decadence: our modern conception of "freedom" is one more proof of the degeneration of the instincts.

In other words, Nietzsche renounces one of the colloquial connotations of the idea of "freedom," namely, freedom from constraints. The point here is obviously of a piece with the concern in *Beyond Good and Evil*, Section 188, where Nietzsche says:

> [E]verything there is, or was, of freedom, subtlety, boldness, dance, or masterly assurance on earth, whether in thinking itself, or in ruling, or in speaking and persuading, in artistic just as in ethical practices has only developed by virtue of the "tyranny of such arbitrary laws"... Every artist knows how far removed this feeling of letting go [*laisser aller*] is from his "most natural" state, the free ordering, placing, disposing and shaping in the moment of "inspiration"—he knows how strict and subtly he obeys thousands of laws at this very moments, laws that defy conceptual formulation precisely because of their hardness and determinateness [*Bestimmtheit*].

So freedom in Nietzsche's sense does not mean "freedom from constraint," but its opposite: being subject to "hard" and "determinate" laws! (Given that Nietzsche is a Hard Incompatibilist, this should hardly be surprising.) Section 213 of *Beyond Good and Evil* continues this line of thought:

> Artists... are the ones who know only too well that their feeling of freedom, finesse and authority, of creation, formation, and control only reaches its apex when they have stopped doing anything "voluntarily" [*willkürlich*] and instead do everything necessarily [*nothwendig*]—in short, they know that inside themselves necessity and "freedom of the will" have become one.

Notice that *freedom of the will* is placed in quotes by Nietzsche himself in this passage: it is not, after all, *real* freedom of the will, since it involves nothing voluntary, only action which is necessary, actions bound, as he says, by hard laws.

[10] It also provides no support to the Gemes/Poellner view of freedom in Nietzsche discussed earlier.
[11] Thanks to Gabriel Zamosc for raising this issue.

These passages resonate, in turn, with the famous Section 335 of *The Gay Science*, which appears to suggest that people can "create" themselves. Here is the bit of the passage emphasized by Poellner (and also Miles): "We... want to *become who we are*—human beings who are new, unique, incomparable, who give themselves laws, who creates themselves!" Yet this passage then continues as follows—a continuation about which most scholars are, alas, silent:[12]

To that end [of creating ourselves] we must become the best learners and discoverers of everything that is lawful and necessary in the world: we must become *physicists* in order to be *creators* in this sense [*wir müssen Physiker sein, um, in jenem Sinne, Schöpfer sein zu können*]—while hitherto all valuations and ideals have been based on *ignorance* of physics... Therefore: long live physics! (GS 335)

Creation "in this sense" is, then, a very special sense indeed: for it presupposes the discovery of what is "lawful and necessary" as revealed by empirical science (if not *literally* physics). (This recalls the earlier theme about the equivalence of freedom and necessity.) In context, what Nietzsche has in mind becomes clearer (cf. Leiter 2002: 96–7): for in the preceding part of GS 335, he explains that while the particular cause of any action is "indemonstrable" [*unnachweisbar*], we do know that values are "among the most powerful levers in the involved mechanism of our actions." Thus the task for the sciences is to discover the laws of cause-and-effect governing particular values and particular actions, a more refined version of the task that Nietzsche later calls for in the "Note" at the end of GM I: namely, for the human sciences to examine the *effects* of different kinds of valuations on "the good of the majority" and "the good of the minority," as he puts it there.

So what textual evidence of Nietzsche's putative "positive" view of freedom remains? Section 347 of *The Gay* Science—which equates "freedom of the will" with *freedom from* the need for certainty, the need that drives people, Nietzsche says, to "faith" and "fanaticism"—obviously tells us nothing about agency or free will, and is a wholly revisionary usage of the concept. There is, in addition, the openly revisionary account of freedom in the first chapter of *Beyond Good and Evil* (discussed in detail in Chapter 5), according to which,

"Freedom of the will"—that is the word for the multi-faceted state of pleasure of one who commands and, at the same time, identifies himself with the accomplished act of willing. As such, he enjoys the triumph over resistances, but thinks to himself that it was his will alone that truly overcame the resistance. (BGE 19)

As I argued in the last chapter, the analysis of the will and freedom in the first section of BGE is fully of a piece with his general denial of free will and moral responsibility (as even Gemes [2009: 48] has acknowledged).[13]

[12] Rutherford (2011) is an illuminating exception, connecting the passage with Spinozistic themes and offering an alternative reading to the one I sketch in the text. I return to Rutherford's reading, below.

[13] Clark and Dudrick (2009) challenge my reading of BGE 19, and so I should say something briefly about why I find their alternative unpersuasive. The crux of their argument is to deem Nietzsche's "phenomenology [of willing] simply implausible" (251), which then opens the door for them to re-read the passage as limited to "actions performed in opposition to temptation," and thus as implicating "one's

That leaves us, then, with just two passages in the published corpus that interpreters of his "positive" theory of freedom point towards. In one passage, GM III:10, in which Nietzsche considers how the ascetic ideal validates the conditions under which philosophers can flourish, he concludes by noting that even in the modern world, the obstacles to being a philosopher remain great: "Is there [even now] enough pride, daring, courage, self-confidence, will of spirt, will to take responsibility, *freedom of will* [emphasis in original], for 'the philosopher' on earth to be really—*possible*?" This passing reference to "freedom of will" is revealing, since it makes clear that Nietzsche views it as interchangeable with dispositions of character like pride [*Stolz*],courage [*Tapferkeit*], and self-confidence [*Selbstgewissheit*], all traits one can possess without being responsible for having them, without, in short, having developed them *freely*. Here "freedom of will" is simply equated with psychological states essential to the higher type—pride, daring, courage etc.—without any suggestion that the higher type's agency must satisfy other conditions.

That brings us to perhaps the most interesting Nietzschean passage mentioning freedom, from Chapter VIII of *Twilight of the Idols*, a passage on Goethe. It bears quoting at some length:

> *Goethe*—not a German event but a European one: a magnificent attempt to overcome the eighteenth century by returning to nature, by coming towards the *naturalness* of the Renaissance, a type of self-overcoming on the part of that century... He made use of history, science, antiquity, and Spinoza too, but above all he made use of practical activity... [H]e did not remove himself from life, he put himself squarely in the middle of it; he did not despair, and he took as much as he could on himself, to himself, in himself. What he wanted was *totality*; he fought against the separation of reason, sensibility, feeling, will (—preached in the most forbiddingly scholastic way by *Kant*, Goethe's antipode), he disciplined himself to wholeness, he *created* himself... In the middle of an age inclined to unreality, Goethe was a convinced realist: he said yes to everything related to him,—his greatest experience was of that *ens realissimum* [the most real thing] that went by the name of Napoleon. Goethe conceived of a strong, highly educated, self-respecting human being, skilled in all things physical and able to keep himself in check, who could dare to allow himself the entire expanse and wealth of naturalness, who is strong enough for this freedom... A spirit like this who has *become free* stands in the middle of the world with a cheerful and trusting fatalism in the *belief* that... everything is redeemed and affirmed in the whole... *he does not negate any more*... But a belief like this is the highest of all possible beliefs: I have christened it with the name *Dionysus*. (TI VIII:49)

There are two striking *motifs* in this passage: first, the emphasis on an ideal of *naturalness* and *realism*, which is explicitly associated with Napoleon; and second, the equation of

commitments or values" (251). This reading, alas, finds no support in the text at all, and is motivated entirely by the claim that as a phenomenology of willing *simpliciter*, Nietzsche's account is implausible, *and so must be read otherwise*. I do not find the account implausible (phenomenology does require careful introspection!), but even if one concurred with Clark and Dudrick about this, it would not follow that the passage has a meaning not to be found in the text: perhaps it is just bad phenomenology. But the evidence that Nietzsche holds the view of the will I attribute to him (see Chapter 5) is overwhelming, and BGE 19 as I read it is certainly of a piece with that (Clark and Dudrick confine their attention to this one passage).

commitment to this ideal with "freedom," an attitude of fatalism, and ultimately Dionysus. How are we to understand these motifs and their relation?

The immediately preceding section (VIII: 48) of *Twilight* in fact concerns Napoleon, and his "high, free, even terrible nature and naturalness"—indeed, Napoleon is declared by Nietzsche to be "a piece of 'return to nature,' as I understand it"—exactly the "return" Nietzsche attributes to Goethe. If we understand the sense in which Napoleon returns to "nature" and exemplifies the "natural," we will understand something about the meaning of "freedom" in the following section.

Napoleon's "return to nature" in Section 48 is explicitly contrasted with Rousseau's conception of man's "natural" state, which Nietzsche deems the "idealistic" fantasies of the rabble, meaning, in particular, their "doctrine of equality." "No poison is more poisonous than this," says Nietzsche, and Section 48 concludes that "only one person . . . perceived it correctly: with *disgust*," namely Goethe. Since "this freedom" for which Goethe is strong enough is equated with "the entire expanse and wealth of naturalness" of which Napoleon is the exemplar, it would seem to follow that the *freedom* of a Goethe is, *in part*, an acceptance of the reality of the natural inequality between people and a renunciation of the Rousseauian illusions about what persons are like in a truly natural state.

But Goethe's kind of "freedom," his "becom[ing] free," is also explicitly equated with an attitude of "cheerful and trusting fatalism," which, in turn, is equated with the Dionysian attitude that is clearly recognizable as *amor fati*, that is, acceptance and affirmation of the way things *really* are, rather than falling prey to the fantasies of the "idealist and rabble rolled into one," namely, Rousseau. To be free, in this sense, then, is to be free of the wish that reality be other than it is—namely, unequal, terrible, and cruel, (as Napoleon, of course, was). It is not, needless to say, to be a free agent as conceived by Kant or Hume. Nietzsche would rather persuade select readers to the fatalism of a Goethe by co-opting the language of freedom itself to commend to them an attitude that is premised on its denial in the most profound sense: a denial of the Enlightenment ideal that men, through free will and their rational capacities, can all become equal. Like the illiberal idea that *Der Frei Mensch ist Krieger* or that to be free is to be big, brave and indifferent to suffering, this key passage from *Twilight* persuasively redefines "freedom" in the service of Nietzschean values: in this case, the illiberal idea that to be *truly* free is to be not just reconciled to, but to affirm, the essential inequality of persons.

3. Nietzsche, Spinoza, Fate, and Freedom

If the psychologically unified agent is just a natural artifact, another consequence of fate, as Nietzsche plainly believes, is there any philosophical pedigree in the canon for associating such a state of affairs with "freedom"? Donald Rutherford (2011) has argued that we can locate Nietzsche's admittedly revisionary sense of freedom, one that reconciles it with fatalism, in the vicinity of the philosophical views of the Stoics and Spinoza. For all these philosophers, Rutherford claims, while "all actions have prior causes, such causes can be distinguished in terms of whether they reflect the inherent power of an agent or the power of external forces" (2011: 514). Rutherford recognizes that "shadows of theology" (2011: 514) loom over the views of both the Stoics and Spinoza, and acknowledges that "the position [Nietzsche] defends goes beyond anything found within the tradition" they define (2011: 525).[14] It seems fair to conclude, as I argued earlier in this chapter, that Nietzsche's sense of freedom really is highly revisionary of any in the philosophical traditions; at the same time, Rutherford has identified the closest cousins.

Rutherford acknowledges Nietzsche's vituperative criticisms of Stoicism (2011: 520–1), which contrast markedly with his general (though not uniformly) favorable attitude towards Spinoza (as in a famous letter Nietzsche wrote to his friend Franz Overbeck in 1881, quoted in Rutherford 2011: 521). As Rutherford observes, "Spinoza's conception of fate, or causal necessity, is even more uncompromising than that of the Stoics: things happen as they do, because they happen necessarily. No set of ends, human or divine, offers any justification for *why* the world unfolds as it does" (2011: 517), a view central to Nietzsche's fatalism. Indeed, it is in this respect[15] that Nietzsche's view is closest to Spinoza's.

"[L]iberating oneself from the influence of external circumstances" (Rutherford 2011: 526) is crucial for Spinoza and also Nietzsche, who, as Rutherford observes, commends, in many passages, the "struggle to become free of external circumstances, to stand alone, unmoved by the opinions and expectations of others" (2011: 526), a familiar theme of Nietzsche's radical individualism. (Rutherford aptly cites BGE 212: "Today the concept of greatness [not freedom, however] entails being noble, wanting to be by oneself, being able to be different, standing alone and having to live independently.")

[14] As Rutherford notes later, "The emphasis that the Stoics and Spinoza place on the lawful order of the universe and its comprehension by rational minds is an obvious way in which Nietzsche diverges from them" (2011: 534).

[15] Freedom in the revisionary tradition Rutherford associates with the Stoics and Spinoza has three elements: "*autonomy*, which presupposes *knowledge* of nature and the truth of *fatalism*" (2011: 524). For Spinoza, "'freedom' designates the mode of acting in which a thing is necessitated to act by its own nature, or power, and not by the action of other things on it" (2011: 517). For Spinoza, this is "reason," though obviously not for Nietzsche, as Rutherford notes (2011:521). "[F]reedom is identified as the condition of an individual who, through reason, has escaped the bondage of the passions and thereby attained a measure of independence from fortune, or those things outside his power" (2011: 519). Rutherford also notes that "there is one principle of order that Spinoza does not expel from his system, that of *law*, or determination in accordance with intelligible, universal principles" (2011: 522). Rutherford notes that Nietzsche seems to reject nomic ordering, but then suggests, based only on *Nachlass* material, that Nietzsche believes only in "the brute necessity of power relations". There is *Nachlass* material to this effect, but it constitutes what I have previously called, with good reason, Nietzsche's speculative forays into "crackpot metaphysics" (Leiter 2013a: 594), which does not infect the work Nietzsche actually published. Regarding the "knowledge" component, Rutherford, correctly in my view, points to GS 335, and notes that, "If we are to be self-determining agents, we cannot live in a fantasy world: we must know nature and culture can constrain our activity. This is a decisive rebuke to those who would read Nietzsche as a radical creationist with respect to the self" (530). But he goes on to treats Nietzsche's idea of perspectival "knowledge" in a way I find implausible (2011: 530–1), for reasons that are made clear in Chapter 4.

The demand for "independence" is particularly stark in Nietzsche's claim that higher human beings create their own standards of value; again, as Rutherford puts it, "Nietzsche envisions a more radical way in which value judgments depend upon the individual... She [the individual] is someone who recognizes that she herself, and not reason, community, or God, is the ultimate arbiter of persons, actions and things" (2011: 527).

Rutherford, unfortunately, glosses this idea of evaluative independence as "entail[ing] normative authority" (2011: 527). Despite the Kantian connotations of that way of formulating it, Rutherford is equally clear this does not, for Nietzsche, involve any assumption about evaluative judgments being answerable to "objective standards of correctness" (*id.*). He describes the relevant Nietzschean idea of "normative authority" as follows: "The authority of... a principle [of action an independent person assigns herself] consists simply in the fact that it is the will of the autonomous person: it is a law that she cannot fail to observe insofar as she acts from her own power, as opposed to being determined to act by the effects of external things on her" (2011: 528). Rutherford, who is otherwise a scrupulous scholar, cites no passage in Nietzsche inviting this reading, and I can think of none. Nietzsche does not think that agents, even higher human beings, do what they do because of "principles" of action: that is a Kantian, not a Nietzschean picture, even allowing that the principles do not answer to objective standards of correctness (see especially the discussion in Chapter 7). We could make sense of talk about "a law that [the agent] cannot fail to observe," but only in a descriptive, not normative, sense of law, i.e., as describing a regularity about a particular kind of person's actions, given the type-facts about them.

I thus agree with Rutherford that Nietzsche calls "autonomous" those whose judgments of value are not products of their environment or the pressures of the "herd," but rather arise from their own standard of value, but disagree that this "autonomous" agent should be described as governed by "principles of action," except in a wholly descriptive sense.[16] So understood, I also agree with Rutherford that the autonomous agent's judgments of value "are causally the result of facts about what one is essentially, as opposed to facts about the circumstances in which one finds [oneself]. Yet, for Nietzsche, facts about what one is essentially are given in terms of what one is *fated* to be" (2011: 532), precisely as I argued in Chapter 5. In Rutherford's useful summation of his reading:

> The person who becomes free is the person whom fate favors with the ability to regiment in herself a principle of action that is expressive of her power... [O]ne must recognize that the success one may have achieved in becoming autonomous is not owed to oneself; it is fate. How and under what circumstances one is able to act from one's own power, is not up to one; it is fate. Fate stands over everything we do. No life can be one in which everything flows from its own locus of power. How one is *able* to act is a consequence not just of what one is, but of what everything is and does. (2011: 533)

[16] In the end, I think Rutherford should agree with this recharacterization of his point.

The only point, again, on which the interpretation defended in this book dissents concerns the first sentence: the person who becomes "free"—autonomous of the herd and the environment—is not someone who legislates a "principle of action" but simply someone who, by fate, is able to act and value in such a way that is independent of the environment and the herd. I also concur with Rutherford's further suggestion that, "Nietzsche envisions a freedom that assents to fate as a condition of its own possibility" (2011: 533), which I take it is something like Nietzsche's recommendation of *amor fati*, and which certainly describes Nietzsche's Goethe, discussed at the end of the last section.

So Spinoza, like Nietzsche, is a kind of fatalist, yet still embraced a notion of autonomy: an agent is autonomous on this view when he is not simply the vector through which various external forces operate, but instead his actions arise from his real nature (i.e., his type-facts), even if that nature is barely known by the agent.[17] "Autonomy" is, as I've written previously, "Nietzsche's name for a certain kind of causal determination, namely, when the primary determinant of one's actions and beliefs are internal to the person, rather than external or environmental factors, such as the values prevalent in the society at large" (2015a: 181). But that possibility itself is determined by fate. One might think this yet another example of Nietzsche's distinctive brand of "naturalized Kantianism." Kant thought the true self or will could stand outside the causal order (Nietzsche obviously denies that), but on Nietzsche's view, some wills or selves can stand outside *not the causal order*, but the external causal order, as it were, "of their time and place." In that regard, they still satisfy something like Kant's ideal of enlightenment.

4. Conclusion

Someone might be tempted to suggest that Nietzsche's view of "autonomy" (or "freedom"), in which one is free to the extent one's actions follow essentially from who one really is, rather than being the causal product of external influence, is really a kind of "Control" view of free will that that we discussed in Chapter 5. Recall that on "Control" views of free will, the agent has to have the right kind of control over his or her actions such that s/he counts as their "real source": candidates in the philosophical literature of recent decades include "identifying" with the desires on which one acts, or being responsive to the "reasons" that bear on how one ought to act. Of course, neither possibility is available to Nietzsche. First, Nietzsche thinks we generally do not know what the drives are that cause us to act, which precludes identification. Second, Nietzsche has no use for the idea of "reasons" for how one *ought* to act, given his anti-realism about value discussed in Part I of this book. What is missing, in short, from Nietzsche's

[17] Notice how remote this is from the Watson's (1996) sense of "attributability," which he treats Frankfurt (1971) and Watson (1975) as explicating. Agents are free or autonomous on this view in virtue of causal facts about the genesis of their actions that have nothing to do with their hierarchy of desires, or their judgments about what is good or valuable.

view, as described in Section 3 of this chapter, is any idea of "control" (after all, this is fate) and, more importantly, any idea that actions that arise from one's type-facts are ones for which one is morally responsible and blameworthy (or praiseworthy). Nietzsche's ideal of autonomy, on the Rutherford reading (suitably amended as I proposed above), is one about the causal connections between type-facts and subsequent actions, not about the exercise of control.

Since Nietzsche says so little that suggests he holds out the hope of a freedom or free will that would be recognizable to the philosophical tradition, or common sense, as such; if his skepticism about freedom and responsibility is so resolute; if what he *actually* says about freedom and free will is so clearly revisionary, so plainly an exercise in persuasive definition that means to exploit his readers' antecedent emotional investment in "freedom" on behalf of very different Nietzschean ideals, even quite illiberal ones; then how are we to explain the recent scholarly "consensus"—criticized earlier in this chapter—with which we began? It is, I fear, a manifestation of the fault against which Nietzsche often railed, and which we have seen so many times before in the Nietzsche literature, in Heidegger's transformation of Nietzsche into the last metaphysical philosopher, in Kaufmann's rendering of him as a harmless secular humanist, in Nehamas' defanging of him as an aestheticist (cf. Leiter 2002). In each case, the aim is to make Nietzsche less appalling to us delicate modern readers than he really is: for Nietzsche does *not* believe in freedom or responsibility; he does not think we exercise any meaningful control over our lives; he does not think that his revisionary sense of "freedom"—the "long, protracted will" as he puts in the passage from GM II:2—is in reach of just anyone, that anyone could "choose" to have it; indeed, in the important passage from *Twilight* quoted at the end of Section 2, "freedom" is rather clearly invoked on behalf of Nietzsche's illiberal vision of the inescapable reality of human inequality. The resistance to these points in the recent scholarly literature, I conclude, reflects the continuing malign influence of moralizing readings of Nietzsche, of the failure to remember what he says about his conception of Renaissance virtue, namely, that we understand it, and him, "moraline-free" (A 2).

7

The Case for Nietzschean Moral Psychology

Brian Leiter and Joshua Knobe

1. Introduction

Until fairly recently (e.g., Doris 2002; Nichols 2004; Prinz 2007), most Anglophone philosophers writing about moral psychology tended to approach their questions "from the armchair," and without regard to pertinent empirical findings about human psychology.[1] Indifference to empirical findings probably also explains another striking feature of the moral psychology literature, namely, that the field has been so dominated by a small number of historical figures, the two most prominent being Aristotle and Kant.[2] From Aristotle has come to us the tradition of virtue ethics, which emphasizes the importance of stable characterological dispositions to act in morally appropriate ways, dispositions which it is the task of a sound moral education to inculcate in children. From Kant, by contrast, has come the rationalist tradition in moral psychology, according to which reason is the source of moral motivation, and the mechanism for moral action is one in which rational agents legislate for themselves certain principles on the basis of which they consciously act.

In this Chapter, Joshua Knobe and I argue that we need to add a neglected figure to this debate, namely Nietzsche; we hope to show that a fair reading of the relevant empirical sciences strongly favors the broad outlines of his moral psychology as against the Aristotelian and Kantian traditions. The primary concern in this chapter is not interpretive (the interpretive burden has been discharged in the prior chapters), but philosophical: to show that neglect of Nietzsche in moral psychology is no longer an option for those philosophers who accept that moral psychology should be grounded in *real* psychology. Admittedly, not all philosophers accept that constraint on their

[1] Moral psychologists influenced by Freud, like Deigh (1996), are also an exception to the inattention to empirical psychology, though even Deigh does not spend time investigating the empirical evidence for Freudian moral psychology. But the Freudian theory is an empirical one, and support does exist (e.g., Westen [1998]).

[2] Humean views have also been extremely influential of course, and, in fact, have certain structural similarities to Nietzsche's as we have seen throughout the book.

moral psychology. Indeed, some contend that issues in moral psychology are not really empirical ones at all. Thus, certain Kantians might say: "Kant's theory is not intended as a psychological hypothesis. It should be understood rather as a statement of the conditions of possibility of moral agency. Hence, if we find that no one actually meets the conditions set out by the theory, we should not conclude that the theory itself was mistaken. Instead, we should conclude that no one ever truly is a moral agent." Let us call philosophers who adopt such a posture *Above-the-Fray Moral Philosophers*. Such philosophers are indeed invulnerable to the empirical results: they tell us how moral agents *ought* to be, and they are indifferent to how moral agents actually are or can be. We reject such an approach in this chapter. We assume that *ought implies can* is a reasonable aspiration in moral psychology; indeed, that *ought implies realistically can* is an even better aspiration (cf. Flanagan 1991).

2. Three Views in Moral Psychology

The Aristotelian and Kantian traditions in moral psychology are historically and philosophically complex. The ambition here is plainly not to do justice to the history or even all the philosophical permutations. Rather, we want to extract certain *core* and *distinctive* elements of these traditions, ones that are, on almost any rendering, important to the views so named, and which, at the same time, involve or presuppose psychological claims that admit of empirical evaluation. Just as there are a multitude of "Humean" views in ethics and action theory that are traceable to Hume, but do not necessarily have the full texture of Hume's actual views, so too, we claim, there are Kantian and Aristotelian views in moral psychology that are traceable to their distinguished historical forebears, but which we do not claim are Kant's or Aristotle's *precise* views. What we do claim, in each case, is that the views in question are important views in moral psychology *to the present* and that these views do not fare well when compared to the, hitherto, under-appreciated "Nietzschean" approach to moral psychology.

2.1 Aristotle

In the Aristotelian tradition of moral psychology, morally good agents are *virtuous* agents, that is, agents possessed of stable dispositions to act in morally appropriate ways as different situations require. The agent who acts morally, according to Aristotle, has three attributes: "he must act knowingly, next he must choose the actions, and choose them for themselves, and thirdly he must act from a firm and unalterable character" (*NE* 1105a29–33).

But Aristotle does not merely suggest that moral action stems from a certain type of character; he also advances a series of specific hypotheses about the nature and origin of that type of character. In particular, he claims that good character consists in certain *habits* (*NE* 1103a25), that these habits are acquired during *childhood* (*NE* 1103b25) and that the key to their acquisition is proper *upbringing* (*NE* 1095b5–10). Ultimately, then, we are left with a definite picture of how virtuous character is acquired. This picture says that people are encouraged to perform certain virtuous behaviors during childhood and that they gradually come to acquire the corresponding dispositions, leading eventually to a full-fledged possession of the relevant virtue.

Richard Kraut (2001) provides a more nuanced discussion of this hypothesis:

> All free males [according to Aristotle] are born with the potential to become ethically virtuous and practically wise, but to achieve these goals they must go through two stages: during their childhood, they must develop the proper habits; and then, when their reason is fully developed, they must acquire practical wisdom (*phronêsis*). This does not mean that first we fully acquire the ethical virtues, and then, at a later stage, add on practical wisdom. Ethical virtue is fully developed only when it is combined with practical wisdom (1144b14–17). A low-grade form of ethical virtue emerges in us during childhood as we are repeatedly placed in situations that call for appropriate actions and emotions; but as we rely less on others and become capable of doing more of our own thinking, we learn to develop a larger picture of human life, our deliberative skills improve, and our emotional responses are perfected. Like anyone who has developed a skill in performing a complex and difficult activity, the virtuous person takes pleasure in exercising his intellectual skills. Furthermore, when he has decided what to do, he does not have to contend with internal pressures to act otherwise. He does not long to do something that he regards as shameful; and he is not greatly distressed at having to give up a pleasure that he realizes he should forego.

"To keep such destructive inner forces [or pressures] at bay," notes Kraut, "we need to develop the proper habits and emotional responses when we are children, and to reflect intelligently on our aims when we are adults."

This "process of training" through which a virtuous agent is produced is not, as John Cooper emphasizes, "purely mechanical":

> Aristotle holds that we become just (etc.) by being repeatedly made to act justly (etc.) ... [S]ince he emphasizes that the outcome of the training is the disposition to act in certain ways, knowing what one is doing and choosing to act that way, the habituation must involve also ... the training of the mind. As the trainee becomes gradually used to acting in certain ways, he comes gradually to understand what he is doing and why he is doing it: he comes, to put it vaguely, to see the point of the moral policies which he is being trained to follow, and does not just follow them blindly. (Cooper 1975: 8; citations omitted)

Of particular importance for our purposes are two features of Aristotle's moral psychology of the virtuous agent: first, the morally good agent, properly raised, must have "a firm and unalterable character"; second, this type of character is typically the product of *childhood upbringing*.[3] Although there has been a great deal of excellent work on the

[3] Although these two themes have been central to the "Aristotelian" tradition within contemporary moral psychology, Aristotle himself appears to have had a more complex and multi-faceted view. He attributes the development of character to a broad process of "acculturation" (trophē) which includes more than just treatment from one's caregivers, and he mentions at a number of points that there are innate differences between individuals in their capacity for virtue, even to the point of suggesting that women and slaves are not capable of true virtue regardless of their childhood experiences. Since modern philosophers working in the tradition of Aristotelian moral psychology have no reason to accept Aristotle's view about

proper interpretation of Aristotle's account of the origin of virtue, there has been surprisingly little discussion of the question as to whether or not Aristotle's views are actually correct. Our concern here will be with this latter question. We want to know whether there actually is any evidence for the view that people's dispositions are shaped primarily by childhood upbringing or whether people's dispositions might arise through some other process entirely.

2.2 Kant

In the Kantian tradition of moral psychology, moral obligations are grounded in principles that each agent consciously chooses. But it is not enough for an agent simply to perform behaviors that happen to accord with these moral principles. If an agent's behavior is merely the product of emotion or habit, then no matter how well that behavior fits with her moral principles, she can never truly be acting morally. Genuine moral action must actually be chosen *because* it is morally right. Or, as Kant famously puts it, genuine moral action is not merely *in accordance with* duty; it is done *out of* duty.

Here is how J.B. Schneewind (1992) usefully summarizes the Kantian view:

> At the center of Kant's ethical theory is the claim that normal adults are capable of being fully self-governing in moral matters. In Kant's terminology, we are "autonomous." Autonomy involves two components. The first is that no authority external to ourselves is needed to constitute or inform us of the demands of morality. We can each know without being told what we ought to do because moral requirements are requirements we impose on ourselves. The second is that in self-government we can effectively control ourselves. The obligations we impose upon ourselves override all other calls for action, and frequently run counter to our desires. We nonetheless always have a sufficient motive to act as we ought. (Schneewind 1992: 309)

So on the Kantian view of moral psychology, (1) agents impose moral requirements on themselves, and (2) these self-imposed requirements are motivationally effective. In order for the self-imposition of moral requirements to be genuinely autonomous it must presumably be a conscious process of self-imposition. And for these consciously imposed principles to be motivationally effective it must be the case that conscious moral principles are motivationally effective.[4]

who has the potential to be virtuous, we may assume that a credible modern Aristotelian moral psychology must be committed to the proposition that everyone is potentially "brought up" properly such that they can become virtuous agents.

[4] We take Schneewind's summary, and the points we emphasize, to comport reasonably well with more elaborate treatments of Kantian ethics and moral psychology, such as that in Korsgaard (1996). So, e.g., Korsgaard says that for Kant, "principles of practical reason" are "principles that govern choice" (xii) and that Kant demonstrates "the reality of moral obligation" in the *Critique of Practical Reason* by appeal to "our consciousness of the moral law and its capacity to motivate us whenever we construct maxims. We are conscious of the law not only in the sense that it tells us what to do, but in the sense that we know we *can* do what it tells us, no matter how strong the opposing motives" (26).

2.3 Nietzsche

The Nietzschean account of moral psychology differs from the Aristotelian and Kantian accounts along almost every dimension as we have seen throughout the book. What is decisive is not upbringing, particular habits, or conscious choice; what matters most are type-facts, i.e., heritable psychological and physiological traits, which operate below the level of conscious deliberation. These type-facts play a powerful (but not exclusive) role in determining one's behavior and values, though a far more powerful role than education or upbringing or conscious choice; indeed, a person's crucial conscious choices and values are themselves explicable in terms of these type-facts. *That* one is a "moral" agent is explained by one's biological inheritance, the type-facts; *that* one is not a moral agent is similarly explained.

3. The Empirical Evidence in Moral Psychology

So which of the three rival views in moral psychology provides the best account of how people actually come to perform moral (or immoral) behaviors? In addressing this question, we make use of an extremely straightforward methodology: we turn to studies that directly measure the extent to which different factors appear to be influencing behavior. Now while the issue here is an empirical one, we should also emphasize that it is not the kind of issue that could ever be resolved by a single crucial experiment. In essence, the problem here is that none of the three views can be refuted by a single isolated case. Virtue ethicists in the Aristotelian tradition do not typically claim that *everything* about a person's character was determined by the way in which he or she was brought up. Nor does Nietzsche need to say that *everything* about a person's character is determined at birth. The three positions differ primarily in their understanding of what *typically* happens in cases where a person acts in a way that is appraised as valuable. Our question is whether the existing empirical evidence favors one of these positions over the others.

To address this question, we turn to the literature in empirical psychology. We will proceed by reviewing psychological research that will enable us to assess the plausibility of the Aristotelian, Kantian, and Nietzschean assumptions about what people are like. The evidence strongly suggests, we shall argue, that the Nietzschean view is far more likely to be correct than either of the others.

We should emphasize that the empirical results we will be discussing here are not those of a few maverick scientists drawing on some small number of scattered experiments. Rather, we will be focusing on some of the major lessons of personality and social psychology, replicated in numerous experiments using a wide variety of methodologies and subject pools. Occasionally, we will describe a specific experiment and report its results, but the importance of these specific experiments is not that they themselves provide evidence for the theories discussed but rather that they serve as *examples*—giving the reader a sense for the kinds of techniques and results to be found in the relevant literatures. In addition to descriptions of specific experiments, we therefore rely heavily on reviews that summarize large numbers of relevant studies. Thus, to take just one example, we briefly mention a paper by Feingold (1992) on the impact of attractiveness on personality. That paper is a review of more than ninety studies including a total of more than *fifteen thousand* subjects. What makes Feingold's theory convincing is the fact that such a wide variety of studies have converged on a single basic result. The same could be said of each of the other theories we discuss.

In Sections 3.1 and 3.2, we adduce empirical evidence that supports the broad outlines of the two central features of Nietzschean moral psychology: first, that individuals are simply born with a certain psycho-physical package of traits (the person's distinctive type-facts); and second, that heritable traits play a powerful role in determining behavior and values. In Sections 3.3 and 3.4, we consider empirical evidence at odds with essential presuppositions of the Aristotelian and Kantian approaches: first (*contra* Aristotle), that character is shaped by upbringing; and second (*contra* Kant), that conscious principles determine action.

3.1 Type-facts and heredity (for Nietzsche)

As we have seen, Nietzsche puts forward the view that a person's traits are determined, to a great extent, by type-facts, many of which are fixed at birth.[5] This view has gone more or less unexplored in the contemporary philosophical literature on moral psychology. (No one suggests, e.g., that the secret to becoming a compassionate person might lie in part in inheriting a genetic propensity of compassion.) And yet, although the Nietzschean view has not found much favor among philosophers, it is receiving an ever-growing mountain of support from empirical studies.

The most important evidence here comes from studies in behavioral genetics. Typically, these studies are conducted either by looking at twins (comparing monozygotic to dizygotic) or by looking at adopted children. The results of such studies are as consistent as they are shocking. Almost every personality trait that has been studied by behavioral geneticists has turned out to be heritable to a surprising degree. So, for example, a recent review of five studies in five different countries (comprising a total sample size of 24,000 twins) estimates that genetic factors explain 60 percent of the variance in extraversion and 50 percent of the variance in neuroticism (Loehlin 1992).

It is difficult to convey just how astoundingly high these numbers are, but perhaps one can get a better sense for the issue by considering the effect sizes obtained in some classic social psychology experiments. The Festinger and Carlsmith (1959) study of cognitive dissonance found an effect that explained 13 percent of the behavioral variance; the Darley and Batson (1973) study of bystander intervention and the diffusion of responsibility found an effect that explained 14 percent of the behavioral variance;

[5] Particular drives may wax and wane, of course, over the course of a life, and some may even be acquired later on, but we shall focus here on the plausibility of the idea that people are born being a certain *type*.

the Milgram (1975) study of obedience and proximity showed an effect that explained 13 percent of the behavioral variance.[6] These are among the most influential and important experiments in all of social psychology. In each case, the fact that researchers were able to explain 13–14 percent of the variance led to a veritable revolution in our understanding of the relevant phenomena. Now consider, by contrast, the fact that behavioral geneticists routinely find effects that explain *fifty percent* of the variance in trait measures. Effect sizes of this magnitude are beyond the range that would previously have been considered possible.

Having said that, we should emphasize that it would be a mistake to attach too much importance to the exact percentages obtained in these studies. On the one hand, adoption studies generally yield lower heritabilities than twin studies do, and one might therefore suspect that the true heritabilities are lower than those reported here. On the other hand, our ability to measure traits is quite limited, and one might therefore suspect that we would obtain even higher heritabilities if we could develop a more accurate trait measure. Whatever the resolution of these various difficulties, it seems clear that most traits have extremely high heritabilities.

Here we should pause to avert a potential misunderstanding of what it means for a trait to be "heritable." When we say that a trait is heritable, we do not mean that it is produced entirely by a person's genes, without any intervention from the environment. All we mean is that the differences between different people's scores on this trait can be explained in part by differences in those people's genetic material. This effect may not be direct. Differences in people's genes might lead to differences in their environments, which in turn lead to differences in their scores on certain traits. Often the result will be a self-reinforcing cycle in which early behaviors that express a given trait lead the person to possess that trait to ever greater degrees. For example, a person's initial extraverted behavior might leave her with a reputation for extraversion, which in turn makes her even more extraverted.

At least in principle, then, it is possible that heritable differences in personality are caused by heritable differences in some non-psychological characteristic. For example, it might turn out that heritable differences in physical appearance lead to differences in treatment by parents and peers, which in turn lead to differences in personality traits (Hoffman 1991). In actual fact, however, it is highly unlikely that any substantial portion of the variance in personality traits can be explained in this way. To take one striking example, physical attractiveness appears to have almost no impact at all on personality: it explains around 2 percent of the variance in dominance, 0 percent of the variance in sociability, 2 percent of the variance in self-esteem, and so forth (Feingold 1992).

[6] A note for the statistically inclined: no effect sizes are reported in the original papers, but Funder and Ozer (1983) have shown that it is possible to compute additional analyses based on information that the authors do report. (All effect sizes given here are calculated by taking the square of the relevant correlation coefficient.)

Of course, the impact of genetics is not confined to morally neutral traits like extraversion and neuroticism; it also extends to traits that lie at the heart of moral psychology. Consider the tendency to use violence (what psychologists sometimes call "aggressive antisocial behaviour"). A number of studies have examined the causes of violent behavior among children, and all show a strong influence of genetics. One recent study using 1,523 pairs of twins found a heritability of 70 percent (Eley, Lichtenstein, and Stevenson 1999). Other studies yield percentages that are lower but still surprisingly high—60 percent (Edelbrock, Rende, Plomin, and Thompson 1995) 49 percent (Deater-Deckard and Plomin 1999) and 60 percent (Schmitz, Fulker, and Mrazek 1995). These huge effect sizes cannot plausibly be ascribed to experimental artifacts or measurement error. Clearly, genetic factors are playing a substantial role in the etiology of certain kinds of violence.

Studies like these confirm the commonsense view that morally-relevant traits, like most other traits, are the product of not only environmental factors but also of heredity. This is the view we find assumed (commonsensically enough) in the works of Nietzsche. "It is simply not possible that a human being should *not* have the qualities and preferences of his parents and ancestors in his body," as Nietzsche quips, "whatever appearances may suggest to the contrary" (BGE: 264).

Subsequent philosophical work, in both the Aristotelian and Kantian traditions, has more or less ignored the role of heredity, focusing either on environmental factors like culture and upbringing, or ignoring questions about the genesis of motivation altogether. Yet all available evidence points to the view that heredity plays a major role in the development of morally-relevant traits, and if we want our moral psychology to be defensible and empirically sound, we need to grapple seriously with the philosophical issues this evidence raises. Of the historical figures we are considering, only Nietzsche has come to terms with the issue.

3.2 Type-facts and fatalism (for Nietzsche)

Thus far, we have been concerned with questions about how people come to have certain traits rather than others. But Nietzsche also makes very strong claims about the *importance* that these traits—however they are acquired—actually have in people's lives. A person's character, he seems to suggest, has a substantial and pervasive impact on the whole course of that person's life. This claim may seem so banal and obviously correct as not even to be worthy of discussion. In actual fact, however, aspects of it have been the object of a long-standing controversy within social and personality psychology.

Personality psychologists have performed numerous studies in which subjects first engage in some task designed to measure their personality traits (typically, filling out a questionnaire[7]) and then are given an opportunity to perform a behavior that ought to

[7] This is not a very Nietzschean way of determining personality traits, however, given the extent to which humans are both often ignorant of themselves and prone to self-deception, but since that is the method in the existing psychological literature, we utilize it here.

be influenced by those traits. One surprising result of such studies is that correlations between a trait measure and an actual behavior rarely exceed .30. In other words, the trait measure rarely allows us to explain more than 9 percent of the variance in the behavior.[8] This is an important finding, that has been discussed in detail by both personality and social psychologists.

In his groundbreaking discussion of the phenomenon, Mischel (1968) suggested that perhaps broad traits do not really exist at all. The suggestion was that it might be more accurate to posit only extremely narrow traits (e.g., a tendency to cheat on exams by copying other people's answers) and stop looking for broad traits like "extraversion" and "neuroticism." This suggestion spurred a great deal of debate throughout the 1970s (e.g., Bem and Allen 1974; Jones and Nisbett 1972), but that debate is now over. Almost all psychologists now believe that broad traits do exist.[9] The key question is how important they are—whether they actually have a large impact on people's behavior or whether they turn out to be far less powerful than certain subtle situational forces. This issue is surprisingly complex. Ross and Nisbett (1991) have offered sophisticated arguments for the view that traits have only a small impact on behavior, but Funder and Ozer (1983) and Epstein (1979) have offered arguments of equal sophistication for the view that traits can have quite large impacts on behavior.

To get a sense for the complexity of the issue, consider what would happen if we tried to predict a basketball player's performance using some measure of his or her ability. Clearly, our predictive power would depend in part on how much of the player's behavior we were trying to predict. If we tried to predict the player's success in getting one particular randomly-selected rebound, our measure of ability would give us only very limited predictive power. (The most important factor would be the difficulty of that particular rebound.) On the other hand, if we were trying to predict the quality of the player's overall performance across the course of an entire season of play—including numerous different kinds of tasks performed in a wide variety of situations—our ability measure would probably prove extremely useful. So should we say that ability has only a small impact on performance or that it has a very large impact? Ultimately, our answer will depend on the precise nature of our concern: whether we

[8] Note on statistics: Although results in behavioral genetics are normally reported as percentages of variance, results in personality psychology are normally reported as correlation coefficients. For the sake of consistency, we therefore transform each correlation coefficient (r) into a coefficient of determination (r^2), which is equal to the percentage of variance explained. The reader can obtain correlation coefficients by taking the square root of each percentage of variance given in the text.

[9] By "broad traits," we simply mean traits that produce a wide variety of different types of behavior. Belief in the existence of broad traits should be carefully distinguished from what Doris (2002) has called *globalism*—namely, belief in the existence of traits that are stable, evaluatively integrated, and yield consistent behavior. (A trait that explains, say, 9 percent of the variance in a wide range of morally-relevant behaviors could be extremely broad but would not yield consistent behavior and would therefore provide no evidence at all for globalism.) When we say that the existence of broad traits is no longer a matter of controversy in social and personality psychology, we certainly don't mean to imply that all psychologists are globalists. Far from it: as we shall see, trait-relevant behaviors are often surprisingly inconsistent.

are concerned with success on one particular occasion or with success over the course of a whole season (as we will see, Nietzsche's interest is with an analogue of the latter).

As Epstein (1979) has argued, a similar conundrum arises in the domain of moral psychology. For example, suppose we wanted to know whether a broad trait of "honesty" can be used to predict the degree to which children will engage in a broad array of different kinds of honesty-related behaviors. If we try to predict just *one* such behavior on the basis of one other behavior, we obtain a correlation that explains only 5 percent of the behavioral variance. However, if we look at the overall honesty that a child shows across a whole battery of tests and then try to predict the honesty that the same child will show in another battery of tests, we obtain a much higher correlation—this time, explaining a full 81 percent of the variance (Hartshorne and May 1928).

Doris (2002) and Harman (1999) have argued that traditional virtue ethics can only be tenable if we have some way to predict specific behaviors on the basis of broad personality traits. A number of philosophers have argued that virtue ethics can still be viable even in the face of the Doris-Harman critique (see, e.g., Kamtekar 2004; Merritt 2000; Sabini and Silver 2005; Sreenivasen 2002). Our aim here is not to resolve this controversy but rather to emphasize that the problem Doris and Harman have identified for virtue ethics does not also apply to Nietzsche's account. Since Nietzsche is interested in the *structure of a life*, and not in isolated, particular instances of conduct, it would seem that Epstein's approach offers strong support. What matters for Nietzsche is that heritable traits structure the *course of a life*, not that they enable one to predict any particular instance of conduct in that life. That was clear enough in the case of Cornaro discussed in Chapter 5: what was at issue was explaining his *overall diet* in terms of type-facts, not every bit of food he consumed. Or as Nietzsche puts it elsewhere, "Wherever a *cardinal* problem is at stake, there speaks an unchangeable 'this is I'" (BGE: 231; emphasis added). Or similarly: "Our *most sacred convictions*... are judgments of our muscles" (WP: 314; emphasis added). It is the *central* features of moral belief and action—the recurring ones that mark the distinctive features of a life—that Nietzsche wants to understand in terms of type-facts, not any particular belief or action on any particular occasion. As we shall see in a moment, though heritable traits may not predict people's behavior on any individual occasion, a wide variety of studies show that they do have a quite substantial impact on the long-run path of an individual's life.

3.3 The role of upbringing (against Aristotle)

In contrast to Nietzsche, philosophers working in the Aristotelian tradition tend to assume that upbringing plays a major role in the shaping of people's character traits. Here it is essential to distinguish two related claims. First, there is the bland and relatively uncontentious claim that a person's environment has an important influence on his or her character (recall the role of culture, for example, in shaping the meta-affects discussed in Chapter 3). Second, there is the more specific and largely unsubstantiated claim that character is shaped by *upbringing*, i.e., by the ways in which person is treated by his or her parents or caregivers. This latter claim is usually put forward without argument, but as we shall see, recent empirical research gives us quite substantial reasons to be suspicious of it.

In thinking about this issue, it may be helpful once again to consider what percentage of the variance in personality traits is explained by each of a number of different factors. We saw above that heredity explains around one-third to two-thirds of the variance in most traits, with the rest presumably explained by environmental factors. Our question now is: of the variance explained by the environment, how much is explained by upbringing and how much is explained by other environmental factors?

To begin with, we should note that socialization researchers have uncovered numerous correlations between childrearing practices and personality development (e.g., the classic studies of Baumrind 1967, 1991). In other words, it can be shown that children who have been raised in particular ways tend to have particular personality traits. But the existence of correlations is not in question here; the only question is about whether particular childrearing practices actually *cause* people to have particular personality traits. For example, it is widely assumed that there is a correlation whereby people who are beaten as children tend to be more violent as adults.[10] One possible explanation of this correlation would be that childhood beatings actually cause people to develop more violent personalities. But there are other plausible interpretations. It could be that certain people have more violent personalities even as children and that these people are more likely to misbehave and then to be beaten by their parents. Alternatively, it could be that a genetic propensity for violence is passed down from parents to children and that, since violent people are especially likely to have violent parents, such people are especially likely to be beaten as children.

The key contribution of behavioral genetics to this question has been in distinguishing between variance explained by the *shared environment* and variance explained by the *non-shared environment*. The "shared environment" is made up of those aspects of the environment that are shared by all children growing up in the same family, while the "non-shared environment" is made up of those aspects of the environment that differ even between two children growing up in the same family. Thus, suppose that two children are brought up by the same parents but have different peer groups. The traits of the parents would then be part of the shared environment, while the traits of the peers would be part of the non-shared environment. We can now ask how much of the variance in personality traits is explained by the shared environment. The surprising answer is: *very little* (only 5 percent to 10 percent in most studies). This is truly a shocking result, but it has been replicated in an enormous variety of studies and is now the basis of a wide-ranging consensus among researchers (see, e.g., Bouchard 1994; Loehlin 1992; Plomin and Daniels 1987).

[10] Widom (1989) reviews dozens of studies on the etiology of violence and concludes that there is actually surprisingly little empirical support for this assumption. Still, the balance of evidence does seem to suggest a correlation between being beaten as a child and being violent as an adult, and we will assume for the sake of argument that the correlation is really there.

To see the force of this finding, it may be helpful to engage in a quick thought experiment. Suppose we know that a given child is going to be adopted by a pair of particularly kind, loving, and open parents. What should we predict about the development of this child's personality? The answer appears to be that our knowledge of the parents gives us almost no predictive power at all. If these parents adopt three different children, those three children will be hardly any more similar than three randomly selected individuals.

As usual, the findings obtained for morally neutral personality traits hold for morally relevant personality traits as well. We noted above that one recent study finds that 70 percent of the variance in children's aggressiveness is explained by genetic differences. That same study finds that only 5 percent of the variance is explained by the shared environment (Eley, Lichtenstein, and Stevenson 1999). But as the authors themselves point out, this result is methodologically suspect, since the study had parents themselves assessing the degree to which their children behaved violently. When the violence of children is assessed by their teachers, heredity accounts for 49 percent of the variance and shared environment has no impact at all (Deater-Deckard and Plomin 1999). Of course, results like these do not call into question the widespread assumption that there is a correlation whereby violent parents are especially likely to rear violent children—but they do suggest another possible interpretation of that correlation. Perhaps the observed correlation has almost nothing to do with parents serving as "bad role models" or "perpetuating a cycle of violence." The effect might be almost entirely genetic, the product of genetic similarity between parents and children.

Reading the works of behavioral geneticists, it is easy to get the impression that no study has ever found the shared environment to have a substantial impact on anything of importance. But that is not quite right. Some studies have indicated a substantial impact of shared environment; however, the vast majority of studies have shown no substantial impact, and even when shared environment does have a substantial impact, this impact is usually far smaller than that of either heredity or nonshared environment.

For a case in which shared environment really has sometimes been shown to make a difference, let us consider the study of criminality. As one might expect, there is a correlation whereby criminal parents are more likely to have criminal children. But what explains this correlation—nature or nurture? To find the answer, we can look at studies of adopted children. Our question will be whether criminality in the children is best predicted by criminality in the adoptive parents or by criminality in the biological parents. A number of early studies using this methodology found that criminality in the biological parents predicted criminality in the children but that criminality in the adoptive parents had no significant impact (Schulsinger 1972; Crowe 1974). Later studies, however, did show that children of criminal adoptive parents had somewhat higher rates of criminality. This is an important victory for the significance of shared environment. Yet, even here, the importance of genetics ends up dwarfing the importance of shared environment. To give one striking example, Cloninger and colleagues showed that children of criminal adoptive parents did have higher rates of criminality, but they also showed that children of criminal biological parents were *twice* as likely to become criminals as were children of criminal adoptive parents (Cloninger, Sigvardsson, Bohman, and Knorring, 1982). Thus, of the total explained variance, 59 percent was explained by the criminality of the biological parents and only 19 percent was explained by the criminality of the adoptive parents.

In light of the repeated failure of shared environment to explain a large portion of the variance in personality, we seem forced to choose between three possible views. One view would be that parental treatment has only a very small impact on the development of personality, with other environmental factors playing a much more important role (Harris 1995, 1998). A second view would be that, although the similar treatment received by children raised together has very little impact, the respects in which such children are raised differently actually do have considerable impact (Plomin and Daniels 1987). A third would be that the very same kinds of parental treatment can have radically different impacts on different kinds of children (Maccoby and Martin 1983). The debate among these three views continues to rage on.

In sum, we have overwhelming evidence that heredity plays a major role in the shaping of personality, whereas the claim that upbringing plays a major role is contentious at best. It is, of course, correct that psychologists have not studied the role of upbringing with respect to the specifically Aristotelian virtues such as "courage," but it is reasonable to assume that if upbringing has little effect on morally relevant behaviors like criminality, it probably has little impact on the more fine-grained virtues that interested Aristotle. Hence, it may somehow be possible to vindicate Aristotle's moral psychology against its Nietzschean rival, but in light of the empirical evidence, there is plainly no reason for optimism that the Aristotelian account is more plausible.

3.4 Conscious decision and behavior (against Kant)

Recall that on the Kantian view, moral agents impose motivationally effective moral requirements upon themselves. This process of rational moral self-legislation is presumably a conscious one, and thus we must presume that these consciously imposed moral "laws" have a substantial impact on behavior if the Kantian view is correct. On the Nietzschean view, by contrast, conscious beliefs play little role in moral (or immoral) agency.[11] People's behaviors are determined not so much by their conscious beliefs as by certain underlying type-facts (cf. Chapter 5).

To see the key difference between these two views, consider the case of a professor who devotes a great deal of time to her students. One explanation of the professor's behavior would be that she has a conscious belief about the importance of devoting time to one's students and that she is acting on that belief. This is the type of explanation that Nietzsche wants to reject; it is the mundane analogue of Cornaro's self-understanding,

[11] Conscious perceptions may play a causal role in explaining agency, but self-conscious beliefs do not: see the discussion in Chapter 5, Section 6.1.

according to which it was his "free" choice to follow a certain kind of diet that explained his long life. A second type of explanation would be that the professor is simply the type of person who feels compelled to help her students and that, although she may have various conscious beliefs about how she ought to live, these beliefs have very little impact on the way she actually treats other people. It is this sort of explanation that one frequently finds in Nietzsche's works and that we saw illustrated, in Chapter 5, in Nietzsche's account of Cornaro.

At least at first glance, it may seem that one way to decide between these two types of explanations would be to see whether there were substantial correlations between certain types of conscious attitudes and certain types of behaviors. For example, we could check whether there was a correlation between the degree to which professors believed they were obligated to spend time with their students and the degree to which those professors actually did spend time with their students. After all, it does appear that we would have a certain kind of *prima facie* evidence that attitudes were influencing behavior if we found a substantial correlation here.

It should be clear, however, that this sort of test is not sufficient to settle the question. The mere existence of a correlation plainly does not establish causality. Just as it is possible that people's attitudes influence their behavior, it is possible that people's behavior influences their attitudes. Thus, it might turn out that certain professors just happen to be the kinds of people who spend time with their students (for reasons that have nothing to do with their conscious beliefs) and that these professors then come to have the belief that they have an obligation to spend time with their students as a result of the fact that they are already performing the relevant behavior. Accordingly, we proceed in two steps: first, with the question as to whether conscious attitudes are *correlated* with behavior and second, asking whether conscious attitudes actually *cause* behavior.

Let us start, then, with the issue of correlation. In the early decades of the twentieth century, most researchers simply assumed that attitudes were highly correlated with behavior. It was assumed, for example, that any program that decreased racist attitudes would thereby also decrease racist behavior. This initial assumption was called into question by the influential work of LaPiere (1934). LaPiere went on a long car trip with a Chinese couple. Along the way, he took careful notes about how his companions were treated at each of the hotels and restaurants they visited. Despite the widespread prejudice against Chinese people in America at the time, LaPiere found that he and his companions were generally treated quite well and that they were refused service on only one occasion. Later, he wrote to all 250 hotels and restaurants listed in his notes, asking the employees whether or not they would be willing to serve Chinese guests. Over 90 percent of respondents said that they would not serve Chinese, in spite of the fact that they had just done exactly that. This finding seemed to suggest that attitudes and behavior were not quite as closely linked as had previously been thought.

The ensuing decades saw an enormous profusion of studies testing the degree to which attitudes and behavior were correlated. The results of this initial wave of research were extremely surprising. In almost every domain studied, the correlation between attitudes and behavior was shockingly low. By 1969, Wicker was able to draw on a wide variety of studies for the influential review in which he argued that there was little convincing evidence for a substantial attitude–behavior correlation (Wicker 1969).

Wicker's review served as a challenge to the next generation of researchers. The goal was to find specific circumstances in which attitudes truly were substantially correlated with behavior. As it happened, researchers were quite successful at this task, devising ever more clever ways to create a situation in which attitudes and behavior were correlated. (To give one particularly striking example, it has been shown that behavior is more highly correlated with attitudes when subjects are looking at themselves in a mirror [Carver 1975].) In a summary of this next generation of research, Kraus reviewed eighty-eight studies and showed that the attitude–behavior correlation was explaining, on average, 14 percent of the total variance (Kraus 1995).

As might be expected, there has been a fair amount of debate about whether a correlation of this size should be regarded as large or small (e.g., McGuire 1985; Kraus 1995). But the size of the correlation is not our primary concern here. Our concern is with the question as to whether or not attitudes actually *cause* behavior. If we find, for example, that there is a substantial correlation between attitudes toward a given race and actual behavior toward that race, we still cannot be sure whether the attitudes are causing the behavior, the behavior is causing the attitudes, or some third factor is causing both the attitudes and the behavior.

In fact, systematic experiments suggest that a substantial portion of the observed correlation is due to the impact of behavior on attitudes rather than other way around. For a simple example, consider the results reported in Fendrich (1967). Subjects were (a) given a questionnaire regarding their attitudes toward black people and (b) asked to participate in a meeting of the National Association for the Advancement of Colored People (NAACP), a civil rights group advocating for the interests of black people. The key question was whether there would be any correlation between subjects' attitudes (as measured by the questionnaire) and their behavior (actual participation in the meeting). There were two conditions in the experiment. In one condition, subjects were *first* given the questionnaire and *then* asked to participate in the meeting. In this first condition, there was no significant correlation between attitude and behavior—indicating that, whatever attitude was measured by the questionnaire, that attitude had very little impact on actual attendance at NAACP meetings. The second condition was exactly the same as the first, except that the order of the tasks was reversed: subjects first decided whether or not to attend the meeting and then filled out a questionnaire regarding their attitudes toward black people. In this second condition, there was a significant and substantial correlation between attitude and behavior. The overall pattern of the results thus points to a surprising conclusion. In this experiment at least, it appears that attitudes had very little impact on behavior *but that behavior had a substantial impact on attitudes*. In particular, subjects appeared to be modifying their attitudes toward black people in such a way as to justify a prior decision to attend or not attend a meeting of a civil rights organization.[12]

Fendrich's experiment is just one of the many that have demonstrated the surprising impact of behavior on attitudes. In a typical experiment of this type, psychologists find some way to manipulate subjects into performing a behavior that goes against their pre-existing attitudes. The result—as psychologists have found again and again—is that subjects modify their attitudes to fit the behavior they have been manipulated into performing. The examination of this phenomenon has been a major preoccupation of the field of social psychology, and a number of competing theories have been proposed to explain it (Aronson 1969; Bem 1972; Festinger 1957; Steele 1988). Although there is no clear consensus as yet, the dominant view seems to be that people are motivated to believe that their own behaviors are justified and that they therefore tend to adopt attitudes that justify the behaviors they have already performed.

Given that the correlation between attitudes and behavior is not overwhelmingly high and that a substantial portion of this correlation can be explained in terms of the impact of behavior on attitudes (rather than the other way around), a number of researchers have concluded that attitudes actually have only a very minimal influence on behavior. So, for example, Haidt (2001) has argued that, although people often have conscious attitudes regarding very general moral questions, these attitudes actually have little impact on people's feelings about the rightness or wrongness of specific acts. Perhaps people's feelings about specific acts are derived not from their conscious moral attitudes but rather from a set of non-conscious mental states (Wilson 2002). Thus, it might be thought that the degree to which an individual discriminates against black people is affected, not so much by that individual's conscious attitudes regarding black people in general, as by certain purely non-conscious prejudices over which the person's conscious attitudes have little causal influence.

In light of the empirical data, it seems rather improbable that conscious principles, adopted on Kantian grounds, would actually motivate most people to act. By the same token, though, the empirical evidence does not show that there are *no* moral agents who act on the basis of consciously adopted moral principles. The problem for the Kantian, however, is that there is no reason to think that the class of people (however small) who do act on the basis of consciously chosen principles is coextensive with the class of people who perform actions that otherwise comport with deontological principles, even if they do not act on the basis of those principles. To be sure, such agents may lack the kind of motivation (e.g., respect for the moral law) Kant himself thought morally significant, but they may well be agents whose conduct otherwise manifests respect for the dignity and autonomy of other persons and comports with the categorical imperative. What the evidence from empirical psychology suggests is that

[12] This result correlates well with the finding, discussed in Achen and Bartels (2016), that party identification drives political views rather than political views affecting choice of political party.

Kantians, insofar as they follow Kant in treating motive as morally decisive, are likely to have to treat as immoral a lot of apparently moral individuals because of the largely unrealistic demands of Kant's moral psychology.

4. A Puzzle about Moral Diversity on the Nietzschean View of Moral Psychology

Suppose Nietzsche is right that individuals have a certain psycho-physical package of traits (the person's distinctive type-facts), and that these type-facts play a powerful role in determining one's central behavior and values, a far more powerful role than education or upbringing or conscious choice. Suppose, in short, that the fact *that* one is a so-called "morally good" or "bad" agent is to a large extent explained by one's biological inheritance (the type-facts), and *that* one is not such an agent is similarly explained. This explanation seems to fly in the face of the apparent diversity of moral opinions across cultures. So, for example, most Americans think it is acceptable for a woman to walk down the street with her hair exposed, while in some Islamic countries, people would disagree. Canada and Spain have recognized a legal right to gay marriage—reflecting a kind of moral consensus in those societies—while in the United States, leading political figures have expressed resolute opposition to the morality of such unions. Examples like this could, of course, be multiplied ad nauseam, and it is reasonable to think that they reflect the pervasive influence on moral opinion of non-biological differences, that is, differences in culture and environment of some sort. Surely it is incredible to think that there is a difference in biological "type-facts" that makes people of different cultures differ in their views about gay marriage or women who expose their hair!

Nothing in the preceding argument should be construed as endorsing this latter incredible proposition. As we emphasized earlier in discussing the notion of "heritable" traits, the choice is *not* between "genes" and "environment." Environmental factors *of course* play an important role.[13] The real issue concerns how we individuate the morally relevant attitudes and how we explain them. At a certain level of cultural specificity, one must necessarily recognize that certain "moral" views are not biologically determined: the view that women should not expose their hair in public, for example, is obviously a product of culture and environment. But the crucial question, for our purposes, is what more *general* moral attitude underlies the specific views which manifest environmental and cultural influences. If the Nietzschean view has bite, it must be at this more general level.

[13] Note that our certainty about the importance of culture does not conflict with our doubts about the importance of upbringing. The key question is whether the transmission of culture takes place primarily through *upbringing* (i.e., through the activities of the caregivers who bring us up) or through other sources (peers, television, etc.). The evidence we reviewed earlier suggests that upbringing actually plays a surprisingly small role here.

When Nietzsche observes, for example, in the *Genealogy* that "the earth is the *ascetic planet* par excellence, a nook of discontented, arrogant, and repulsive creatures who could not get rid of a deep displeasure with themselves, with the earth, with all life and who caused themselves as much pain as possible out of pleasure in causing pain" (GM III:11), and then tries to offer an explanation for why this kind of "ascetic ideal" should be so prevalent,[14] he necessarily abstracts away from all the many culturally particular manifestations of asceticism, whether it is Islamic or Orthodox Jewish proscriptions on women's dress and appearance in public, or Mormon prohibitions on drinking alcohol, or Catholic views of "original sin." Nietzsche thinks there is a psychology (and a kind of psycho-biology) of asceticism that is adequate to explaining why "the earth is the ascetic planet," even though the psychological story told will not illuminate the local differences in how the ideal expresses itself. In other words, the suggestion is that each particular ascetic practice is the product of a complex interaction between certain type-facts (which yield a general drive toward asceticism) and certain cultural constructs (which determine the specific form in which this drive will express itself).

Recent work in social and personality psychology lends some support to this basic perspective. Consider the concept of *need for closure* (Kruglanski and Webster 1996). People who are high in need for closure (NFC) feel a strong need to arrive at very definite views. They tend to be intolerant of ambiguity and uncertainty, preferring always to have an answer to the questions at hand. In American culture, high NFC people are more likely to be conservative than liberal (Jost, Glaser, Kruglanski, and Sulloway 2003), more likely to be accountants than artists (Webster and Kruglanski 1994). It seems, however, that high NFC people do not perform the very same kinds of behaviors in all cultures. What one finds is rather that high NFC people tend to believe strongly in the traditional values of whichever culture they grew up in. Thus, high NFC people in America tend to subscribe to traditional American values, whereas high NFC people in China tend to subscribe to traditional Chinese values. Under certain conditions, one therefore finds that high NFC people in China perform exactly the *opposite* sort of behavior from what we find in high NFC people in America (Chiu, Morris, Hong, and Menon 2000). Here we seem to have a case of exactly the pattern described above—a complex interaction between an underlying type-fact (which yields a drive for quick answers to complex questions) and certain features of the cultural context (which determine the specific form in which this drive expresses itself).

Cases like this one illustrate the promise of Nietzschean moral psychology. It is not that we expect to find certain type-facts that are correlated, in all possible cultural contexts, with the very same specific behaviors. Rather, the type-facts serve (along with various other factors) to produce certain basic drives, but the precise form in which these drives express themselves will often be determined in large part by the cultural context.

[14] See the account in Leiter (2002: 254–63) and Leiter (2015a: 203–11).

5. Conclusion

We have been concerned with three rival views in moral psychology—one that emphasizes habits acquired through childhood upbringing, one that emphasizes conscious moral principles, and one that emphasizes heritable psychological traits. Philosophers have devoted considerable time and thought to the first two of these views, and partisans of each of these views have shown great theoretical sophistication in clarifying the relevant concepts and working out the key ethical implications. But this philosophical ingenuity is never accompanied by any empirical evidence showing that the factors under discussion actually play any important role in people's lives, and when one looks to the empirical literature, one finds shockingly little evidence that either childhood upbringing or conscious moral principles have a substantial impact on people's moral behavior. It seems likely, then, that much of the recent work on these issues has been taken up with an attempt to work out the implications of a moral psychology that is not actually instantiated in many real human beings.

By contrast, the third view—the one that we find in Nietzsche and that has been defended at length in this book—garners support from a growing body of empirical evidence. This evidence suggests that heritable psychological traits influence many aspects of people's lives, including their behavior that is the object of moral assessment. Nietzsche complained, with justification, that great philosophers were really advocates for a moral cause they did not want to acknowledge; Nietzsche by contrast, was an advocate for, we might say, an amoral cause that he was quite happy to acknowledge and which actually wins support from all the available empirical evidence. Serious moral psychology going forward will have to be moral psychology with Nietzsche.

Bibliography

References to Nietzsche

Over the many years of writing this volume, I have consulted a variety of English translations by Walter Kaufmann, R.J. Hollingdale, Maudemarie Clark and Alan Swensen, Carol Diethe, and Judith Norman. I have sometimes followed the lead of more than one translator and I have also sometimes made modifications based on Friedrich Nietzsche, *Sämtliche Werke: Kritische Studienausgabe in* 15 *Bänden*, ed. G. Colli and M. Montinari (Berlin: de Gruyter, 1980); where there is no existing English edition, the translation is my own (sometimes with advice from William Leiter). Nietzsche's works are cited as follows, unless otherwise noted: roman numerals refer to major parts or chapters in Nietzsche's works; Arabic numerals refer to sections, not pages. I use the standard abbreviations for Nietzsche's works, as follows: *The Antichrist* (A); *Beyond Good and Evil* (BGE); *The Birth of Tragedy* (BT); *Daybreak* (D); *Ecce Homo* (EH); *The Gay Science* (GS); *Thus Spoke Zarathustra* (Z); *Twilight of the Idols* (TI); *The Will to Power* (WP).

Other References

Achen, Christopher, and Larry Bartels. 2016. *Democracy for Realists.* Princeton, NJ: Princeton University Press.

Ackeren, Marcel van (ed.). 2018. *Philosophy and the Historical Perspective.* Oxford: Oxford University Press.

Alfano, Mark. 2018. "A Schooling in Contempt: Emotions and the Pathos of Distance," in Paul Katsafanas (ed.), *The Nietzschean Mind.* London: Routledge.

Anscombe, Elizabeth. 1958. "Modern Moral Philosophy," *Philosophy* 33: 1–19.

Anscombe, Elizabeth. 1966. "A Note on Mr. Bennett," *Analysis* 26: 208.

Aronson, E. 1969. "The Theory of Cognitive Dissonance: A Current Perspective," in Leonard Berkowitz (ed.), *Advances in Experimental Social Psychology*, Vol. 4. New York: Academic Press.

Awad, Edmond, et al. 2018. "The Moral Machine Experiment," *Nature* 563: 59–64.

Ayer, A.J. 1936. *Language, Truth and Logic.* London: Victor Gollancz Ltd.

Barrett, R.B., and R.F. Gibson (eds.). 1990. *Perspectives on Quine.* Cambridge, MA: Blackwell.

Baumrind, D. 1967. "Child Care Practices Anteceding Three Patterns of Preschool Behavior," *Genetic Psychology Monographs* 75: 43–88.

Baumrind, D. 1991. "The Influence of Parenting Style on Adolescent Competence and Substance Use," *Journal of Early Adolescence* 11: 56–95.

Beiser, Frederick. 2005. *Hegel.* London: Routledge.

Bem, Daryl J. 1972. "Self-Perception Theory," in Leonard Berkowitz (ed.), *Advances in Experimental Social Psychology*, Vol. 6. New York: Academic Press.

Bem, Daryl J., and Andrea Allen. 1974. "On Predicting Some of The People Some of the Time: The Search for Cross-Situational Consistencies in Behavior," *Psychological Review* 81: 506–20.

Berkowitz, Leonard (ed.). 1969. *Advances in Experimental Social Psychology*, Vol. 4. New York: Academic Press.

Berkowitz, Leonard (ed.). 1972. *Advances in Experimental Social Psychology*, Vol. 6. New York: Academic Press.

Berkowitz, Leonard (ed.). 1988. *Advances in Experimental Social Psychology*, Vol. 21. New York: Academic Press.

Bernoulli, Carl Albrecht. 1908. *Franz Overbeck und Friedrich Nietzsche: Eine Freundschaft*. Jena: Eugen Diederichs Verlag.

Berry, Jessica. 2011. *Nietzsche and the Ancient Skeptical Tradition*. New York: Oxford University Press.

Blackburn, Simon. 2011. "Morality Tale," (Review of Parfit [2011]) Financial Times (August 6): www.ft.com/content/2bf7cf30-b9e1-11e0-8171-00144feabdc0.

Bloomfield, Paul. 2004. *Moral Reality*. New York: Oxford University Press.

Bouchard Jr., Thomas. 1994. "Genes, Environment and Personality," *Science* 264: 1700–1.

Boyd, Richard. 1988. "How to be a Moral Realist," in Geoffrey Sayre-McCord (ed.), *Essays on Moral Realism*. Ithaca, NY: Cornell University Press.

Brady, Michael S. (ed.). 2010. *New Waves in Metaethics*. Basingstoke: Palgrave.

Brennan, Tad. 2003. "Stoic Moral Psychology," in Brad Inwood (ed.), *The Cambridge Companion to the Stoics*. Cambridge: Cambridge University Press.

Brink, David O. 1989. *Moral Realism and the Foundations of Ethics*. Cambridge: Cambridge University Press.

Brobjer, Thomas. 2008. *Nietzsche's Philosophical Context: An Intellectual Biography* Urbana, IL: University of Illinois Press.

Büchner, Ludwig. 1870. *Force and Matter*, trans. J.G. Collingwood. London: Trubner.

Carver, C. S. 1975. "Physical Aggression as a Function of Objective Self-Awareness and Attitudes toward Punishment," *Journal of Experimental Social Psychology* 11: 510–19.

Chiu, C.Y., M.W. Morris, Y.Y. Hong, and T. Menon. 2000. "Motivated Cultural Cognition: The Impact of Implicit Cultural Theories on Dispositional Attribution Varies as a Function of Need for Closure," *Journal of Personality and Social Psychology* 78: 247–59.

Christensen, David. 2007. "The Epistemology of Disagreement: The Good News," *Philosophical Review* 116: 187–217.

Clark, Maudemarie. 1990. *Nietzsche on Truth and Philosophy*. Cambridge: Cambridge University Press.

Clark, Maudemarie, and David Dudrick. 2007. "Nietzsche and Moral Objectivity: The Development of Nietzsche's Metaethics," in Brian Leiter and Neil Sinhababu (eds.), *Nietzsche and Morality*. Oxford: Oxford University Press.

Clark, Maudemarie, and David Dudrick. 2009. "Nietzsche on the Will: An Analysis of BGE 19," in Ken Gemes and Simon May (eds.), *Nietzsche on Freedom and Autonomy*. Oxford: Oxford University Press.

Clark, Maudemarie, and David Dudrick. 2012. *The Soul of Nietzsche's* Beyond Good and Evil. Cambridge: Cambridge University Press.

Clark, Maudemarie, and Brian Leiter. 1997. "Introduction," in *Nietzsche's Daybreak*. Cambridge: Cambridge University Press.

Clarke-Doane, Justin. 2014. "Moral Epistemology: The Mathematics Analogy," *Noûs* 48: 238–55.

Cloninger, C.R., S. Sigvardsson, M. Bohman, and A. Knorring. 1982. "Predisposition to Petty Criminality in Swedish Adoptees," *Archives of General Psychiatry* 39: 1242–7.

Cohen, Joshua. 1997. "The Arc of the Moral Universe," *Philosophy & Public Affairs* 26: 91–134.
Colquhoun, David. 2014. "An Investigation of the False Discovery Rate and the Misinterpretation of P-Values," *Royal Society Open Science* (November 19): http://rsos.royalsocietypublishing.org/content/1/3/140216.
Cooper, John M. 1975. *Reason and Human Good in Aristotle*. Cambridge, MA: Harvard University Press. Page references are to the reprint edition (Indianapolis, IN: Hackett, 1986).
Crowe, R. 1974. "An Adoption Study of Antisocial Personality," *Archives of General Psychiatry* 31: 785–91.
Cushman, Fiery, Liane Young, and Joshua Greene. 2010. "Multi-System Moral Psychology," in John M. Doris and the Moral Psychology Research Group (eds.), *The Moral Psychology Handbook*. Oxford: Oxford University Press.
Darley, John. M., and C. Daniel Batson. 1973. "'From Jerusalem to Jericho': A Study of Situational and Dispositional Variables in Helping Behavior." *Journal of Personality and Social Psychology* 27: 100–08.
Deater-Deckard, K., and R. Plomin. 1999. "An Adoption Study of the Etiology of Teacher Reports of Externalizing Problems in Middle Childhood," *Child Development* 70: 144–54.
Deigh, John. 1994. "Cognitivism in the Theory of the Emotions," *Ethics* 104: 824–54.
Deigh, John. 1996. *The Sources of Moral Agency: Essays in Moral Psychology and Freudian Theory*. Cambridge: Cambridge University Press.
Della Rocca, Michael. 2013. "The Taming of Philosophy," in Mogens Laerke, Justin E. Smith, and Eric Schliesser (eds.), *Philosophy and its History: Aims and Methods in the Study of Early Modern Philosophy*. New York: Oxford University Press.
Dodds, E.R. 1959. "Socrates, Callicles, and Nietzsche," in *Plato's Gorgias*. Oxford: Clarendon Press.
Doris, John M. 2002. *Lack of Character: Personality and Moral Behavior*. Cambridge: Cambridge University Press.
Doris, John M., and Alexandra Plakias. 2007. "How to Argue about Disagreement: Evaluative Diversity and Moral Realism," in Walter Sinnott-Armstrong (ed.), *Moral Psychology, Volume 2: The Cognitive Science of Morality: Intuition and Diversity*. Cambridge, MA: MIT Press.
Doris, John M. and the Moral Psychology Research Group (eds.). 2010. *The Moral Psychology Handbook*. Oxford: Oxford University Press.
Dries, Manuel (ed.). 2017. *Nietzsche on Consciousness and the Embodied Mind*. Berlin/Boston: de Gruyter.
Duhem, Pierre. 1914. *La Théorie Physique: Son Objet et sa Structure*. Paris: Marcel Riviera & Cie.
Dworkin, Ronald. 1996. "Objectivity and Truth: You'd Better Believe It," *Philosophy & Public Affairs* 25: 87–139.
Edelbrock, C., R.D. Rende, R. Plomin, and L.A. Thompson. 1995. "A Twin Study of Competence and Problem Behavior in Childhood and Early Adolescence," *Journal of Child Psychology and Psychiatry* 36: 775–85.
Ekman, Paul, and W.V. Friesen. 1989. "The Argument and Evidence about Universals in Facial Expressions," in H.L. Wagner and A. Manstead (eds.), *Handbook of Social Psychophysiology*. New York: John Wiley & Sons.
Eley, Thalia C., Paul Lichtenstein, and Jim Stevenson. 1999. "Sex Differences in the Etiology of Aggressive and Nonaggressive Antisocial Behavior: Results from Two Twin Studies," *Child Development* 70: 155–68.

Emden, Christian. 2014. *Nietzsche's Naturalism: Philosophy and the Life Sciences in the Nineteenth Century*. Cambridge: Cambridge University Press.

Enoch, David. 2006. "Agency, Shmagency: Why Normativity Won't Come from What is Constitutive of Agency," *Philosophical Review* 115: 169–98.

Enoch, David. 2009. "How is Moral Disagreement a Problem for Realism?" *The Journal of Ethics* 13: 15–50.

Enoch, David. 2010. "Shmagency Revisited," in Michael S. Brady (ed.), *New Waves in Metaethics*. Basingstoke: Palgrave.

Epstein, Seymour. 1979. "The Stability of Behavior: On Predicting Most of the People Much of the Time," *Journal of Personality and Social Psychology* 37: 1097–126.

Fechner, Gustav Theodor. 1848. "Über das Lustprinzip des Handelns," *Zeitschrift für Philosophie und philosophische Kritik* 19: 163–94.

Feingold, Alan. 1992. "Good-Looking People Are Not What We Think," *Psychological Bulletin* 111: 304–41.

Fendrich, James. 1967. "A Study of the Association among Verbal Attitudes, Commitment and Overt Behavior in Different Experimental Situations," *Social Forces*, 45: 347–55.

Festinger, Leon. 1957. *A Theory of Cognitive Dissonance*. Stanford, CA: Stanford University Press.

Festinger, Leon, and James M. Carlsmith. 1959. "Cognitive Consequences of Forced Compliance," *Journal of Abnormal and Social Psychology* 58: 203–10.

Fieve, R.R., D. Rosenthal, and H. Brill (eds.). 1975. *Genetic Research in Psychiatry*. Baltimore, MD: Johns Hopkins University Press.

Flanagan, Owen. 1991. *Varieties of Moral Personality*. Cambridge, MA: Harvard University Press.

Fodor, Jerry. 1975. "Introduction: Two Kinds of Reductionism," in *The Language of Thought: a New Direction*. Cambridge, MA: Harvard University Press.

Foot, Phillipa. 1973. "Nietzsche: The Revaluation of Values," in Robert Solomon (ed.), *Nietzsche: A Collection of Critical Essays*. South Bend, IN: University of Notre Dame Press.

Foot, Phillipa. 1991. "Nietzsche's Immoralism," in *New York Review of Books* 38/11: 18–22.

Förster-Nietzsche, Elisabeth. 1907. *Das Nietzsche-Archiv, seine Freunde und seine Feinde*. Berlin: Marquardt.

Forster, Michael N. 2017. "Moralities are a Sign-Language of the Affects," *Inquiry* 60: 165–88.

Fowles, Christopher. 2019. "Nietzsche on Conscious and Unconscious Thought," *Inquiry* (forthcoming).

Frankfurt, Harry. 1971. "Freedom of the Will and the Concept of a Person," reprinted in Gary Watson (ed.), 2003. *Free Will, 2nd edition (Oxford Readings in Philosophy)*. New York: Oxford University Press.

Frede, Michael. 2011. *A Free Will: Origins of the Idea in Ancient Thought*. Berkeley, CA: University of California Press.

Funder, D.C., and D.J. Ozer. 1983. "Behavior as a Function of the Situation," *Journal of Personality and Social Psychology* 44:107–12.

Gemes, Ken, and Simon May (eds.). 2009. *Nietzsche on Freedom and Autonomy*. Oxford: Oxford University Press.

Gemes, Ken. 2009. "Nietzsche on Free Will, Autonomy, and the Sovereign Individual," in Ken Gemes and Simon May (eds.), *Nietzsche on Freedom and Autonomy*. Oxford: Oxford University Press.

Gemes, Ken, and Christopher Janaway. 2005. "Naturalism and Value in Nietzsche," *Philosophy and Phenomenological Research* 71: 729–40.

Gemes, Ken, and John Richardson (eds.). 2013. *The Oxford Handbook of Nietzsche*. Oxford: Oxford University Press.
Gendler, Tamar Szabó, and John Hawthorne (eds.). 2005. *Oxford Studies in Epistemology*, Volume 1. Oxford: Oxford University Press.
Goldie, Peter. 2002. *The Emotions: A Philosophical Exploration*. Oxford: Clarendon Press.
Greene, Joshua. 2007. "The Secret Joke of Kant's Soul," in Walter Sinnott-Armstrong (ed.), *Moral Psychology, Volume 3: The Neuroscience of Morality: Emotion, Disease, and Development*. Cambridge, MA: MIT Press.
Gregory, Frederick. 1977. *Scientific Materialism in Nineteenth-Century Germany*. Dordrech: D. Reidel.
Guthrie, W.K.C. 1971. *The Sophists*. Cambridge: Cambridge University Press.
Guyer, Paul. (ed.). 1992. *The Cambridge Companion to Kant*. Cambridge: Cambridge University Press.
Haddock, Geoffrey, Gregory R. Maio, Karin Arnold, and Thomas Huskinson. 2008. "Should Persuasion Be Affective or Cognitive? The Moderating Effects of Need for Affect and Need for Cognition," *Personality and Social Psychology Bulletin* 34: 769–78.
Haidt, Jonathan. 2001. "The Emotional Dog and its Rational Tail: A Social Intuitionist Approach to Moral Judgment," *Psychological Review* 108: 814–34.
Harman, Gilbert. 1977. *The Nature of Morality*. New York: Oxford University Press.
Harman, Gilbert. 1999. "Moral Philosophy Meets Social Psychology: Virtue Ethics and the Fundamental Attribution Error," *Proceedings of the Aristotelian Society* 99: 315–31.
Harris, Judith Rich. 1995. "Where is the Child's Environment? A Group Socialization Theory of Development," *Psychological Review* 102: 458–89.
Harris, Judith Rich. 1998. *The Nurture Assumption: Why Children Turn Out the Way They Do*. New York: Free Press.
Hartshorne, H., and M.A. May. 1928. *Studies in Deceit*. New York: Macmillan.
Heidegger, Martin. 1982. *Nietzsche, Volume IV: Nihilism*, trans. D.F. Krell. San Francisco, CA: Harper & Row.
Hempel, Carl. 1965. *Aspects of Scientific Explanation and other Essays in the Philosophy of Science*. New York: Free Press.
Hetherington, E. Mavis (ed.). 1983. *Handbook of Child Psychology, Vol. 4: Socialization, Personality, and Social Development*. New York: Wiley.
Hoffman, Lois. 1991. "The Influence of the Family Environment on Personality: Accounting for Sibling Differences," *Psychological Bulletin* 110: 187–203.
Hollingdale, R. J. 1985. *Nietzsche: The Man and his Philosophy*. London: Ark Paperbacks.
Holton, Richard. 2004. "Review of Daniel Wegner, The Illusion of Conscious Will," *Mind* 113: 218–21.
Huddleston, Andrew. 2014. "Nietzsche's Meta-Axiology: Against the Sceptical Readings," *British Journal for the History of Philosophy* 22: 322–42.
Huddleston, Andrew. 2017. "Normativity and the Will to Power: Challenges for a Nietzschean Constitutivism," *Journal of Nietzsche Studies* 47: 435–56.
Hunt, Lester. 1991. *Nietzsche and the Origin of Virtue*. London: Routledge.
Hussain, Nadeem. 2011. "The Role of Life in the Genealogy," in Simon May (ed.), *Nietzsche's On the Genealogy of Morality: A Critical Guide*. Cambridge: Cambridge University Press.
Hussain, Nadeem. 2013. "Nietzsche's Metaethical Stance," in Ken Gemes and John Richardson. (eds.), *The Oxford Handbook of Nietzsche*. Oxford: Oxford University Press.

Inwood, Brad (ed.). 2003. *The Cambridge Companion to the Stoics*. Cambridge: Cambridge University Press.

Janaway, Christopher (ed.). 1998. *Willingness and Nothingness: Schopenhauer as Nietzsche's Educator*. Oxford: Oxford University Press.

Janaway, Christopher. 2007. *Beyond Selflessness: Reading Nietzsche's Genealogy*. Oxford: Oxford University Press.

Janaway, Christopher. 2017. "Attitudes to Suffering: Parfit and Nietzsche," *Inquiry* 60: 66–95.

Janaway, Christopher, and Simon Robertson (eds.). 2012. *Nietzsche, Naturalism & Normativity*. Oxford: Oxford University Press.

Jaspers, Karl. 1965. *Nietzsche: An Introduction to the Understanding of His Philosophical Activity*, trans. C. Wallraff and F. Schmitz. South Bend, IN: Regnery/Gateway Inc.

Jech, Thomas. 2002. "Set Theory," in E. Zalta (ed.), Stanford Encyclopedia of Philosophy: http://plato.stanford.edu/entries/set-theory/.

Jenkins, Scott. 2008. Review of Leiter & Sinhababu (2007), *Notre Dame Philosophical Reviews* (January 3): https://ndpr.nd.edu/news/nietzsche-and-morality/.

Jones, Edward E., David E. Kanouse, Harold H. Kelley, Richard E. Nisbett, Stuart Valins, and Bernard Weiner (eds). 1972. *Attribution: Perceiving the Causes of Behavior*. Morristown, NJ: General Learning Press.

Jones, Edward E., and Richard. E. Nisbett. 1972. "The Actor and the Observer: Divergent Perceptions of the Causes of Behavior," in Edward E. Jones, David E. Kanouse, Harold H. Kelley, Richard E. Nisbett, Stuart Valins, and Bernard Weiner (eds). 1972. *Attribution: Perceiving the Causes of Behavior*. Morristown, NJ: General Learning Press.

Jost, J.T., J. Glaser, A.W. Kruglanski, and F.J. Sulloway. 2003. "Political Conservatism as Motivated Social Cognition," *Psychological Bulletin* 129: 339–75.

Kail, Peter. 2007. *Projection and Realism in Hume's Philosophy*. Oxford: Oxford University Press.

Kail, Peter. 2009. "Nietzsche and Hume: Naturalism and Explanation," *Journal of Nietzsche Studies* 37: 5–22.

Kamtekar, Rachana. 2004. "Situationism and Virtue Ethics on the Content of Our Character," *Ethics*, 114: 458–91.

Kane, Robert. 2005. *A Contemporary Introduction to Free Will*. Oxford: Oxford University Press.

Katsafanas, Paul. 2013a. *Agency and the Foundations of Ethics: Nietzschean Constitutivism*. Oxford: Oxford University Press.

Katsafanas, Paul. 2013b. "Nietzsche's Philosophical Psychology," in Ken Gemes and John Richardson (eds.), *The Oxford Handbook of Nietzsche*. Oxford: Oxford University Press.

Katsafanas, Paul. 2016. *The Nietzschean Self: Moral Psychology, Agency, and the Unconscious*. Oxford: Oxford University Press.

Katsafanas, Paul. (ed.). 2018. *The Nietzschean Mind*. London: Routledge.

Kaufmann, Walter. 1974. *Nietzsche: Philosopher, Psychologist, Antichrist*, 4th edition. Princeton, NJ: Princeton University Press.

Kelly, Thomas. 2005. "The Epistemic Significance of Disagreement," in Tamar Szabó Gendler and John Hawthorne (eds.), *Oxford Studies in Epistemology*, Volume 1. Oxford: Oxford University Press.

Kim, Jaegwon. 1988. "What is Naturalized Epistemology?" *Philosophical Perspectives* 2: 381–405.

Kitcher, Philip. 1993. *The Advancement of Science*. New York: Oxford University Press.

Knobe, Joshua, and Brian Leiter. 2007. "The Case for Nietzschean Moral Psychology," in Brian Leiter and Neil Sinhababu (eds.), *Nietzsche and Morality*. Oxford: Oxford University Press.

Kögel, Fritz. 1893. "Friedrich Nietzsche. Ein ungedrucktes Vorwort zur Götzendämmerung," *Das Magazin für Literatur* 62: 702–4.

Korsgaard, Christine. 1996. *Creating the Kingdom of Ends*. Cambridge: Cambridge University Press.

Korsgaard, Christine. 2012. Interview with Richard Marshall. "Treating People as Ends in Themselves," *3AM* MAGAZINE: www.3ammagazine.com/3am/treating-people-as-ends-in-themselves/.

Kraus, Stephen. 1995. "Attitudes and the Prediction of Behavior: A Meta-Analysis of the Empirical Literature," *Personality and Social Psychology Bulletin* 21: 58–75.

Kraut, Richard. 2001. "Aristotle's Ethics," in E. Zalta (ed.), *The Stanford Encyclopedia of Philosophy*: http://plato.stanford.edu/entries/aristotle-ethics/.

Kruglanski, A.W., and D.M. Webster. 1996. "Motivated Closing of the Mind: 'Seizing' and 'Freezing.'" *Psychological Review* 103: 263–83.

Kusch, Martin. 1995. *Psychologism: A Case Study in the Sociology of Philosophical Knowledge*. London: Routledge.

Laerke, Mogens, Justin E. Smith, and Eric Schliesser (eds.). 2013. *Philosophy and its History: Aims and Methods in the Study of Early Modern Philosophy*. New York: Oxford University Press.

Lange, Friedrich. 1950. *History of Materialism*, 2nd book, trans. E.C. Thomas. New York: Humanities Press. Org. published in German in 1865.

LaPiere, R. 1934. "Attitudes vs. Actions," *Social Forces* 13: 230–7.

LeDoux, Joseph. 1998. *The Emotional Brain: The Mysterious Underpinnings of Emotional Life*. New York: Simon & Schuster.

Leiter, Brian. 1994. "Perspectivism in Nietzsche's Genealogy of Morals," in Richard Schacht (ed.), *Nietzsche, Genealogy, Morality*. Berkeley, CA: University of California Press.

Leiter, Brian. 1997. "Nietzsche and the Morality Critics," *Ethics* 107: 250–85.

Leiter, Brian. 1998. "The Paradox of Fatalism and Self-Creation in Nietzsche," in Christopher Janaway (ed.), *Willingness and Nothingness: Schopenhauer as Nietzsche's Educator*. Oxford: Oxford University Press.

Leiter, Brian. 2000. "Nietzsche's Metaethics: Against the Privilege Readings," *European Journal of Philosophy* 8: 277–97.

Leiter, Brian. 2001. "Moral Facts and Best Explanations," *Social Philosophy & Policy* 18: 79–101. Reprinted in Leiter (2007b) (page citations are to the reprinted version).

Leiter, Brian. 2002. *Nietzsche on Morality*. London: Routledge.

Leiter, Brian. 2007a. "Nietzsche's Theory of the Will," *Philosophers' Imprint* 7: 1–15.

Leiter, Brian. 2007b. *Naturalizing Jurisprudence: Essays on American Legal Realism and Naturalism in Legal Philosophy*. Oxford: Oxford University Press.

Leiter, Brian. 2013a. "Nietzsche's Naturalism Reconsidered," in Ken Gemes and John Richardson (eds.), *The Oxford Handbook of Nietzsche*. Oxford: Oxford University Press.

Leiter, Brian. 2013b. "The Boundaries of the Moral (and Legal) Community," *Alabama Law Review* 64: 511–31.

Leiter, Brian. 2013c. "Moralities are a Sign-Language of the Affects," *Social Philosophy & Policy*, 30: 237–58.

Leiter, Brian. 2014. "Moral Skepticism and Moral Disagreement in Nietzsche," in Russ Shafer-Landau (ed.), Oxford Studies in Metaethics, Volume 9. New York: Oxford University Press.

Leiter, Brian. 2015a. *Nietzsche on Morality*, 2nd edition. London: Routledge.

Leiter, Brian. 2015b. "Normativity for Naturalists," *Philosophical Issues: A Supplement to Noûs* 25: 65–79.

Leiter, Brian. 2017. "Nietzsche's Naturalism and Nineteenth-Century Biology," *Journal of Nietzsche Studies* 48: 71–82.

Leiter, Brian. 2018. "The History of Philosophy Reveals that 'Great' Philosophy is Disguised Moral Advocacy: A Nietzschean Case Against the Socratic Canon in Philosophy," in Marcel van Ackeren (ed.), *Philosophy and the Historical Perspective*. Oxford: Oxford University Press.

Leiter, Brian, and Neil Sinhababu (eds.). 2007. *Nietzsche and Morality*. Oxford: Oxford University Press.

Lindzey, G., and E. Aronson (eds.). 1985. *The Handbook of Social Psychology*. New York: Random House.

Loeb, Don. 1998. "Moral Realism and the Argument from Disagreement," *Philosophical Studies* 90: 281–303.

Loehlin, J. C. 1992. *Genes and Environment in Personality and Development*. Newberry Park, CA: Sage.

MacIntyre, Alasdair. 1981. *After Virtue*. Notre Dame, IN: University of Notre Dame Press.

Maccoby, E. E., and J.A. Martin. 1983. "Socialization in the Context of the Family: Parent-Child Interaction," in E. Mavis Hetherington (ed.), *Handbook of Child Psychology, Vol. 4: Socialization, Personality, and Social Development*. New York: Wiley.

Mackie, John. 1977. *Ethics: Inventing Right and Wrong*. London: Penguin.

Magnus, Bernd. 1988. "The Use and Abuse of The Will to Power," in Robert Solomon and Kathleen Higgins (eds.), *Reading Nietzsche*. New York: Oxford University Press.

May, Simon (ed.). 2011. *Nietzsche's On the Genealogy of Morality: A Critical Guide*. Cambridge: Cambridge University Press.

McGuire, W. J. 1985. "Attitudes and Attitude Change," in G. Lindzey and E. Aronson (eds.), *The Handbook of Social Psychology*. New York: Random House.

McKenna, Michael, and Derk Pereboom. 2016. *Free Will: A Contemporary Introduction*. London: Routledge.

Mele, Alfred. 2006. *Free Will and Luck*. Oxford: Oxford University Press.

Merritt, Maria. 2000. "Virtue Ethics and Situationist Personality Psychology," *Ethical Theory and Moral Practice* 3: 365–83.

Miles, Thomas. 2007. "On Nietzsche's Ideal of the Sovereign Individual," *International Studies in Philosophy* 39: 5–25.

Milgram, Stanley. 1975. *Obedience to Authority*. New York: Harper Colophon.

Mill, John Stuart. 1979. *Utilitarianism*. Indianapolis, IN: Hackett. Org. published in 1861.

Mischel, Walter. 1968. *Personality and Assessment*. New York: Wiley.

Montinari, Mazzino. 1982. "Nietzsches Nachlass von 1885 bis 1888 oder Textkritik und Wille zur Macht," in *Nietzsche Lesen*. Berlin: de Gruyter.

Morgan, George Allen. 1941. *What Nietzsche Means*. Cambridge, MA: Harvard University Press.

Müller-Lauter, Wolfgang. 1971. "Nietzsches Lehre vom Willen zur Macht," *Nietzsche-Studien* 3: 1–61.

Nagel, Thomas. 1986. *The View from Nowhere*. New York: Oxford University Press.

Nagel, Thomas. 1997. *The Last Word*. New York: Oxford University Press.

Nehamas, Alexander. 1985. *Nietzsche: Life as Literature*. Cambridge, MA: Harvard University Press.

Nichols, Shaun. 2004. *Sentimental Rules: On the Natural Foundations of Moral Judgment*. New York: Oxford University Press.

Oakley, David A., and Peter W. Halligan. 2017. "Chasing the Rainbow: The Non-Conscious Nature of Being," *Frontiers in Psychology* 8: 1924.

Owen, David, and Aaron Ridley. 2003. "On Fate," *International Studies in Philosophy* 35: 63–78.

Parfit, Derek. 2011a. *On What Matters, Volume 1*. Oxford: Oxford University Press.

Parfit, Derek. 2011b. *On What Matters, Volume 2*. Oxford: Oxford University Press.

Paul, Ellen F., Fred D. Miller, and Jeffrey Paul (eds.). 1990. *Foundations of Moral and Political Philosophy*. Oxford: Basil Blackwell.

Pereboom, Derk. 2001. *Living Without Free Will*. Cambridge: Cambridge University Press.

Plomin, Robert, and Denise Daniels. 1987. "Why are Children in the Same Family So Different from One Another?" *Behavioral & Brain Sciences* 10: 1–16.

Poellner, Peter. 2009. "Nietzschean Freedom," in Ken Gemes and Simon May (eds.), *Nietzsche on Freedom and Autonomy*. Oxford: Oxford University Press.

Poellner, Peter. 2012. "Aestheticist Ethics," in Christopher Janaway and Simon Robertson (eds.), *Nietzsche, Naturalism & Normativity*. Oxford: Oxford University Press.

Prinz, Jesse. 2007. *The Emotional Construction of Morals*. Oxford: Oxford University Press.

Prinz, Jesse, and Shaun Nichols. 2010. "Moral Emotions," in John M. Doris and the Moral Psychology Research Group (eds.), *The Moral Psychology Handbook*. Oxford: Oxford University Press.

Putnam, Hilary. 2004. *The Collapse of the Fact/Value Dichotomy and Other Essays*. Cambridge, MA: Harvard University Press.

Quine, W.V.O. 1951. "Two Dogmas of Empiricism," *The Philosophical Review* 60: 20–43.

Quine, W.V.O. 1975. "On Empirically Equivalent Systems of the World," *Erkenntnis* 9: 313–28.

Quine, W.V.O. 1981. *Theories and Things*. Cambridge, MA: Harvard University Press.

Quine, W.V.O. 1990. "Three Indeterminacies," in R.B. Barrett and R.F. Gibson. (eds.), *Perspectives on Quine*. Cambridge, MA: Blackwell.

Quine, W.V.O. and Joseph Ullian. 1978. *The Web of Belief*, 2nd edition. New York: Random House.

Railton, Peter. 1986a. "Facts and Values," *Philosophical Topics* 14: 5–31.

Railton, Peter. 1986b. "Moral Realism," *Philosophical Review* 95: 163–207.

Railton, Peter. 1990. "Naturalism and Prescriptivity," in Ellen F. Paul, Fred D. Miller, and Jeffrey Paul (eds.), *Foundations of Moral and Political Philosophy*. Oxford: Basil Blackwell.

Riccardi, Mattia. 2015. "Inner Opacity: Nietzsche on Introspection and Agency," *Inquiry* 58: 221–43.

Riccardi, Mattia. 2017. "Nietzsche on the Superficiality of Consciousness," in Manuel Dries (ed.), *Nietzsche on Consciousness and the Embodied Mind*. Berlin/Boston: de Gruyter.

Richardson, John. 1996. *Nietzsche's System*. Oxford: Oxford University Press.

Richardson, John. 2009. "Nietzsche's Freedoms," in Ken Gemes and Simon May (eds.), *Nietzsche on Freedom and Autonomy*. Oxford: Oxford University Press.

Robertson, Simon. 2017. "Rescuing Nietzsche from Constitutivism," *Journal of Philosophical Research* 42: 353–77.

Rorty, Richard. 1989. *Contingency, Irony and Solidarity*. Cambridge: Cambridge University Press.

Rosenthal, David. 2008. "Consciousness and Its Function," *Neuropsychologia* 46: 829–40.

Ross, Lee, and Richard E. Nisbett. 1991. *The Person and the Situation: Perspectives of Social Psychology*. New York: McGraw Hill.

Rutherford, Donald. 2011. "Freedom as a Philosophical Ideal: Nietzsche and his Antecedents," *Inquiry* 54: 512–40.

Sabini, John, and Maury Silver. 2005. "Lack of Character? Situationism Critiqued," *Ethics* 115: 535–62.

Sandis, Constantine. 2011. "Review of On What Matters, Volumes I and II," *The Times Higher Education* (June 9): www.timeshighereducation.co.uk/416411.article.

Sayre-McCord, Geoffrey (ed.). 1988. *Essays on Moral Realism*. Ithaca, NY: Cornell University Press.

Scanlon, T.M. 2014. *Being Realistic about Reasons*. Oxford: Oxford University Press.

Schacht, Richard. 1983. *Nietzsche*. London: Routledge & Kegan Paul.

Schacht, Richard (ed.). 1994. *Nietzsche, Genealogy, Morality*. Berkeley, CA: University of California Press.

Schmitz, S., D.W. Fulker, and D.A. Mrazek. 1995. "Problem Behavior in Early and Middle Childhood: An Initial Behavior Genetic Analysis," *Journal of Child Psychology and Psychiatry* 36: 1443–58.

Schnädelbach, Herbert. 1983. *Philosophy in Germany: 1831–1933*, trans. E. Matthews. Cambridge: Cambridge University Press.

Schneewind, J.B. 1992. "Autonomy, Obligation, and Virtue: An Overview of Kant's Moral Philosophy," in Paul Guyer (ed.), *The Cambridge Companion to Kant*. Cambridge: Cambridge University Press.

Schopenhauer, Arthur. 1985. *On the Freedom of the Will*, trans. K. Kolenda. Oxford: Blackwell. Org. published in German in 1839.

Schroeder, Mark. 2008. *Being For: Evaluating the Semantic Program of Expressivism*. Oxford: Oxford University Press.

Schroeder, Mark. 2009. "Hybrid Expressivism: Virtues and Vices," *Ethics* 119: 257–309.

Schroeder, Mark. 2011. Review of Derek Parfit's On What Matters, Volume 1 and 2, Notre Dame Philosophical Reviews (August 1): http://ndpr.nd.edu/news/25393-on-what-matters-volumes-1-and-2/.

Schroeder, Timothy, Adina L. Roskies, and Shaun Nichols. 2010. "Moral Motivation," in John M. Doris and the Moral Psychology Research Group (eds.), *The Moral Psychology Handbook*. Oxford: Oxford University Press.

Schulsinger, F. 1972. "Psychopathy: Heredity and Environment," *International Journal of Mental Health* 1: 190–206.

Shafer-Landau, Russ. 2005. *Moral Realism: A Defence*. Oxford: Oxford University Press.

Shafer-Landau, Russ (ed.). 2014. *Oxford Studies in Metaethics, Volume 9*. New York: Oxford University Press.

Silk, Alex. 2015. "Nietzschean Constructivism: Ethics and Metaethics for All and None," *Inquiry* 58: 244–80.

Sinhababu, Neil. 2007. "Vengeful Thinking," in Brian Leiter and Neil Sinhababu. (eds.), *Nietzsche and Morality*. Oxford: Oxford University Press.

Sinhababu, Neil. 2009. "The Humean Theory of Motivation Reformulated and Defended," *Philosophical Review* 118: 465–500.
Sinnott-Armstrong, Walter. (ed.). 2007a. *Moral Psychology, Volume 2: The Cognitive Science of Morality: Intuition and Diversity*. Cambridge, MA: MIT Press.
Sinnott-Armstrong, Walter. (ed.). 2007b. *Moral Psychology, Volume 3: The Neuroscience of Morality: Emotion, Disease, and Development*. Cambridge, MA: MIT Press.
Smart, J.J.C. 1973. "An Outline of a System of Utilitarian Ethics," in B. Williams and J.J.C. Smart, *Utilitarianism: For and Against*. New York: Cambridge University Press.
Smith, Robin. 2007. "Aristotle's Logic," in E. Zalta (ed.), Stanford Encyclopedia of Philosophy (December 14): http://plato.stanford.edu/entries/aristotle-logic/.
Solomon, Robert (ed.). 1973. *Nietzsche: A Collection of Critical Essays*. South Bend, IN: University of Notre Dame Press.
Solomon, Robert and Higgins, Kathleen (eds.). 1988. *Reading Nietzsche*. New York: Oxford University Press.
Sommers, Tamler. 2007. "The Objective Attitude," *The Philosophical Quarterly* 57: 321–41.
Sosa, David. 2001. "Pathetic Ethics," in B. Leiter (ed.), *Objectivity in Law and Morals*. Cambridge: Cambridge University Press.
Sreenivasan, Gopal. 2002. "Errors about Errors: Virtue Theory and Trait Attribution," *Mind* 111: 47–68.
Steele, C. M. 1988. "The Psychology of Self-Affirmation: Sustaining the Integrity of the Self," in Leonard Berkowitz (ed.), *Advances in Experimental Social Psychology*, Vol. 21. New York: Academic Press.
Stegmaier, Werner. 2012. *Nietzsches Befreiung der Philosophie: Kontextuelle Interpretation des V. Buchs der "Fröhlichen Wissenschaft."* Berlin: de Gruyter.
Stevenson, Charles. 1938. "Persuasive Definitions," *Mind* 47: 331–50.
Stich, Stephen. 1978. "Could Man Be an Irrational Animal?" Reprinted in Stephen Stich. 2012. *Collected Papers, Volume 2: Knowledge, Rationality, and Morality, 1978–2010*. New York: Oxford University Press.
Stich, Stephen. 2012. *Collected Papers, Volume 2: Knowledge, Rationality, and Morality, 1978–2010*. New York: Oxford University Press.
Strawson, Galen. 1994. "The Impossibility of Moral Responsibility," *Philosophical Studies* 75: 5–24.
Street, Sharon. 2006. "A Darwinian Dilemma for Realist Theories of Value," *Philosophical Studies* 127:109–66.
Stroud, Barry. 1977. *Hume*. London: Routledge.
Thucydides. *History of the Peloponnesian War*, in [1993] *On Justice, Power and Human Nature*, trans. P. Woodruff. Indianapolis, IN: Hackett.
Vaihinger, Hans. 1876. *Hartman, Dühring und Lange: Zur Geschichte der deutschen Philosophie im XIX. Jahrhundert; ein kritischer Essay*. Iserlohn: J. Baedeker.
Velleman, David. 1992. "What Happens When Someone Acts?" *Mind* 101: 461–81.
Vitzthum, Richard C. 1995. *Materialism: An Affirmative History*. Amherst, NY: Prometheus Books.
Wagner, H.L., and A. Manstead (eds.). 1989. *Handbook of Social Psychophysiology*. New York: John Wiley & Sons.

Watson, Gary. 1975. "Free Agency," Reprinted in Gary Watson (ed.). 2003. *Free Will, 2nd edition (Oxford Readings in Philosophy)*. New York: Oxford University Press.

Watson, Gary. 1996. "Two Faces of Responsibility," reprinted in Gary Watson 2004. *Agency and Answerability: Selected Essays*. Oxford: Clarendon Press.

Watson, Gary (ed.). 2003. *Free Will, 2nd edition (Oxford Readings in Philosophy)*. New York: Oxford University Press.

Watson, Gary. 2004. *Agency and Answerability: Selected Essays*. Oxford: Clarendon Press.

Webster, D.M., and A.W. Kruglanski. 1994. "Individual Differences in Need for Cognitive Closure," *Journal of Personality and Social Psychology* 67:1049–62.

Wedgwood, Ralph. 2007. *The Nature of Normativity*. Oxford: Clarendon Press.

Wegner, Daniel. 2002. *The Illusion of Conscious Will*. Cambridge, MA: MIT Press.

Wegner, Daniel, and Thalia Wheatley. 1999. "Apparent Mental Causation: Sources of the Experience of Will," *American Psychologist* 54: 480–92.

Westen, Drew. 1998. "The Scientific Legacy of Sigmund Freud: Toward a Psychodynamically Informed Psychological Science," *Psychological Bulletin* 124: 333–71.

Wicker, A. W. 1969. "Attitudes vs. Actions: The Relationship of Verbal and Overt Behavioural Responses to Attitude Objects," *Journal of Social Issues* 22: 41–78.

Widom, C.S. 1989. "Child Abuse, Neglect, and Violent Criminal Behavior," *Criminology* 27: 251–71.

Wiggins, David. 1988. "Truth, Invention, and the Meaning of Life," in Geoffrey Sayre-McCord (ed.), *Essays on Moral Realism*. Ithaca, NY: Cornell University Press.

Wilcox, John. 1974. *Truth and Value in Nietzsche*. Ann Arbor, MI: University of Michigan Press.

Wilson, Timothy. 2002. *Strangers to Ourselves: Discovering the Adaptive Unconscious*. Cambridge, MA: Harvard University Press.

Wolf, Susan. 1981. "The Importance of Free Will," *Mind* 90: 386–405.

Wright, Crispin. 1988. "Realism, Anti-Realism, Irrealism, Quasi-Realism," *Midwest Studies in Philosophy* 12: 25–49.

Wright, Crispin. 1992. *Truth and Objectivity*. Cambridge, MA: Harvard University Press.

Young, Julian. 2010. *Friedrich Nietzsche: A Philosophical Biography*. Cambridge: Cambridge University Press.

Index